Hot Stove Economics

Hot Stove Economics

Understanding Baseball's Second
Season

J.C. Bradbury

Copernicus Books

An Imprint of Springer Science + Business Media

© Springer Science+Business Media, LLC 2011

Published in the United States by Copernicus Books,
an imprint of Springer Science+Business Media.

Copernicus Books
Springer Science+Business Media
233 Spring Street
New York, NY 10013
www.springer.com

Library of Congress Control Number:
2010922994

Manufactured in the United States of America.
Printed on acid-free paper.

ISBN 978-1-4419-6268-3   e-ISBN 978-1-4419-6269-0

To my mother,
who gives more than necessary.

Additional Praise for *Hot Stove Economics*

In *Hot Stove Economics*, J.C. Bradbury delves into important questions of how professional baseball franchises value the talent of players. The questions are of interest to baseball fans who can and do argue the merits of specific trades, established player for established player or established player for prospects. The questions and their answers may also be interesting to people who bemoan the large salaries paid to grown men playing a game, people who want to know on what basis a ball player can be worth millions of dollars a year. J.C. addresses all these questions and all these readers in an engaging and easy style that manages to inform barroom sports debates and teach some basic economics all at the same time.

–Dennis Coates, University of Maryland, Baltimore County and past President of the North American Association of Sports Economists

Reviews of *The Baseball Economist*

Bradbury would be the first guy to tell you that baseball fans are the most statistically minded sports fans out there. And he should know: he is an economics professor and a baseball addict (and a popular blogger, too). Here, he tackles some of the game's most cherished truisms and controversies. Is being left-handed really a disadvantage for a catcher? What role, really, do steroids play in being a home-run king? (You may be surprised at the answer.) How can we effectively evaluate a player's value to his team? Ball fans may be shocked at how relevant economics is to their favorite game, and economists may find an exciting new application for their specialty. Like John Allen Paulos, author of such "popular math" books as *A Mathematician Reads the Newspaper* (1995), Bradbury writes with a smooth, accessible style and makes the tricky game of numbers seem both straightforward and exciting. Like *Bill James' Abstracts* (2003), this volume could become essential reading for baseball fans.

–Booklist, David Pitt

Subjecting recent baseball debates to plentiful regression analyses, Kennesaw State economist, Bradbury, gamely fuses our national pastime and the "dismal science" somewhat in the spirit of Steven Levitt (*Freakonomics*), Michael Lewis (*Moneyball*), and Bill James (*Baseball Between the Numbers*). Like the latter, Bradbury offers a front-office perspective on labor (that's the players), salaries, managerial influence, steroids, market size, and the like. Like a scrappy role player, Bradbury's enthusiasm is evident (he's a Braves supporter); he offers a chapter on managers' ability to work the umps ("it appears that most managers don't seem to have any real impact in arguing balls and strikes") and investigates top pitching coach Leo Mazzone's contributions. A blogger at his website sabernomics.com (a play on the acronym SABR, the Society for American Baseball Research), Bradbury, while not forging new ground, shines in the closing chapters, in which he convincingly bucks the conventional wisdom that Major League Baseball behaves like a monopoly. While the numbers crunched are more of the *Financial Times* than the box score kind, the issues the book deals with are those discussed in many a barroom.

–Publisher's Weekly

Acknowledgments

I would like to thank several people for their help with this project. First, I offer a special thanks to Sean Forman for providing access to much of the data I used in this project. His website Baseball-Reference.com is an amazing resource for baseball data, and he was kind enough to put forth extra effort to help me with this project. My former Sewanee colleague Doug Drinen discussed ideas with me and provided some data assistance, but most of all I owe him a debt of gratitude for putting me on my current research path. I would also like to thank Matt Zarin for his valuable research assistance and feedback on early drafts of this manuscript.

Thanks to many individuals for useful comments on issues relating to ideas in this book, which were presented in parts over several years: Dave Berri, Mary Jo Bryan, Dennis Coates, Brad Humphreys, John McLester, Phil Porter, Skip Sauer, Frank Stephenson, Bob Tollison, and several anonymous referees. I know that I received comments from many other individuals whose exact contributions I cannot directly recall; please know that I appreciate your help. Also, thanks to the many volunteers and employees who collected and published baseball data with Baseball Info Solutions, Baseball-Databank.org, Cot's Baseball Contracts, Retrosheet, and the Society for American Baseball Research.

Thanks to my editor Jon Gurstelle for having confidence in my project, and his comments greatly improved the book. Also, thanks to Gillian Greenough and the other folks at Copernicus/Springer for their help in producing the book.

Finally, and most importantly, I want to thank my family for their time and support. My parents, in-laws, and extended family provided practical support and advice that allowed me to write this book. My wife Rachael, who wrote her own book as I wrote this one, and my daughters Rebekah and Sarah saw less of their husband and father as I worked on the manuscript. You are my inspiration, and I love you all.

List of Abbreviations

Abbreviation	Name
AL	American League
AVG	Batting average
BABIP	Batting average on balls in play
BB	Walks
BB9	Walks per nine innings pitched
BFP	Batters faced by pitcher
BRA	Batter's run average
DIPS	Defense-independent pitching statistics
DPT	Doubles-plus-triples
ERA	Earned run average
ERA+	ERA plus
GCL	Gulf Coast League
GM	General Manager
HR	Home runs
HR9	Home runs per nine innings pitched
K	Strikeouts

K9	Strikeouts per nine innings pitched
LSLR	Least squares linear regression (regression-estimated runs)
LWTS	Linear weights
MLB	Major League Baseball
MRP	Marginal revenue product
MVP	Most-valuable player
NL	National League
OBP	On-base percentage
OPS	On-base-plus-slugging
PA	Plate appearance
PV	Present value
RA	Runs allowed average
RBI	Runs batted in
RC	Runs created
RISP	Runners in scoring position
SABR	Society for American Baseball Research
SLG	Slugging average
VAM	Value approximation method
VORP	Value over replacement player
W	"Win" as earned by a pitcher
WAR	Wins above replacement
WPA	Win probability average

Preface

I am in a business called professional baseball where no quarter is asked and no quarter is given,—highly competitive, where we put a dollar mark on the muscle...

—Branch Rickey[1]

As much as I like watching the action on the baseball diamond, I have to admit that I enjoy the space between the World Series and spring training nearly as much. And I am not alone. Popular websites like MLBTradeRumors.com experience their highest traffic of the year when teams aren't even on the field. Newspapers, websites, and friendly gatherings erupt with exchanges that have nothing to do with tape-measure homers or web-gems that normally spur baseball chatter. The MLB Network replaces its signature television program MLB Tonight with Hot Stove.

The off-season marks the beginning of the "hot stove league," when fans follow a different type of game. In this league, it's not the athletic feats of baseball players that attract fans; instead, players are individual parts, which when properly assembled, produce a championship contender. Journalists and fans aren't just spectators; they're participants who discuss the moves that teams make, don't make, or should make. Each team has different needs: an ace starter, shoring up the bullpen, acquiring a back-up catcher, etc.; and, every fan thinks he/she has identified the missing puzzle pieces to complete the team.

The main event of the hot stove league is the opening of free agency, where teams purchase player services on the open market. While most people I know don't normally enjoy watching other people shop, baseball's free-agent market draws significant attention. It is easy for fans to ponder the contents of the free-agent pool and imagine what each player might do for their team. Players compete against players to sell their services to the highest bidder, and owners compete against owners to purchase the best players for the lowest possible price. The players flirt with many teams as player agents plant rumors in the media about their clients' desires and expectations, often playing general managers off each other in the hope of bidding up salaries. At some point, all a player's suitors but one are gone. The general manager with the highest bid calls a press conference where he drapes a new jersey on the back of his smiling prize.

The off-season is also a time when teams tinker with their rosters by swapping players between clubs, a tradition from the old days of baseball when bartering was the main way that players switched major-league teams. Trades are often more exciting to fans than free-agent acquisitions; because, while the expected financial worth of players is not immediately obvious, comparisons between traded players are simple to make.

No matter the course of a player's arrival, fans are generally excited when their team lands a new weapon; yet, some fans can't help but feel the sting of the winner's curse. "If we were willing to pay more for this player than any other team, did we overpay?" Or, "if this guy's so good, why was another general manager willing to give him up for players we didn't want?" A general manager might be incompetent or genius, but how can fans know?

Economists are a curious breed of thinkers. We tend to be quite imperialistic in wielding our methods to answer questions in all aspects of life. The tools that economists use to study important but mundane topics like financial crises, budget deficits, and unemployment can be applied to other, more-interesting aspects of daily life. Baseball's labor market has been a frequent topic of analysis among economists for more than half a century. The methods economists have used to analyze this market provide tools useful for informing hot stove debates.

Whether the transaction is a $100 million free-agent contract or a three-team trade, judging the deal requires knowing the value of the player(s) involved; but, putting precise dollar values on the things players do on the field is no simple task. This book presents the steps needed to answer the hot stove league's most pertinent question: *what is a player worth?* The methods I use provide general ballpark (pardon the pun) estimates of player worth in real dollar terms. Each transaction has its own characteristics that makes capturing precise values difficult; however, the estimates can serve as a guide to curious fans as well as provide practical advice to general managers, player agents, and fantasy-team owners. The valuation process requires identifying how the things players do on the field translate into dollars in owners' wallets. The methods I employ are grounded in a rich economic literature on baseball's labor market—largely unknown to the general public—modifying past analyses with more-detailed data, advanced techniques, and an updated understanding of how baseball performance translates into winning and revenue.

An analytical approach to baseball may be new to some readers, but there exists a group of fans who have been thinking about baseball in this manner for many years. As Alan Schwarz details in his book *The Numbers Game*, researchers have been using data from baseball games to examine strategy and tactics since the mid-twentieth century. George Lindsey, Earnshaw Cook, and Harlan and Eldon Mills all used the game of baseball as a laboratory; however, Bill James is the Johnny Appleseed of this type of analysis.

James dubbed his work and the similar work of his contemporaries *sabermetrics*, in homage to the Society for American Baseball Research, which is more commonly known by its acronym SABR. The field of sabermetrics spawned a large following of stat-savvy baseball fans who soon found the Internet to be a conduit for sharing their unique passion for the game. The discussion has greatly enhanced our knowledge of the game in many areas, with a few sabermetric discoveries infiltrating mainstream commentary. The metrics I use to evaluate player performance in this book were largely developed and popularized by sabermetricians. However, when it comes to valuing players—a frequent topic among sabermetricians—I rarely see the work of economists Simon Rottenberg, Gerald Scully, or Anthony Krautmann mentioned, despite the fact that their analyses of baseball's labor market are the gold standard for economists. Their work will receive significant attention in this book, because understanding their models is an important first step in properly valuing players. I believe my contribution will help us better value players—benefiting the economics and baseball analysis communities—while entertaining and informing curious baseball fans.

Organization of the Book

The book begins by explaining the players-as-assets framework for valuing players. It is a mistake to value players solely on their athletic contributions, because some players excel while drawing small salaries, and other players have been signed to contracts (mistakenly) that well-exceed their revenue-generating contributions. To teams, players are assets—a bundle of rights to probabilistic income streams. Converting performance into dollars requires a basic framework for evaluating players as financial instruments. Chapter 1 explains why it is important to consider the financial obligations to players along with their on-field performance in order to estimate expected returns. Failure to incorporate both aspects can result in erroneous declarations of one team getting the better end of a trade. In this framework, one seemingly lopsided trade—Johnny Estrada for Kevin Millwood—doesn't seem so unbalanced.

The task of valuing players requires properly assessing player performance on the field. While baseball fans often rely on traditional measures of player performance like batting average and earned run average, other metrics do a better job of gauging the things that players do to generate wins and revenue for their teams. Incorrectly measuring performance means that any estimated dollar values based on these evaluations will improperly value player contributions. Chapter 2 presents criteria for judging the usefulness of player performance metrics to aid in the selection of the most appropriate measures of player performance for translating on-field play into dollars.

Valuing players as assets also requires knowing how player performance changes over time as a result of aging. Chapter 3 discusses the importance of age on players' careers—going all the way back to little league—and uses historical performance records to identify aging patterns of players. The results support the conventional wisdom that players gradually improve through their 20s peaking just before 30, when they begin a gradual descent.

With the basic framework for valuing players in place, Chapter 4 presents the method for the converting performance into dollars so that players are valued according to the revenue they generate for their teams. Chapter 5 offers a critical examination of the estimates and identifies baseball's best and worst deals. Though some players may outperform their peers on the field, the labor rules governing player compensation sometimes cause less-experienced inferior play-ers to be more valuable as assets than more-experienced superior players. The estimates reveal why baseball players tend to earn seemingly exorbitant salaries and that many players consistently earn salaries less than their worth.

Beyond evaluating individual deals, estimates of individual players' worth also shed light on how well ballclubs manage their rosters. Is your favorite team putting a good team on the field at the cheapest possible price? Winning and winning efficiently are the signs of a well-managed organization. Chapter 6 rates teams according to how wisely they spend their resources, and uses the information to identify the best- and worst-managed franchises of the past decade.

Player contracts are not normally annual agreements, renewed every season according to each player's performance. In most cases, players and teams reach long-run deals that require taking into account factors that affect player value over time; therefore, it is important to project how players' values are expected to change during the contract term. Chapter 7 incorporates aging and other factors that affect players' long-run value in order to project players' expected worth. C.C. Sabathia's recent seven-year, $161 million deal with the New York Yankees provides an example for demonstrating how factors such as aging, league revenue growth, and team quality affect players' long-term value.

Another frequent type of transaction among clubs is the trade of veteran major-leaguers for minor-league talent. How can a player who has never played a day in the big leagues net a proven major-league regular? The answer lies in the probabilistic value of unproven talent, whom baseball insiders often refer to as "prospects." Major baseball news outlets like *Baseball America, Baseball Prospectus*, and ESPN devote significant resources to covering players who have yet to don a major-league uniform. In the bowels of farm clubs, prospects gen-erate short-term negative returns, which organizations gladly suffer as good long-term investments. Not every prospect pans out, which means the returns are uncertain. Chapter 8 presents a model for estimating the expected worth of these volatile assets and reveals that the development costs may explain why players agree to below-market wages during their early years in the league.

The chapters are also accompanied by brief asides labeled "Hot Stove Myths." In my many years of following the hot stove league, I've come across several mistaken ideas that are sometimes expressed as conventional wisdom. I discuss a few of these notions at the end of each chapter and explain why they are misguided. Though they draw on information presented in the main chapters, they can be read on their own.

After completing the book, it is my hope that readers will understand not only how much baseball players are worth, but also how I arrived at these values. The book is written for a wide audience that ranges from casual fans, who are just curious as to what baseball players are worth, to experienced researchers, who wish to know the intricacies of the analysis. Being as open about my methods sometimes requires going into technical details that may not interest some readers. Therefore, where the explanations become complicated I report the intuition behind the technical details so that readers will not become overwhelmed, but I include further details in endnotes and appendices. In addition, each chapter concludes with a brief summary of the main findings.

This book is the culmination of several years of research: building up, tearing down, and rebuilding models for estimating player worth. What began as a last-minute one-chapter inclusion in my previous book *The Baseball Economist* turned into what seems like an epic quest. Though the book contains many tables, figures, and equations I have tried not only to keep the analysis fun, including anecdotes that demonstrate the relevance of the results, but also to keep the mood light. I follow baseball because its a fun game to watch, and it is my hope that this book will add to your appreciation of the national pastime.

J.C. Bradbury

Contents

Part I
Getting Started

Chapter 1
Why Johnny Estrada Is Worth Kevin Millwood: Valuing Players As Assets

In the fall of 2002, Kevin Millwood was on top of the world. He had just completed his fifth full season as a regular in the Atlanta Braves starting rotation, helping lead the team to its eleventh consecutive Division crown. After posting the tenth best ERA in the National League he was poised take over as the staff ace from sure-to-be Hall-of-Fame rotation mates Greg Maddux and Tom Glavine, who would soon depart the club. At 27, he had already made one All-Star team (1999) and more trips to the mid-season classic seemed inevitable as he looked to be budding into one of the game's most dominant pitchers entering the prime of his career.

At the same time, Johnny Estrada's career was on a different track. He was a 26-year-old catcher just finishing up his second tour of duty for the Phillies Triple-A farm club. Though his minor-league career had been less than stellar, he had been called up to the majors for parts of the previous two seasons, where his performance had been dismal. At best, Estrada projected to be a career back-up catcher, who couldn't run, and wasn't particularly capable on offense or defense. His major-league career appeared to be closer to its end than its beginning.

Until late December 2002, there was no reason to mention Estrada in the same sentence as Millwood. That is when the Braves traded a former All-Star pitcher coming off an 18-win season for a back-up catcher who appeared to have stalled out in Triple-A. Suddenly, the world had been turned on its head. Braves General Manager John Schuerholz—a man revered for being one of the architects of his team's eleven-year playoff run—had been bested by Phillies General Manager Ed Wade, who would be fired three years later after failing to guide Phillies to the playoffs. The joke at the time was that when the Phillies told

J.C. Bradbury, *Hot Stove Economics*, DOI 10.1007/978-1-4419-6269-0_1,
© Springer Science+Business Media, LLC 2011

Estrada that he'd been traded for Kevin Millwood that even he responded, "and who else is going to Atlanta?"

The Braves were quick to spread a tale of financial woe as an explanation for the move. After Greg Maddux unexpectedly accepted the Braves offer to go to arbitration—which meant that the Braves would have to pay him nearly $15 million for his services in 2003—the team was going to be over budget. Schuerholz was up against a hard budget constraint and was forced to ship Millwood out. But even fans sympathetic to Schuerholz's predicament complained that the Braves should have been able to get more in return for Millwood than Johnny Estrada. Schuerholz even admitted that Estrada was not the club's top choice, "We did not initiate this to get Johnny Estrada. ... We were unable to finalize anything else."[2]

A budget crisis may have pushed Millwood out the door, but it did not mean that the team had to accept Estrada in return. The Philadelphia Phillies were not the only team in baseball that coveted starting pitchers; and, I'm reasonably certain that Schuerholz made calls to the 28 other teams. At the end of his search the Braves GM felt that the best option on the table was Johnny Estrada.

Possible Explanations

If Millwood was such a superior player to Estrada—as many critics of Schuerholz believed—how could all these other teams have passed on Millwood? I can think of three possible explanations:

1. Kevin Millwood was not as good as fans perceived.
2. Johnny Estrada was better than fans perceived.
3. The players involved in this transaction were valued for reasons other than their baseball abilities.

I can see how fan expectations of Millwood may have exceeded his ability. He had been a major contributor to a good team that had just won 101 games, while coming off the second-best season of his career. His best season occurred just three years prior—still fresh in the minds of fans—when Millwood was named to the All-Star team and had the second-best ERA in the National League. Braves fans had come to expect good pitching from their farm, and Millwood appeared

Year	Team	ERA+	Strikeouts per 9 IP	Walks per 9 IP	Home Runs per 9 IP
1998	Atlanta Braves	102	8.4	2.9	0.9
1999	Atlanta Braves	167	8.1	2.3	0.9
2000	Atlanta Braves	99	7.1	2.6	1.1
2001	Atlanta Braves	103	6.2	3.0	1.5
2002	Atlanta Braves	128	7.4	2.7	0.7
2003	Philadelphia Phillies	99	6.9	2.8	0.8
2004	Philadelphia Phillies	92	8.0	3.3	0.9
2005	Cleveland Indians	146	6.8	2.4	0.9
2006	Texas Rangers	102	6.6	2.2	1.0
2007	Texas Rangers	87	6.4	3.5	1.0
2008	Texas Rangers	87	6.7	2.6	1.0
2009	Texas Rangers	127	5.6	3.2	1.2

TABLE 1-1   Kevin Millwood's Performance (1998–2009)

to the next ace in a routine process that recently had yielded Tom Glavine, John Smoltz, and Steve Avery. But, it was premature to put Millwood in that category just yet.

Table 1-1 lists Millwood's performance during his first eleven seasons as a full-time starter in the major leagues in several areas. ERA+, calculated by Baseball-Reference.com, is a useful metric analyzing pitchers over time and across teams, because it adjusts for the effects of run scoring that may differ across ballparks and change from year to year. The baseline for ERA+ is 100, so that in any year that a pitcher performs above average his ERA+ is greater than 100, and when he performs worse than average his ERA+ is less than 100. The table also includes his strikeout, walk, and home run rates per nine innings pitched, because they reveal some useful information about pitcher performance that I explain in Chapter 2.

Outside of his 1999 and 2002 seasons, Millwood had been a rather ordinary pitcher. In his first five full seasons, he had two seasons that were well above average (1999 and 2002) and three that were about average (1998, 2000, and 2001). In the years that would follow, he would have some up and down years, indicating that he probably was not an elite or average pitcher, but somewhere in between. It is possible that baseball fans may have been enamored with his peaks and, therefore, thought he was better than he was.

Despite not blossoming into a classic number-one starter, Millwood has had a productive career, and players of Millwood's caliber are valuable. Though baseball fans may have thought Millwood was going to step into the Hall-of-Fame shoes of Maddux and Glavine, baseball insiders were likely aware that Millwood was not as good as his public reputation; therefore, teams were not willing to offer much compensation in a trade.

As for Johnny Estrada, whether he needed a change of scenery or had just had some bad luck in the Phillies organization is difficult to know. With the Braves, Estrada blossomed into much more than an adequate back-up that many scouts assumed would be his ceiling. In his first season in the Braves organization he earned the club's Triple-A Player-of-the-Year honor for his stellar play in Richmond. The following season he replaced Atlanta catching veteran Javy Lopez on the big-league roster. He earned the Braves' only All-Star selection and received the National League's Silver Slugger Award for being the best hitter at his position. The remainder of Estrada's career would not be as impressive as his 2004 season, but he remained a decent backstop who would play for several teams over the next few years before being released by the Washington Nationals in 2008.

Thus, just as Millwood appeared to be overrated a bit, so too was Estrada underrated. In my view, the biggest surprise in this deal was not that Millwood regressed from his 2002 form, but that Johnnny Estrada became a decent major-league catcher. In fact, had the Phillies known what Estrada would become, I doubt that they would have been willing to give him up for Millwood.

Even though fans and media may not have properly judged the talent of the two players involved in the trade, the third factor—that the players were valued for something other than their play on the field—has to be the biggest reason that this exchange took place. No matter how you crunch the numbers, Millwood has been a far better major-league player than Estrada. It is not necessary to bring in star status, charitable contributions, or bad-boy antics to explain why the teams were willing to swap these players. The financial obligations owed to the players, which were heavily influenced by Major League Baseball's salary rules, played a significant role in determining the players' values.

A Quick Primer on MLB's Compensation System

Major-league players fall into one of three categories based on their service time in the league: purely-reserved players, arbitration-eligible players, and free-agent players. In general, during the first six years of a player's major-league career, the rights to his play are owned by his parent club. That is, if he wants to play baseball in Major League Baseball, he can play for his assigned club or no other club. The owning club can also trade the rights to its players' baseball services to other teams.

The contract status of young players gives clubs strong *monopsony* power over them. A monopsony exists in a market when there is a single buyer for a product, which is similar to a monopoly market where there is a single seller. Like a monopolist, a monopsonist can use its market power to extract wealth from its trading partners. In this case, teams receive wealth in the form of baseball talent that is more valuable than the price that they must pay for it. Because there are few other employment opportunities to play baseball outside of Major League Baseball, teams can get away with offering players lower salaries than they would otherwise offer in a competitive market.

Prior to the 1976 Collective Bargaining Agreement between the players union and the owners, teams permanently owned the rights to their players under a provision in all player contracts known as the "reserve clause," which allowed teams to pay their players significantly less than their financial worth. Economist Gerald Scully estimated that under the reserve system players received salaries that were approximately 80 to 90 percent less than their gross revenue contributions from their play on the field. The new agreement and subsequent modifications set new rules that created labor-market classifications that reduced team control over player salaries.

In the first three years of service, a player has the least bargaining power of his career. A purely reserved player must accept whatever salary his club is willing to offer, which means most players with less than three years of service earn close to the league's minimum salary, which is currently $400,000 for an entire season.

In the second three years of service, a player becomes eligible to have his salary governed by a neutral third party, which increases his bargaining power by a small amount. The arbitration process begins with the team and player proposing salaries for the upcoming season. The parties are free to negotiate a contract on their own; however, if the team and player cannot agree on a salary, then each side argues its case before a panel of three arbitrators. The arbitration panel selects the salary offer—not a mid-way compromise—that it considers to be closest to player salaries of a similar ability and service time. This method, known as final offer arbitration, is preferred over having a third party set a level of compensation because it encourages both sides to reach a compromise on their own—for fear of having to pay/receive the winning side's figure—and thus not incur the costs of the arbitration hearing. The method has been successful at limiting the number of hearings to a handful of cases each year.

The arbitration rules permit players and teams to compare players to other players' salaries with similar service time, but players cannot be compared to players with more than one additional year of service. Because the comparison group includes purely-reserved players with severely depressed salaries, arbitration-eligible players tend to make less than what they would earn on the open market. Only after achieving "special accomplishments" are players allowed to compare themselves to players outside their service-time cohorts. Baseball agent Randy Hendricks was the first person to exploit this clause to win Pittsburgh Pirates pitcher Doug Drabek a $3.35 million contract in only his fourth year of service in 1991, arguing that Drabek's Cy Young Award should trigger the exception.[3] More recently, Ryan Howard used his MVP, Silver Slugger, and All-Star selections to win a $10 million arbitration award in his first year of arbitration eligibility in 2008. In most cases, the bargaining power provided by arbitration increases salaries above those of purely-reserved players, but salaries remain below what similarly-talented free agents earn.

After six years of service, a player becomes a free agent. A free agent is allowed to shop his services to any major-league club willing to employ him; thus, wages tend to rise dramatically once players enter free agency. Competition among teams causes salaries to rise, because offers below a player's expected worth typically will be matched by another club. The competitive bidding process drives wages toward the player's expected worth to the team.

Players as Assets

This is where the exchange of Kevin Millwood and Johnny Estrada begins to make more sense. Team owners do not value players as athletes, but as financial assets that generate revenue for them. These men were not just players, they represented bundles of rights to probabilistic income streams, like equity shares traded on the New York Stock Exchange. The rights to player services are valuable commodities that vary in value along several dimensions. Everyone is aware that good players are worth more than average players, and average players are worth more than bad players; but, the right to pay a player a salary less than his market value is also an important determinant of player value.

As an asset, a player is worth what he generates in revenue to his team minus his expected employment costs. These costs include training, equipment, medical care, etc., but the biggest cost is his salary. Typically, a player yields the most value to his team when he has less than three years of service, because he can be paid close to the league-minimum salary while generating revenue well in excess of his wage. As a player's service time increases, his value begins to decline, because his salary obligation increases and he has fewer years of reduced-salary service available to his parent club. By the time a player reaches his sixth year of service, he will be earning a salary approaching his expected worth and his term of indenture to his parent club is nearly over. Thus, as an asset, a player is valued according his expected net revenue produced each year (revenue − salary) and the amount of time his rights are controlled by his owning club.

As an example, consider the asset value of a hypothetical player who will be worth $4 million per season during the first six years of his career. Table 1-2 lists his expected value over the course of his reserved years. During his first three years, his salary will be the league-mandated minimum of $400,000, thereby generating $3.6 million in net revenue to his team. When he becomes

					Remaining Value at End of Season	
Service Time	Expected Revenue ($)	% Salary < MRP	Expected Salary ($)	Net Revenue ($)	Total Value ($)	Present Value ($)
1	4.00	90	0.40	3.60	16.20	14.29
2	4.00	90	0.40	3.60	12.60	11.34
3	4.00	90	0.40	3.60	9.00	8.25
4	4.00	75	1.00	3.00	6.00	5.62
5	4.00	75	1.00	3.00	3.00	2.87
6	4.00	75	1.00	3.00	0.00	0.00

TABLE 1-2   Expected Value of Hypothetical $4 Million Player
Dollar in millions

arbitration eligible, his salary requirements rise, but he still generates significant net value to the team. The last two columns of the table report the total remaining value of the player's service time at the conclusion of each season, with the last column discounting the expected revenue. Present value discounting is important because it reflects the opportunity cost of alternative investments; instead of compensating a player, the team could generate similar revenue by buying the guaranteed revenue stream from an annuity—a financial instrument that makes payouts over time (see Appendix A for an explanation of discounting). This example demonstrates why players are worth considerably more than their salaries, and when teams trade such assets, they should appropriately value the expected net revenue generated by player performance and contract status.

Returning to the examination of the Millwood-for-Estrada trade, the analysis changes when valuing the players as assets rather than judging them solely by their play on the field. Millwood may have been the better player; however, he would be under his club's control for only one more season, and he wasn't going to be cheap. Estrada had not even completed a full year of service at the time of the trade. The team that acquired Estrada would be able to pay him a salary less than his market value for the next six years. However, given Estrada's past performance at the time of the trade, the potential high returns that Estrada-the-asset might produce were likely only a small part of this deal. I suspect that Braves scouts did see something in Estrada that they liked, and certain difficult-to-identify talents may have been responsible for his success; however, I do not think the Braves had high hopes that he would perform as he did.

Instead, the reason that Kevin Millwood netted only Johnny Estrada was the fact that acquiring Millwood-the-asset was expected to generate a negative return. In the two seasons that preceded his trade, Millwood had been paid $3.1 and $3.9 million by the Braves. He was due a big raise in 2003 for two reasons. First, he was coming off one of the best seasons of his career, and arbitrators are required to give strong weight to the previous season. Second, the players to whom Millwood could compare himself at his arbitration hearing were earning much bigger salaries. For example, at the time, two pitchers similar to Millwood in service time and ability were Matt Morris and Bartolo Colon, who earned $10.5 million and $8.25 million, respectively, in 2003. Every team anticipated that Millwood's agent Scott Boras would use such comparisons to get Millwood a

	Value			
Year	2007 Dollars ($)	Current Dollars ($)	Salary ($)	Net Value ($)
1998	5.97	2.75	0.18	2.57
1999	8.36	4.19	0.23	3.96
2000	5.97	3.27	0.42	2.85
2001	2.60	1.55	3.10	−1.55
2002	8.35	5.43	3.90	1.53
2003	6.82	4.83	9.90	−5.07
2004	4.71	3.63	11.00	−7.37
2005	6.04	5.09	7.00	−1.91
2006	7.18	6.59	7.97	−1.38
2007	4.61	4.61	9.84	−5.23
2008	5.36	5.84	10.37	−4.53
2009	4.93	5.86	12.87	−7.01

TABLE 1-3   Kevin Millwood's Estimated Value (1998–2009)
Dollars in millions

similar salary, and they were right. After being traded to the Phillies, he would sign a one-year, $9.9 million deal, and the following year he agreed to a one-year free-agent deal with the Phillies for $11 million.

Table 1-3 lists several measures of Kevin Millwood's performance value over the course of his career using the method that I explain in the following chapters. The second column lists the values in 2007 dollars (what the performance would be worth in 2007) so that different seasons can be compared in terms of how good his pitching was from season to season—the value of players changes over time, growing approximately nine percent per year. The third column reports the dollar value of his performance in each year, which would have been the figure relevant his team's bottom line at the time the salary was paid out. In 2002, Millwood's performance was worth $5.43 million. In the following year, during which he performed at a lower level but in a year of higher revenue, he was worth $4.83 million. Both of those estimates are significantly less than what the Phillies would pay Millwood in 2003. Strangely enough, the Phillies would agree to a one-year, $11 million contract for 2004. The net value that Millwood would generate for the Phillies (reported in the last column) would be negative in both his years with the Phillies.

In fairness to the Phillies front office, these were not necessarily awful contracts. The estimates of player values are crude and affected by several factors, which I discuss later in this book; and, an injury in 2004—which would have been difficult to anticipate given Millwood's previous record of excellent health—significantly impacted his value. The important point here is that at the time the Braves were attempting to move Millwood, the salary that his acquiring club would have to pay him in 2003 was likely more than what he was generating in revenue, which explains why clubs were unwilling to offer anything more than Johnny Estrada for Millwood. The fact that Johnny Estrada eventually became a useful major-league player was an added bonus for the Braves. By trading Millwood to the Phillies, the team had just rid itself of an asset that was not generating positive value. Had Estrada never played another day in the majors, the Braves were bettered simply by removing Millwood from their roster.

The move was exacerbated by the stagnation of pitcher salaries during this time. From 2002 to 2004 total league pitcher salaries grew at an average rate of 0.6 percent per year. In the preceding three years (1999–2001) pitcher salaries grew at an average rate of 14.6 percent per year, and in the succeeding three years (2005–2007) grew at an average rate of 9.1 percent per year. This was an era of cheap pitching, not a time when a team needed to be paying top dollar for mid-level talent. The Braves would replace Millwood with a series of moves that included promoting minor-league talent and signing some veteran free agents; the latter group was especially cheap. The Braves signed Paul Byrd to a two-year, $10 million contract two days before trading Millwood to replace the expected departure of Greg Maddux. The more-affordable Byrd would be kept over Millwood; though, the deal would not work out as Byrd would miss a season and a half to injury. But still, the acquisition reveals that veteran pitchers of a quality similar to Millwood were available on the free-agent market at a lower price.

The irony of the Millwood-for-Estrada trade is that it is often mentioned as one of John Schuerholz's worst deals, when in fact, it appears to have been a smart move. Not only did he dump Millwood, but he acquired an All-Star catcher who would become a major contributor to the big-league club for two years, then be traded to the Arizona Diamondbacks for pitching help. For all of this, the Braves paid Estrada less than $1 million, or less than ten percent of what the team would have had to pay Kevin Millwood for one season of work.

Other Factors to Consider (or Not) When Valuing Players as Assets

The Millwood–Estrada exchange reveals the importance of non-performance factors that affects players' value as assets, but there are other factors related to asset value that deserve discussion.

In-Kind Compensation

In January 2006, pitcher Bronson Arroyo signed a three-year, $11.2 million contract extension with the Boston Red Sox—this was against the advice of his agents who thought he could get a better offer on the free-agent market. Over the term of his contract, I estimate that his performance was worth just under $19 million; so, it is understandable why his agents did not favor the agreement. But Arroyo wasn't stupid, he just didn't value the money as much as he did playing in Boston.

> I love playing here. I love the fans. I love the city. I want to stay here
> for my whole career. I feel that's going to beneficial for me as well as
> the team. Hopefully, they see it that way and don't trade me.[4]

His payment was *in-kind* instead of monetary compensation, and players frequently prefer such payment in order to stay close to family and friends. In-kind payments sometimes come in the form of lavish suites on road trips or access to the owners' vacation house, but they may also include non-tangible perks. Agents can't be too fond of in-kind payments because they don't get a percentage cut like they do from monetary compensation. Clubs with favorable living conditions or a friendly managers may be able to attract players for less than their going market salary. In this case, Arroyo's fondness for Boston allowed the Red Sox to earn excess financial returns from employing him.

No-Trade Clauses

However, though Arroyo wanted to play in Boston, the Red Sox retained the right to trade him to any other club. Arroyo did not believe this possibility was likely, even though his contract lacked a no-trade clause. Two months later, Arroyo was traded to the Cincinnati Reds for outfield prospect Wily Mo Pena. Soon after the trade, many pundits wondered why Arroyo had not insisted on a no-trade provision in his contract. If playing in Boston was important enough for him to forgo millions of dollars, shouldn't he have insured that he got to throw at least one more pitch for the team?

A no-trade clause isn't free, and it turns out that Arroyo may not have been as altruistic toward the city of Boston as he seemed. A no-trade clause would have limited the team's options as to what it could do with him, lowering his value as an asset and the salary the Red Sox would be willing to pay him. Just as Arroyo was willing to sacrifice income for long-term security and the possibility of playing in Boston, the Red Sox valued Arroyo less as an immovable asset. If another team valued Arroyo more than a prospect that the Red Sox coveted—such as Pena—they would be unable to move Arroyo. I suspect that the Red Sox would gladly have included a no-trade provision if Arroyo agreed to take an even lower salary; however, as much as Arroyo claimed to love Boston, he apparently valued financial security more.

It's ironic that the discount he took to stay in Boston made Arroyo a valuable trade chip, because he was locked down to a below-market contract in the heart of his pitching prime, which likely explains his agents' objection. Players of Arroyo's caliber typically cost far more on the free-agent market. And so, when the Red Sox approached the Reds about Pena, Arroyo represented a valuable asset that the Reds were willing to take on instead of Pena.

Option Clauses

It was probably good that Arroyo got out of Boston, learning a valuable lesson about taking advice from his agents, and learning that Cincinnati wasn't so bad a place to play. In 2007, he signed a two-year extension with the Reds that would pay him a total of $20.5 million for the 2009 and 2010 seasons. In addition to a $2.5 million signing bonus, the contract included a provision that gave the Reds the right to retain Arroyo for the 2011 season at a salary of $11 million. If the team decided it didn't want to retain his services they would have to pay him a $2 million buyout. Arroyo was guaranteed $25 million, but the Reds had the right to extend the deal for $9 million ($11 million minus the $2 million buyout they would have to pay if they didn't pick up the option).

The option clause might seem to be beneficial only to the Reds, because if Arroyo is pitching well enough to command more than $9 million on the free-agent market, the Reds can keep him for less. But Arroyo didn't give away his option year for free. Just as teams expect lower salary demands in return for no-trade clauses, players expect higher salaries up front for agreeing to option years. It's likely that without the option year, Arroyo would have received less guaranteed money in 2009 and 2010.

Some contracts occasionally include player options as well. For example, before the 2005 season, J.D. Drew signed a five-year, $55 million contract with the Los Angeles Dodgers. His contract included an option to void the deal after two seasons and become a free agent. Dodgers General Manager Paul DePodesta was loudly criticized for including this option. "If he's good, then he'll leave!" his critics complained. However, this concession in the contract actually saved the Dodgers money. If the clause was not included, then the team would have had to cough up more money to get him to play in L.A. for two years. Drew would eventually exercise his option and sign a five-year, $70 million deal with the Red Sox. In return, the Dodgers got Drew for two years at a price less than what they would have had to pay without the option clause. Drew got his freedom, but the team now had more payroll to chase other free agents.

Sunk Costs

In June 2006, the Arizona Diamondbacks asked starting pitcher Russ Ortiz to clean out his locker even though he still had $22 million remaining on a four-year, $33 million contract. The team chose to release him and send him paychecks to do anything he wanted other than pitch for the Diamondbacks after coming to an important realization: Russ Ortiz was worse than other options the team had to pitch those same innings. Players like Enrique Gonzalez and Juan Cruz could better cover the innings that Ortiz was supposed to pitch and the team would win more games and earn more revenue. The $22 million that the Diamondbacks owed Ortiz was irrelevant: no matter how well he pitched, he would be paid $22 million. If the Diamondbacks continued to pitch Ortiz in order to justify the salary, he would have increased the organization's losses; hence, the team sent him packing. The salary obligations to Ortiz were a *sunk cost*, a forgone cost that cannot be recovered; therefore, not relevant to economic decisions. Rather than looking at already-set salary obligations, teams should value players according to their expected future production.

However, just because a player is overpaid does necessarily mean that the team would be better off by releasing him. On occasion, teams misunderstand the application of sunk-cost dictum and give up on players too soon, like the Toronto Blue Jay did with Frank Thomas in 2008.

After getting off to a slow start, the Blue Jays asked Thomas to take a lesser bench role with the team. Thomas was not happy about his new assignment, so the Blue Jays simply released him while continuing to pay out the remaining portion of his salary, which was around $7 million. $7 million was a sunk cost to the Blue Jays, and should not have factored into their decision of whether to employ Thomas or not. Releasing Thomas did not erase the initial bad decision of signing him to a big contract. By cutting Thomas, the Blue Jays lost the rights to a diminished, but still productive, hitter. The Oakland A's immediately picked up Thomas, for whom he generated over $2 million for the remainder of the season, which represents revenue that could have been used to help cover Thomas's salary; therefore, Thomas-as-an-asset still had positive value that the Blue Jays gave away.

A lesson from the principles of microeconomics is that shutting down isn't always the correct response to losses. As long as the revenue from production exceeds the operating costs, a portion of the sunk-cost obligations can be covered by continuing to operate; shutting down actually increases losses. Even as a pinch hitter off the bench, Thomas could have helped the Blue Jays win games, as he did for the A's. The Blue Jays did not have to keep Thomas on their roster to get some value out of him. Rather than allowing the Oakland A's to pick up Thomas for virtually no cost, the Blue Jays could have demanded the A's send some cash or another player in return for his services. The A's would not have been willing to pay all of Thomas's salary, but they might have paid more than they did, and that would have softened the blow of losing his services.

Summing Up

The Millwood-for-Estrada exchange reveals how pure performance comparisons between players exclude a crucial element in understanding player value. The remainder of the book focuses on valuing players, mainly focusing on their potential revenue-generating capabilities. When estimating free-agent salary expectations, it is sufficient to assume players ought to be worth what they are paid. However, it is important to consider the financial obligations to players when determining player asset values. Players with below-market contracts are more valuable than players with contracts that require compensation beyond the revenue they generate.

A large portion of the divergence between salary and performance value derives from baseball's compensation rules for young players, but long-run contracts that guarantee a salary above or below a player's expected production also affect players' asset value. Teams who want to trade players with bad contracts cannot just dump them off on another team. When players with excessive contracts are traded, oftentimes the trading club agrees to pay a portion of the salary, or agrees to take a player who also has a bad contract. When a team attempts to trade a player with a good contract, it expects compensation for relinquishing an asset that should generate extraordinary revenue for his owning club.

Valuing players as assets permits us to consider more than a player's performance in contributing to the success of the baseball business; however, properly valuing players does require evaluating on-field performance. The next chapter addresses how we should judge players as baseball players, so that we can put a dollar value on what they do.

Hot Stove Myth: Every Trade has a Winner and a Loser

When a trade goes down, the first question that many fans ask is "who won?" After all, the number of baseball players in the world hasn't changed, they merely swapped places. As if we are balancing budget or a chemistry equation, giving to one side necessarily means taking an equal amount away from the other side. Therefore, baseball trades must be an even swap of players, or one side gains at the expense of the other. But often, when I turn on the television to see the analysis of the trade, the commentator says something like, "this is one of those *few* occasions where both teams benefited from the trade." As an economist, the fact that many people think both parties benefiting from trades is rare makes me chuckle. Intuitively each trade seems to make sense, but they can't get over the seeming contradiction that the number of resources in the world hasn't changed. But to economists, there is no contradiction.

Rarely will you meet an economist who doesn't like trade. And if you are a former student of James Buchanan—as I am—you *really* like trade. Buchanan, winner of the 1986 Nobel Memorial Prize in Economic Sciences, stresses to all his students that economists should begin by studying markets and exchange rather than resource allocation. Classical economists Adam Smith and later David Ricardo demonstrated why specialization and trade leads to outcomes that maximize output for the benefit of society.

But, optimally allocating resources is not the only reason that economists like voluntary exchange. If the parties involved in the exchange are rational, self-interested, and acting of their own volition, then they will only engage in exchange when they think they are made better off. A fair trade isn't a swap of equally valued resources. If the swap is equal, then why even bother with the trouble of trading? Both parties will make the exchange only if they feel what the other party has is more valuable than what they give up. Trade is a positive sum activity, and is, therefore, mutually beneficial. This logic applies to the exchange of baseball players, as well.

Players change teams only because *both* general managers see the new player(s), prospect(s), or cash as superior to what they gave up.

And this doesn't necessarily mean superior playing quality—salary obligations, service time, age, and contract length also play important roles. Player skill-sets may just fit better on different teams, one team may need budget relief while the other is willing to spend, or a team that's out of the pennant race may be willing to give up its star for the potential of prospective future stars. To pick winners and losers in baseball trades is to view one general manager as superior to another, when in fact both individuals are likely improving their teams—they're both winners.

Now, what people mean by winning and losing a trade may differ. Some people like to look backwards to evaluate a trade to see what ultimately happened. I disagree; the future is difficult to project, and I believe that trades should be evaluated according to what the parties knew at the time of the trade. In the long run, every trade will likely turn out to be better for one of the participants. Just because someone wins the lottery doesn't mean that the winner should be praised for his/her investment acumen. It's wrong to punish a general manager for not having information that no one else had either. For example, was it really possible to predict what would happen to Ken Griffey in Cincinnati?

Commentators who begin by asking "who won?" aren't starting in the right frame of mind for analyzing the trade, because trade is not a zero-sum game. Rather than trying to identify winners and losers, it's best to first try to understand why the trade happened. Sometimes after analyzing a trade, I don't get the deal; and, it's OK to say "that team got fleeced." But, I rarely find myself saying this. Most times I find that deals make sense for both sides, as economic theory predicts. Mistakes happen, but as a general rule, all parties to trades are winners. Who says economists aren't touchy-feely?

Chapter 2
Down With The Triple-Crown: Evaluating On-Field Performance

The first step in valuing player performance is figuring out which aspects of performance ought to be rewarded and how to weight them. It might be tempting to borrow from baseball's traditional wisdom to determine which skills that players possess are most important; however, popular notions of what determines success in baseball are not necessarily so. Baseball fans tend to be capable of recalling performance statistics of their favorite players with ease, but there exists widespread innumeracy regarding their interpretation. Despite the available evidence regarding player contributions to winning, most mainstream baseball commentary judges players with antiquated notions of what constitutes good and bad performance.

For example, nearly every time a batter steps to the plate during a televised game, three numbers are posted on the screen below his name: batting average, runs batted in (RBI), and home runs. Like most children who grew up devoting their summers to following the game, I embraced the popular yardsticks for evaluating players without questioning their utility. But the metrics that constitute the "triple-crown" of hitting are not the best measures of batters' abilities to help their teams win, and it does not take much thought to understand why.

The batting average tells us something about one way that a batter can safely reach base: how frequently he gets a hit. This is useful information; however, it can be misleading for two reasons. First, the batting average ignores other ways that a batter can safely reach base without getting a hit. A player who draws many walks or who is hit by many pitches puts a runner on first base for his team and does not make an out, just as a hit does. Reaching base via a hit does

J.C. Bradbury, *Hot Stove Economics*, DOI 10.1007/978-1-4419-6269-0_2,
© Springer Science+Business Media, LLC 2011

have some additional benefits over these other methods of reaching base, such as advancing runners; however, batters who walk frequently have more value compared to batters with the same batting average who rarely walk.

Second, the batting average treats all hits equally, even though hits that allow a hitter to advance multiple bases produce more runs than singles. Between two players with identical batting averages, a player with many doubles and home runs is more valuable than a hitter who hits mostly singles. Managers are obviously aware of this as they frequently keep sluggers with low batting averages in the lineup, because they make up for a lack in consistent hitting with power.

The inclusion of RBI and home runs next to batting average may provide some information about the hitting power of a player, because the more hitting power that a hitter has, the more RBI and home runs he ought to have. This logic is correct as players with many RBI and home runs typically do hit with power, but these metrics are not the best sources of information for measuring extra-base power.

RBI is an especially dangerous statistic to rely upon for measuring power, because it is heavily influenced by factors unrelated to hitting ability. A major determinant of RBI is RBI chances: the more often that a batter steps to the plate with runners in scoring position, the more RBI he ought to have. RBI chances are not random across teams or the batting order. A team that has many hitters that reach base will provide many RBI chances to its team's batters that might not be available on a lesser team. Also, a batter who bats in the middle of the lineup typically bats after several players who frequently reach base and will, therefore, have more RBI opportunities than players at the top and bottom of the order. It's not necessarily an ability (such as power) that causes players to rack up RBI; therefore, crediting hitters for RBI rewards or punishes them for factors beyond their control.

Imagine comparing a child born in an upper-class household in the United States to a child born in a refugee camp in Sudan. Just because the American grew up to be a doctor, while the Sudanese became a bus driver does not mean that the American has more natural ability. Clearly, these children's lives were heavily affected by circumstances beyond their control. It might be that the successful American is the more-talented child; just the high-RBI clean-up hitter might more productive than a low-RBI leadoff hitter, but comparing their overall final outcomes is a poor benchmark for measuring their talent. In the real world, it would be difficult to compare the innate talents of these children. We might give them IQ tests or judge their accomplishments relative to their peers in their environment, but in baseball a comparison between player talents isn't difficult at all.

What about "clutch" hitters who perform better than other players in run-producing situations? RBI might capture this skill, and a player who hits better with runners in scoring position would be more valuable than one who chokes. However, as much as fans like to talk about players who rise to the moment, it doesn't seem that hitters have much control over this type of situational hitting (see the Hot Stove Myth at the end of this chapter for evidence). Therefore, it would be wrong to credit players for any successes or failures that they happen to produce in the clutch.

Nearly every event in baseball is recorded, and has been since Henry Chadwick first invented the box score. A clumsy statistic like RBI isn't the only yardstick available for measuring output that a batter generates beyond his batting average. To gauge hitting power, baseball fans often use a modified batting average that is weighted by the number of bases a batter advances when he gets a hit: two bases for doubles, three bases for triples, and four bases for home runs. This way the hitter receives additional credit for power. This metric is known to most baseball fans as the slugging average (SLG). Slugging average is not a perfect measure of hitting power, but it is much more useful than batting average and RBI. A player's slugging average is not affected by a player's teammates nor by his place in the hitting lineup; thus it permits player comparisons across teams and different lineup slots.[5] The slugging average also has the advantage of including the third leg of the triple-crown, home runs.

The slugging average is just one example of a metric that is superior to the triple-crown statistics for judging hitters. Baseball fans have developed a wealth of statistics for measuring player performance. Determining which of these metrics is the best choice for valuing players requires a developing criteria for choosing the right measures.

Criteria for Evaluating Performance Metrics

A performance metric should be judged according to three criteria: (1) how it correlates with winning, (2) the degree to which it separates true ability from random chance, and (3) whether or not the information it conveys regarding performance matches reasonable intuition about what constitutes good performance.[6]

In baseball, teams strive to win, but assigning responsibility for wins to individual players on the team is difficult. For example, a common statistic used for judging pitchers, erroneously labeled "wins" (to avoid the confusion between a team win and a pitcher win I refer to the latter as "W") does a poor job of evaluating pitchers. I frequently hear television analysts comment that W's are the best metric for judging pitchers, because winning games is the goal of every team. As Hall-of-Fame player and ESPN announcer Joe Morgan recently stated, "The name of the game, people always want to forget, for pitchers is wins and losses."[7] This conclusion results from semantic confusion. A starting pitcher is credited with a W if he pitches at least five innings, his team is winning when he leaves the game, and his team holds a lead until the end of the game. This is very different from the sole criterion for a team win: the team scores more runs than the opposing team.

The problem with equating W's with wins is obvious: to earn a W the pitcher needs help from his offensive players, his relief pitchers, and the defenders behind him. Awarding a pitcher full credit for a win because he met the criteria for a W overestimates his contribution. A pitcher who pitches on a team with good hitters will receive more W's than if he was on a team with bad hitters. Conversely, a pitcher on a team with bad hitters will earn fewer W's than he would on a team with good hitters. Properly crediting pitchers for their contributions to winning requires using other measures that better reflect pitchers' abilities to help their teams win.

In baseball, the task of breaking down the game into components of responsibility is relatively easy compared to other team sports, because the teams take turns on offense and defense, and pitchers and batters engage in one-on-one contests. We can value offensive accomplishments for their run production and

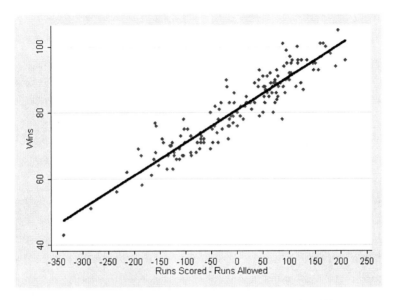

FIGURE 2-1   Relationship Between Wins and Run Differential (2003–2007)

defensive accomplishments for their run prevention. As a hitter produces more runs, or a pitcher prevents more runs, his team's chance of winning increases. Figure 2-1 reveals that there is a tight relationship between team run differential (runs scored – runs allowed) and winning, because the as the run differential rises and falls, so do wins.[8] Evaluating offensive and defensive ability in runs allows us to credit players for the aspects of the game they can control as well as to measure their contributions to winning in a common currency.

Evaluating Hitting

In order to evaluate how well performance metrics meet the first criterion for measuring contributions to winning, let's examine how closely several potential metrics correlate with runs scored on offense and runs prevented on defense, using a sample of team data from 2003 to 2007. The stronger the association between the metric and runs, the better the metric measures player contributions to winning. I chose eight hitting metrics that are sometimes used to judge hitters: batting average (AVG), on-base percentage (OBP), slugging average (SLG), on-base-plus-slugging (OPS), batter's run average (BRA), runs created (RC), regression-estimated runs (LSLR), and linear weights (LWTS).

The first three should be familiar to most baseball fans, and I discussed the batting average and slugging average above. The on-base percentage is the rate at which a player reaches base via a hit, walk, or hit-by-pitch relative to the number of times he steps to the plate. Like the batting average, it does not weight how a player reaches base; but, unlike the batting average, it includes other ways that a hitter can reach base.

The other metrics are commonly used by sabermetricians because they have a stronger correlation with run scoring than the preceding statistics. On-base-plus-slugging, more commonly known by its acronym OPS and popularized by John Thorn and Pete Palmer in *The Hidden Game of Baseball*, is simply the sum of on-base percentage and slugging average. Batter's run average is the product of the two metrics. While adding and multiplying these values together are not intuitive, the combined values correlate strongly with runs scored. Though OPS has its weaknesses, its most-attractive feature is that it is nearly as good an estimator of run production as more complicated metrics while being relatively easy to calculate with information available on the scoreboard.

Runs created, regression-estimated runs, and linear weights are estimators that convert many specific things that players do into expected runs scored, but they differ in their methods for estimating the impact of baseball events. Runs created was developed by Bill James; though, it has many variations I report its simplest formula: the sum of hits and walks, times total bases, divided by the sum of at-bats and walks. Regression-estimated runs uses historical team data to estimate the impacts of singles, doubles, triples, home runs, walks, and hit-by-pitches, stolen bases, and caught stealing on run scoring. The method uses *multiple regression analysis* to weight individual factors according to how much they impact runs. Multiple regression analysis uses changes in many variables across many observations to generate weights to account for the impacts of each factor (see Appendix A for further explanation). For example, the technique estimates that a singe is worth 0.62 runs and a double is worth 0.76 runs.[9]

Linear weights is similar to regression-estimated runs in that it assigns weights to the things that individual players do to produce runs; however, instead of estimating weights of baseball events from team outcomes using regression analysis, it uses play-by-play data to estimate expected runs that typically result from baseball events. This method was developed by operations research analyst George Lindsey. Thorn and Palmer expanded on Lindsey's work to update expected run-value weights from a more recent and larger sample of games. I use the "batting runs" linear weights formula to value hitters in later chapters, because it generates expected run values for nearly all the things that hitters do, including stealing bases.[10]

Figure 2-2 shows the graphs of eight different metrics and their correlations with run scoring. In each graph, the dark trend line maps the direction of the relationship; and, for all the metrics, better performance is associated with more run scoring. The line represents the linear "best fit" of the relationship between performance metric and runs scored calculated by minimizing the prediction error based of metric.[11] In most cases, the actual runs scored and the performance metric for teams do not fall on the line but are close to it. The further the dots are from the line, the weaker the relationship is between the metric and runs scored; dots clustered closely around the line indicate a stronger relationship. The graphs reveal that batting average is the metric least associated with scoring runs. On-base percentage and slugging average have a stronger association with run scoring than batting average, but are less correlated with run scoring than the more-advanced metrics.

The second criterion for choosing a performance metric is how well it reflects skill rather than luck. Though a player may have been involved in events that directly helped or hurt his team's run scoring, his performance was not necessarily the result of an ability, which the market ought to reward.

Imagine that you want to identify the best investment strategist in your neighborhood to handle your retirement. You decide to find your richest neighbor and ask his advice; after all, it's reasonable to assume that a good investor ought to be wealthy if he is good at managing money. However, upon finding this person you learn that he amassed his fortune by hitting the Powerball Jackpot. This doesn't reveal that playing the lottery is a smart business strategy: he got lucky. This example reveals why relying on metrics that are heavily influenced by luck to measure skill can be misleading. It is important not to reward or punish players for outcomes beyond their control when valuing players.

One method for gauging how well a metric captures talent versus luck is to observe how it fluctuates from one year to the next. Real skills should persist over time, while luck ought to fade away.[12] Table 2-1 reports correlation coefficients from season to season for hitters with more than 400 plate appearances in

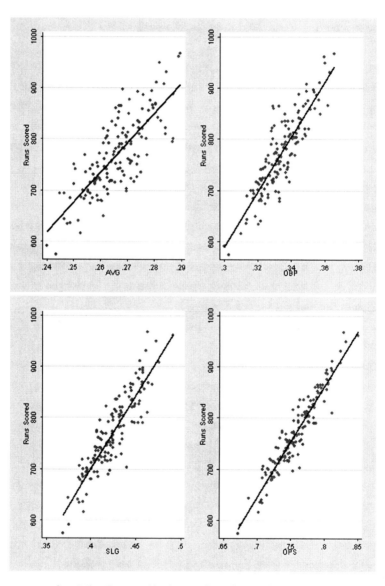

FIGURE 2-2   Correlation Between Metrics and Runs Scored (2003–2007)

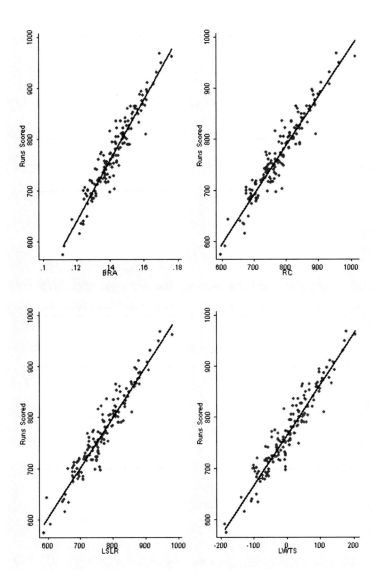

FIGURE 2-2   (continued)

back-to-back seasons. The absolute value of the correlation coefficients range from zero to one as player performances range from less to more similar across seasons.[13] The higher the correlation, the more stable player performance is in this area and the more likely it reflects ability than luck.

Metric	Correlation
AVG	0.4139
OBP	0.6542
SLG	0.6333
OPS	0.6388
BRA	0.6635
RC	0.5782
LSLR	0.5347
LWTS	0.6311

TABLE 2-1   Performance Correlation from Season to Season for Hitters (2003–2007)
>400 PAs for consecutive seasons

All the metrics vary similarly from season to season; however, batting average is the least stable of the bunch. This is not surprising, because hits are heavily influenced by random bounces on the field. Slow bleeders often dribble between fielders, and line drives may be hit directly at defenders, but in most cases bleeders result from bad hitting and "at-'em balls" reflect good hitting. Over a period of time, these occurrences normally even out, but occasionally luck can accrue in one direction. Avoiding volatile performance areas limits potential bias from luck. The high variance of batting average is one of the reasons that I do not like to use it for evaluating players.

Batting average is a major component of on-base percentage and slugging average; therefore, whenever I see a player's numbers in those areas rising above or falling below expectation, I immediately look to the batting average to see if it foretells a coming reversion. If a player's isolated on-base percentage (on-base percentage – batting average) and isolated power (slugging average – batting average) significantly deviate from past performance, then I normally expect the player to return to career form. For example, in 2004, Chipper Jones of the Atlanta Braves batted a measly .248, which was quite a departure from his .309 career batting average. At the time, many commentators thought Jones's career was nearing its end, and that his reduced production was a product of age. Instead, over the next four seasons Jones would bat .332 and win the batting title in 2008. Looking closer at Jones's numbers in 2004, it should have been clear that his down year was an anomaly. He was walking and hitting for power at his career rates; the problem was that his batting average was approximately 60 points below his career norm. Chipper Jones was unlucky on his hits in 2004; and, when all his other numbers remained stable, a rebound should have been expected.

It is important to acknowledge that other metrics being more stable than batting average does not mean that they are immune from luck. Bad and good luck are more likely to be prevalent in the batting average than the other metrics. Other metrics are also subject to random fluctuations; therefore, care must be taken when inferring skills from any performance metric.

At this stage it appears that several offensive metrics are highly correlated with run production and are similarly stable. Any of these metrics would do a fine job at estimating player value, but because I have to choose one metric for valuing hitters, I use the one that makes the most intuitive sense, which the third criterion requires.

OPS, battter's run average, and runs created measure batting skill, but do not include stolen bases. While, stealing bases is not as useful as it is often portrayed in the media, it is a valuable part of many players' games. For example, Carlos Beltran of the New York Mets has attempted to steal over 300 bases in his career, while being caught just twelve percent of the time. Few players can steal at such a high rate, but those who do offer quite a bit of value to their team. Regression-estimated runs and linear weights include stolen bases, but because linear weights uses average outcomes from game states it is better for evaluating individual players.

Regression-estimated runs suffers from a problem known as *omitted variable bias*, which occurs when factors omitted from the analysis are accidentally weighted by factors included in the analysis. Economist Ted Turocy noticed that when stolen bases, caught stealing, and triples are included in the regression model—variables correlated with player speed, and speed is not controlled for explicitly in the model—that the regression estimates assign incorrect weights to the included the factors. Therefore, regression-estimated runs are likely to generate biased weights of player contributions to run production. Linear weights don't suffer from this bias, because it credits the expected value from each event determined from play-by-play outcomes rather than estimating weights from the sum of team performance.

Evaluating Pitching

Measuring pitcher contributions to winning requires a slightly different approach. Unlike hitters, baseball fans typically judge pitchers according to how well they prevent runs using the earned run average, more commonly known as ERA. Denominating performance in runs is an advantage, but ERA is inferior to hitting metrics in other areas. While ERA suffers from some issues in attributing runs to different pitchers, its main problem is that it is heavily polluted by factors beyond the pitcher's control.

First, let's look at the impact of different pitcher performance metrics on run prevention at the team level. Figure 2-3 includes several graphs that map the relationship between runs allowed and several pitching performance metrics: ERA, strikeout rate, walk rate, and home run rate. ERA is far and away the best measure of run prevention, but this is expected. The way runs are credited to teams, only unearned runs—runs that were produced because of errors by the defense—are not included. Earned runs allowed and runs allowed are virtually the same thing at the team level. This is why the second criterion for evaluating performance metrics is so important.

For things that pitchers do to prevent runs without fielders—dish out strikeouts, issue walks, and give up home runs—the relationship with runs allowed is not particularly tight. This occurs because more than 70 percent of plate appearances result in a ball hit into the field of play, which requires the help of fielders. That this is a major component of a pitcher's ERA is unfortunate because pitchers do not appear to have much ability to affect this part of their game. Outcomes from balls in play are heavily random, which makes ERA unstable.

Table 2-2 lists the correlations from season to season for several pitching statistics. In particular, I focus on the main components of ERA: strikeouts (K9), walks (BB9), home runs (HR9), and batting average on balls in play (BABIP). Strikeout and walk rates are much more stable over time than ERA, while the home run rate stability is similar to that of ERA. BABIP measures the percentage of balls handled by fielders that become hits, and it is much less stable than ERA's components.[14]

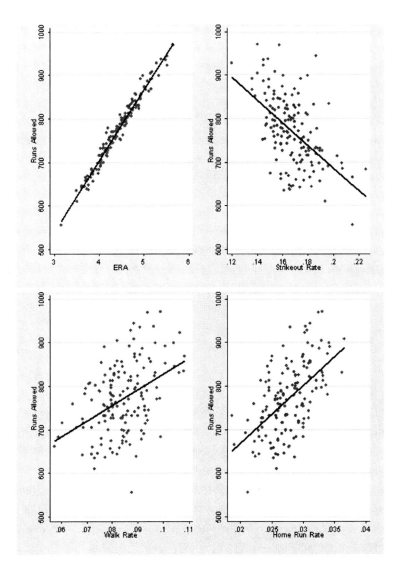

FIGURE 2-3   Correlation Between Metrics and Runs Allowed (2003–2007)

The heavy influence of the unstable BABIP on ERA caused sabermetrician Voros McCracken to develop a new metric for evaluating pitchers without looking at the hits they allow on balls in play: he called it the defense-independent

Metric	Correlation
ERA	0.30
K9	0.77
BB9	0.69
HR9	0.32
BABIP	0.18
DIPS ERA	0.54

TABLE 2-2   Performance Correlation from Season to Season for Pitchers (2003–2007)
>400 BFP for consecutive seasons

pitching statistics (DIPS) ERA. McCracken contended that pitchers had little ability to impact whether or not a ball put in play would become a hit. Because hits allowed on balls in play are a major determinant of ERA, the statistic is misleading. His DIPS ERA uses plays during which fielders do not participate in defense to predict performance of pitchers from season to season. It turns out that a DIPS ERA actually does a better job of projecting a pitcher's future ERA than his past ERA. By removing the noise generated on balls in play, we can better gauge pitcher quality and reward pitchers for ability rather than luck.

The last row of Table 2-2 lists the season-to-season correlation for the DIPS ERA that I use to value pitchers in Chapter 4, and it proves to be more stable than raw ERA. Though the DIPS components appear to be only moderate predictors of run prevention on their own, together they do a decent job, and they convey more information about pitcher quality than ERA. Figure 2-4 maps the predicted runs allowed estimated from the DIPS components relative to actual runs allowed. While the correlation with run prevention isn't as strong as raw ERA, this is expected because ERA is merely reporting what did happen on the field, which was heavily influenced by luck. The information provided by the defense-independent performance provides a sufficient prediction and dampens the impact of luck.[15]

The intuition criterion for pitching metrics is easily met by DIPS ERA. That pitchers who strike out many batters and give up few walks and home runs prevent more runs than pitchers who perform poorly in these areas is consistent with expectations regarding run prevention.

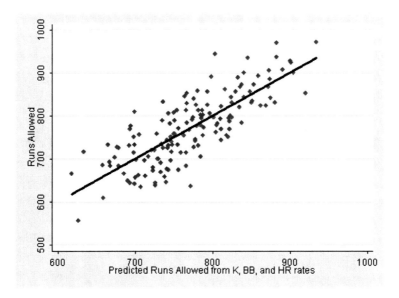

FIGURE 2-4   Predicted Runs Allowed from DIPS ERA

Evaluating Fielding

Defense behind pitchers also plays a role in preventing runs, and many players are prized for their defensive skill at turning likely hits into outs. Unlike hitting and pitching, few metrics exist for quantifying fielder contributions. Errors, the mainstream benchmark for measuring defensive ability, are deeply flawed by the fact that errors are based on the subjective judgment of scorers. Skilled scorers, trained to evaluate defense objectively, might be able to judge the fieldability of all balls hit into play consistently, but that is not how scorers assign errors. The basic criterion for recording an error on a play is that if a fielder looks like he should have made the play and did not record an out, he is credited with an error. This means that there are two ways to avoid errors: make plays or don't make it look like a play could be made. A fielder with stone feet won't come within fielding range of a ball that most average fielders would easily turn into an out; yet, an error won't be recorded because it didn't look like he could have gotten to the ball. On the other side, excellent fielders who flub plays that normal fielders wouldn't come close to making are credited with errors.

There have been a few attempts to generate alternative fielding metrics, but most suffer from inherent biases in their construction or calculation.[16] In 2004, Baseball Info. Solutions began recording a new fielding metric known as plus/minus. To remove some subjectivity from defensive analysis, plus/minus is calculated by mapping batted balls on a television screen using a grid. Players are then held responsible for fielding balls relative to their peers and are graded in terms of plays made above (plus) or below (minus) average. John Dewan, the founder of STATS, Inc. and Baseball Info Solutions, explains the objectivity of the recording:

> Every play is entered into the computer where we record the exact direction, distance, speed, and type of every batted ball. Direction and distance is done on a computer screen by simply clicking the exact location of the ball on a replica of the field shown on the screen . . ..
> The computer totals all softly hit groundballs on Vector 206, for example, and determines that these types of batted balls are converted into outs by the shortstop only 26% of the time. Therefore, if, on this occasion, the shortstop converts a slowly hit ball on Vector 206 into an out, that's a heck of a play, and it scores at +0.74. The credit for the play made, 1.00, minus the expectation that it should be made, which is 0.26. If the play isn't made—by anybody—it's −0.26 for the shortstop . . .
> Add up all the credits the player gets and loses based on each and every play when he's on the field and you get his plus/minus number (rounded to the nearest integer).[17]

According to *The Fielding Bible*, each play that a player makes above/below average costs the team between 0.56 and 0.76 runs, depending on the position played. Thus, the plus/minus numbers can be used to estimate how many runs a player adds or subtracts with his defense. While Dewan continues to tweak his system, and certainly there will be improvements, the basic core of what is being done is correct, and I feel safe using these measures to quantify the fielding prowess of position players. Because of its newness, I cannot evaluate its variance as I have done with the hitting and pitching metrics. However, having reviewed the system and viewing some of the raw data, I am satisfied that plus/minus provides a sufficient proxy for fielding skill, and, therefore, I will use it to value the defensive ability of fielders.

Summing Up

Performance metrics should be evaluated according to three criteria: (1) how well they correlate with winning, (2) the extent to which they measure ability instead of luck, and (3) if they make intuitive sense. Hitters who get on base and move around the bases with power and speed produce runs, and linear weights does a good job of measuring the many things that hitters do to produce runs. Pitchers who keep the other teams' hitters off the bases by striking out batters, preventing walks, and keeping the ball in the ballpark prevent runs. Though recording outs on fielding balls is a major determinant of runs allowed, pitchers appear to have little influence over preventing hits on balls in play. Therefore, a DIPS ERA should be used to estimate pitcher's run-prevention capabilities. Fielding is difficult to evaluate, but the newly developed plus/minus metric provides an objective measure of defense that avoids many of the problems that plague older measures of fielding ability.

Properly quantifying players' on-field contributions to winning is only the first step in valuing players, and there is still a bit more left to be done. Player performance isn't constant over time, it changes in a predictable rise-and-decline pattern due to aging. Valuing players requires knowing not only how good players are now, but how good they will be in the future. The next chapter looks to the past to see how performance tends to change with age. With this information, it's possible to generate long-term projections so that players can be valued over time.

Hot Stove Myth: Some Players are Clutch

Baseball announcers love to praise players for their ability to come through when the game is on the line. The problem is that our identification of players as "clutch" or "chokers" is largely based on inferences drawn from selective sampling of performance. It's true that players have hero and goat moments, but that doesn't mean that players who have them possess some sort of clutch skill that we can count on them to draw upon at the appropriate moment.

Performances in pivotal moments leave lasting memories that we sometimes use to make generalizations about player abilities that are wrong. A walk-off homer may cause us to forget the dozens of other times when player grounded out to end the game in an expected loss. And the pitcher who gave it up maybe never forgiven by fans, even though he's among the league leaders in strikeouts. As a Braves fan, I'll never forget Francisco Cabrera's miraculous single that scored Sid Bream from second base to win the 1992 National League Championship, but I never hope to see the light-hitting Cabrera at the plate or the slow-footed Bream on the base paths when the game is on the line ever again.

Whether some players rise to the moment or shrivel in the spotlight is an empirical question that has been studied by many researchers, and the general conclusion is that players don't seem to have any special clutch ability. For example, statisticians Jim Albert and Jay Bennett find that if any clutch ability exists its impact is small, and it is difficult to identify which players might have clutch skill.[18] Most studies of clutch ability take a set of aggregate performance in clutch and non-clutch situations and compare the outcomes using statistical tools. There is nothing wrong with this method, but it's possible that some of this clutch ability is getting lost in the noise of aggregate data. For example, when we compare hitters in clutch and non-clutch situations, it's difficult to account for the fact that the best pitchers tend to come in the game at that time, and the best players vary from team to team—it's not just pressure that distinguishes the situations. I think it would be better to look at performance at a more granular level to see how players performed in the clutch.

Using a sample of play-by-play data, I estimated the outcome of individual plate appearances while controlling for several potentially influential factors. I looked at three types of outcomes for hitters and pitchers: whether or not the batter gets a hit, whether or not batter gets on-base, and the number total bases the batter advances.[19] As a proxy for any clutch ability that a player might have, I used his performance with runners in scoring position (RISP) during the previous three seasons as an explanatory variable. If clutch performance is a skill, then past performance should be associated with RISP performance in the present. I also controlled for the general ability of the player by including his seasonal overall performance, the quality of the pitcher on the mound, and I identified whether or not the platoon advantage (batter and pitcher have opposite dominant hands) was in effect. The overall performance for hitters and pitchers is measured by batting average for hits, on-base percentage for reaching base, and slugging average for total bases. After accounting for all of these factors, if pitchers or hitters have clutch ability, then past RISP performance should predict present RISP performance.

The results presented in the table below strongly support the hypotheses that neither hitters nor pitchers have clutch ability. The table below reports the estimated impact of each factor on the likelihood of the outcome occurring, where a one-unit change in the predicting variable is associated with an X-unit change in the outcome variable at the average. For example, every one-point (0.001) increase in a batter's batting average is expected to increase a batter's likelihood of getting a hit by 0.00104.

Predicting the Outcome of Plate Appearances

	Hit	On Base	Total Bases
Hitters			
Past RISP	−0.06162	**0.00018**	**0.00012**
Batter Performance	**1.04**	**0.98**	**0.93**
Pitcher Performance	**1.152**	**1.031**	**0.983**
Platoon Advantage	**0.014**	**0.040**	**0.039**
Pitchers			
Past RISP	−0.02390	−0.00220	−0.11920
Pitcher Performance	**1.1801**	**0.8815**	**0.9702**
Batter Performance	**1.0148**	**1.0737**	**0.9816**
Platoon Advantage	**0.017**	**0.033**	**0.043**

Bold font indicates that the estimated relationship is statistically significant, meaning that the estimated effect is likely not zero. For the most part, the variables are statistically significant and fit with the general intuition about how they ought to predict the outcomes (e.g., better performance in the past is associated with positive outcomes). But among the clutch variables, in only one case does a player's past clutch performance appear to predict future clutch performance: getting on base for hitter. However, before we declare clutch "on-basing" to be a real skill, we need to look at more than statistical significance.

The estimate shows that every one-unit increase in RISP on-base percentage is associated with a 0.00018 increase in the likelihood of getting on base; thus, a player increasing his RISP on-base percentage by 0.010 (10 "points") increases his on-base probability by 0.0000018. For practical purposes, there is no effect here; especially when compared to the other factors in the model. The performance variables show a nearly one-for-one relationship with outcomes. The platoon advantage predictably increases the likelihood of getting a hit by 1.4 to 1.7 percent and reaching base by 3.3 to 4 percent—that is, 14 to 17 points in batting average and 33 to 40 points of on-base percentage. The expected number of total bases increases between 0.39 and 0.043 bases or 39 to 43 points of slugging average.

Those who wish to cling to the idea that clutch ability exists may identify imperfections in the analysis to justify their continued faith in clutch players. I admit, this study is imperfect, and so are many others that have been done by other researchers who have not found evidence of clutch skill. But, if clutch hitting is something that is so easy for baseball pundits to identify, then why isn't it showing up under a figurative microscope? The sheer number of observations makes statistical significance simple to achieve, yet, past clutch performance does not seem to predict present clutch performance with any reasonable certainty. If clutch ability exists, it is not readily identifiable among players and is, therefore, useless for evaluating players.

Chapter 3
A Career Guide From Little League To Retirement: Age And Success In Baseball

On July 2, 2006, Washington Nationals manager Frank Robinson grinned as he stood beside Carlos Lugo at a press conference to announce the signing of a 16-year-old shortstop prospect. Team president Stan Kasten could not hide his enthusiasm for his young acquisition, "This is an important signing. We can now compete for the best talent in Latin America. We will have a presence there." General Manager Jim Bowden could already see success in young Lugo's future, "He's a definite starter in the big leagues. He's an incredible shortstop." Nationals officials described him as possibly being capable of fielding like Ozzie Smith and hitting like Miguel Tejada.[20]

Lugo would join the Nationals' Gulf Coast League team for the following two years; in the latter year he posted a .906 OPS and won the league's MVP award. It seemed that Lugo was on the path to become what everyone thought he would be; but, in February 2009, all that changed. Publications that had previously ranked the young shortstop as one of the Nationals' top prospects would drop him off their prospect lists completely. Overnight, Lugo went from hot prospect to roster-filler fodder. Up until that time, Lugo had been known by a different name, Esmailyn Gonzalez, and he was not 19. Carlos Lugo was 23 years old—four years older than he claimed to be.

But what is the big deal? Lugo is not the first player to falsify his age; in fact, the ages of Latin American players have been somewhat of a joke for many years. When Alfonso Soriano was traded to the Rangers from the Yankees, it became known that he was 28, not 26 as he had previously claimed. Rafael Furcal's true age came to light after a drunk-driving conviction, when he aged from 19 to 22 to avoid an underage drinking charge. After being traded from the Orioles to

J.C. Bradbury, *Hot Stove Economics*, DOI 10.1007/978-1-4419-6269-0_3,
© Springer Science+Business Media, LLC 2011

the Astros in 2008, a media investigation uncovered that Miguel Tejada was two years older than his listed age. These cases differed from Lugo's because they happened to veteran players who had already established themselves as bona fide major-league stars.

Lugo wasn't a star yet: to big-league teams, "Esmailyn Gonzalez" wasn't a player, but a probabilistic asset that projected to be something special in the future. Had the age-fibs of Soriano, Furcal, and Tejada been discovered when they were much younger, the consequences probably would have been more severe. It's possible that Lugo will become a major-league talent, but the odds of doing so are much longer than what analysts once thought. Before players have established themselves as major-league caliber players, age is very important for projecting what that players will be. Why Lugo's sin was so great and why it impacted his asset value so severely can be seen as far back as little league.

The Relative-Age Effect

Several years ago, I volunteered as a coach for a youth little-league team in Sewanee, Tennessee. I thought returning to the environment that bread my love of the game would be a good experience, and it was. Our team's league served a small town of 2,000 residents, and thus the league's talent was spread quite thin across its four teams. Players ranged from ages eight to twelve, which was almost too much. The twelve-year olds towered over the youngest competitors whose optimal strategy was to crouch down low, try to earn a walk, and be prepared to dive out of the way of errant fastballs. It was no surprise that the team that won the league championship was the one with four twelve-year olds; and, it was obvious to everyone involved that age was the key determinant of success in this league. The maturity differences across players meant that the best players on the team were not the same as the most-talented players. Age provided such large advantages that younger children with superior abilities could not overtake their older rivals.

In fact, the most-talented player on my team was nine, and it wasn't even close. Timmy was a natural athlete, with dexterity, competitive drive, and intelligence. While most of his teammates cringed in fear as they stepped to the plate,

Timmy ran to the batters box with anticipation. He didn't goof off in the dugout—well, he goofed off less than anyone else—and often made insightful strategy suggestions.

Despite all of Timmy's natural advantages, he was overmatched by the older boys. He could hit the best pitcher's fastest fastball, but the ball wouldn't travel past the outfielders. His puny muscles just couldn't get the job done. And though he had the range to play shortstop, he needed a full running windup to get the ball to first from the hole. If a major-league scout had to pick who on the field might go on to play in the majors, none of the four guys with peach-fuzz mustaches hoisting the league championship trophy would be candidates, but Timmy might, because Timmy was only nine and would grow out of his deficiencies.

The four-year spread between the youngest and the oldest in my league was the same as the difference between Carlos Lugo and Esmailyn Gonzalez; however, the maturity difference between an eight- and a twelve-year-old is far more than the difference from 16 to 20. After all, other major-leaguers went on to have success after exaggerating their youth. It turns out that small age differences matter quite a bit; in fact, even one day can make a huge difference in the likelihood that a player will make it to the big leagues.

Timmy may have been the most-talented player on my team, but Edward was the best hitter. I knew that Edward was two years older than Timmy, because he palled around with Timmy's older brother, who was also on my team. As Edward launched a ball over the plastic orange landscaping barrier that served as the outfield fence for the little-league games, I thought to myself, "we're going to have a good team next year." I should have looked a little closer at the rule book; because, though Edward was only eleven, in the eyes of Little League Baseball he was in his last year of eligibility. Edward was born on July 31, and according to Little League rules, though he was technically eleven and would be entering sixth grade in the fall with all his other eleven-year-old friends, Edward was considered twelve. Edward would end up coming to our games next year to watch all his friends play, while he sat in the stands. He quit playing baseball altogether. If only his mother could have held out for one more day, Edward would have led our team to the league championship, and he might have made it all the way to the majors.

"Come on!" you say. "There was very little chance that he was going to play major-league baseball anyway." While this is true, it turns out that there are many Edwards out there, and this population of almost twelve-year olds who quit baseball includes adolescents who would have been major-leaguers. How do I know this? The evidence is in the distribution of major-league player birthdays.

Figure 3-1 lists the percentage of American-born players in the league by month of birth who debuted in the major leagues between 1970 and 2008.[21] The graph reveals an unusual trend: the months prior to the official Little League Baseball cutoff produce few players while the months just after the cutoff produce many players.[22] August has the highest birth percentage with just over eleven percent of all player birthdays, and the three following months are above the monthly average (8.33 percent, denoted by the horizontal dashed line). The percentage of players per birth-month tends to decline as months progress from August. June and July, the months just prior to the cutoff, are the least-represented birth-moths among major-league players.

The likely cause of the extreme disparity of births by month across major-league baseball players is that many pre-August summer-birthday children just

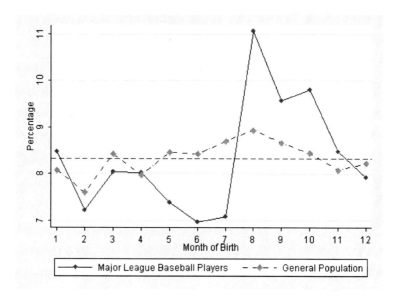

FIGURE 3-1   Percentage of US Births by Month for MLB Players

stopped playing baseball because they were the youngest of their age group, while the fall-birthday children, who were the oldest of their age group, kept playing. Adolescents like Edward have a choice: become the youngest player on a team at a higher level or chose to do something else. As all parents know, even talented children may just give up when tasks become difficult. When you are not good at something, especially relative to your peers, it looses its enjoyment. This is compounded by the fact that you are competing against individuals who enjoy a maturity advantage. You don't put forth the effort to acquire the necessary human capital needed to succeed at a higher level, because you're not having fun. This effect is exacerbated by coaches, players, and parents who are unaware of the relative-age effect—after all, the children are already organized with the same age group—may not offer the proper instruction, support, and encouragement to foster future success.[23]

An alternate explanation is that the birth-month percentages in baseball mirror the distribution in the general population. Fetal gestation would be consistent with conception during colder winter months (and after the World Series), and thus the distribution of births among major-leaguers could occur through natural means. The general population's birth-month distribution depicted on the graph shows that August is also the most frequent birth-month for all Americans. However, the difference from the average is not as extreme as it is for baseball players, and there is an increasing and decreasing trend before and after August. May, June, and July are three of the lowest birth-months for baseball players; however, for the general population, May through July are above-average birth-months. The birth-month distribution in baseball cannot be explained by the distribution of births in the general population.

Another possibility is that for some yet-known reason, children born in late-summer and early-fall have genetic advantages that provide them with superior athletic skills. It's a long-shot, but if this is the case, then among major-league players the birth-month advantages should exist across players. That is, better players should disproportionately come from August-born players relative to July-born players. It turns out that this is not the case. Figure 3-2 shows the birth distribution for American-born players who made an All-Star team during their career. While August produces a high number of All-Star representatives, the pattern is not consistent with the entire baseball population.[24] November

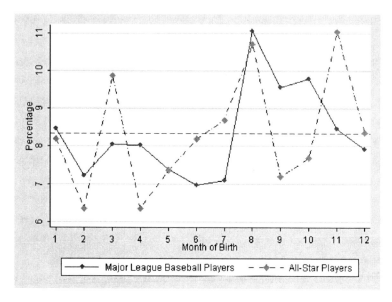

FIGURE 3-2   Percentage of US Births by Month, All-Stars and All Players

is the most common birth-month for All-Stars; July has an above-average num-ber of births, and September and October are below-average birth-months. Thus, your birth-month can help you get into the game, but once you are there it has little effect.

The relative-age advantage phenomenon is neither restricted to baseball, nor just to sports. Both soccer and hockey are populated with players who were born in January, February, and March, just after the standard December 31 cutoff dates for classifying youth participants into age groups for those sports. The relative-age effect has been documented to affect college attendance, confidence, and self-esteem, as well.[25] It is easy to imagine how this might affect a young athlete. Without confidence, it is difficult to muster up enough courage to step up to the plate to learn and improve. So, it appears that for the most whimsical of reasons—schools in Williamsport, Pennsylvania (the birthplace of Little League Baseball) used July 31 as their age-cutoff date—many children capable of playing major-league baseball just quit before they could grow into their talent.

But, as humans grow older, age differences matter less: the age-gap that was important in childhood eventually disappears. Two 18-year-old prospects, one born in July and one born in August, are going to be treated as equals when they show up for rookie ball. When they were younger, the August-born prospect would have been in a lower age group where he could dominate the less-mature competition, and the July-born prospect was disadvantaged by being the youngest of his age cohort. Thus, the prospects in the latter group are less likely to reach the stage where all players are treated equal, regardless of age.

There is some good news for summer-born children who have yet to start their youth baseball careers: in 2006, Little League Baseball changed its age-determination date to April 30. The unfortunate side effect of this change is that children born in March and April will be the new group to suffer from the relative-age effect. Baseball should be dominated by May- and June-born players in a decade or so. This will be a nice natural experiment for an enterprising social scientist to study several decades from now.

How Do Major-League Baseball Players Age?

It's one thing to know how age affects the probability that a child will reach the majors; however, for most fans, the interest is in how players age once they reach the big leagues. Estimating the value of players over time requires knowing how performance changes as players improve and decline with age. If players peak at 27, then a 25-year-old ought to be nearing his best work. If players peak at 30, then there may still be some life in a 32-year-old veteran.

There exists an extensive literature on the effects of age on athletic performance. In general, humans tend to improve into their mid-20s to early-30s before declining. In most athletic activities, athletes can become competitive at the top-level in their late-teens, and some athletes will continue to remain capable into their early-40s. This pattern is sometimes referred to as an "inverted U" to describe the shape of the aging curve. While the general shape of the aging function is similar across all humans, aging trajectories differ by gender and the athletic requirements of the activity. Women tend to peak earlier than men. Explosive speed and power tend to peak in the early-20s, while endurance and knowledge peak later, often into the early-30s.[26]

As baseball skills go, most tasks involve moderate amounts of athleticism; however, some areas of performances employ skills that age differently. Baseball is no doubt athletic, but when compared to other sports on a scale of athleticism, baseball is on the lower end. As veteran manager Jim Riggleman explained, "We're not running up and down a court. We're not playing football with equipment on in 100 degree temperature. It's a baseball game. It's not a physically taxing sport."[27] Thus, it's likely that baseball players peak in their late-20s to early-30s.

Only a few studies have looked directly at baseball, and the peak-age estimates fit within a broad range. In exercise physiology, studies have estimated player peak ages to be around 27 and 28, with some skills peaking earlier (base stealing) and others peaking later (walking).[28] Jim Albert, a statistician who has extensively studied baseball found peak age for hitters to range from 28 to 30, with later peaks occurring in the present relative to the past. Economist Ray Fair, who has studied aging in many athletic contests finds peak age to be 27 to 28 for hitters and 24 to 26 for pitchers. Several studies in the sabermetrics community have identified a peak age near 27, and I examine some of these studies in the Hot Stove Myth at the end of this chapter. Past studies reveal a wide range of ages at which players may peak, which indicates that the subject is in need of further study. Therefore, I conducted a new study to estimate the impact of age on player performance using major-league player careers to estimate the age-performance relationship, while controlling for factors that may bias the measurement of aging.[29]

Selecting a Sample

The first important step required for studying aging in baseball is selecting a sample of players to examine. Looking at every single player who played baseball creates a few problems. First, good players tend to enter the game earlier and leave it later than less-skilled players. This occurs because even before their skills are better developed and even after they have atrophied, good players are capable of playing major-league caliber baseball. This non-random entry and exit may bias the aging estimates, because the less-skilled players who enter the game in their mid-20s and depart by their mid-30s are not around to have their performances measured. If we looked at average player performances by age, players would look to be much better than they are in their early-20s and late-30s, because the players in the majors at these ages includes a sample of mostly excellent players. To remove this bias, I looked at players only during their age 24 to 35 seasons, with age calculated as days from birth to July 1 of the season of analysis divided by the average number of days in a year (365.25). It is important to measure age continuously—as opposed to assigning each player to a whole number "age"—because birthdays are not randomly distributed throughout the year.

Second, the sample must include players with significant playing time over many years to properly capture aging effects. A player who plays sparingly during a short career does not provide much useful information. In any given season, a player with few at-bats may look much better or worse than his true talent. A few lucky bounces and wind gusts can dramatically alter the overall numbers of a player with little playing time. For each season, I included hitters with 300 plate appearances and pitchers with 200 batters faced to provide a sufficient sample size to smooth out random events so that the numbers likely reflect true ability. Also, if a player does not have a long career, there is not a career trajectory to follow; thus, it will be difficult to discern yearly changes in performance from aging and random fluctuations in the data. A long career provides a history to track and establishes a baseline for the quality of each player. Thus, I looked at players who played at least ten years and had a minimum number of batter–pitcher confrontations—5,000 plate appearances for hitters and 4,000 batters faced for pitchers.[30]

The Playing Environment

One of the beloved aspects of baseball is that the playing dimensions are less uniform than in other sports, but this impacts how players perform. A hitter in Colorado will put up better numbers than he would in San Diego because of differences in park shape, weather, and altitude. As players move from team to team, it is necessary to adjust for the bias induced by playing half their games in the same park. Players who play in parks that help or hinder run scoring need to have their performances deflated or inflated to account for the effect. I employed adjustments based on performances of teams at home and on the road to account for park effects, which are applied to hitters and pitchers.[31]

Also, the era in which players play is vital for identifying aging, because baseball has seen drastic changes in its run environment over the course of its history. Figure 3-3 maps the runs per game by year and league since 1901. Imagine a player whose career began in the early-1980s in the National League and ended in late-1990s in the American League. His raw statistics might appear to show rapid improvement without suffering much of a decline simply because of changes in the run environment. First, I ignored seasons prior to 1920, when baseball was still developing, because differences in the rules and style of play were different from what they are today. While there is not an exact discrete point at which we enter the "modern era" of baseball, 1921 is a good place to start because it marks the prohibition of the spit-ball and the rise of the home run.

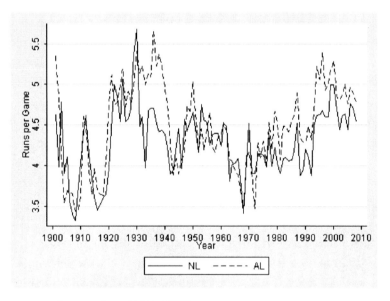

FIGURE 3-3   Runs per Game (1901–2008)

Second, I normalized all player performances to a common run environment, which is of utmost importance for comparing baseball players across eras. To do this, I evaluated each player's performance by season according to a *z-score*. A *z*-score is the difference from the sample average divided by the sample standard deviation (see Appendix A for further explanation). Each player is evaluated according to the distribution of performances by players in the league during each season of observation. Even as the league average rises and falls, each player's performance is adjusted to account for the fluctuation. Thus, a player who is one standard deviation better than average in one season is comparable to a player who is one standard deviation better than average in any other season. The adjustments yield a sample of 450 hitters and 436 pitchers over 86 seasons of play for a total of 4,627 and 4,154 observations of pitchers and hitters to evaluate.

I used multiple regression analysis to isolate the impact of age on performance while controlling for other factors to follow individual careers and estimate typical aging patterns. The effect of age on performance was estimated as a quadratic function—age and age-squared are used—which generates an aging curve that gradually increases to a peak and then gradually declines to produce the hypothesized inverted U shape. I used career performance to ground the performance estimates to the ability of each player, which differs considerably across players. For example, both Alex Rodriguez and Alex Gonzalez are shortstops who began their careers in 1994. The main difference between them isn't that Rodriguez is three years younger: A-Rod is simply a more gifted player, and his gifts are far more important for determining his performance than his age. Failing to include a talent baseline will cause the estimates to attribute changes to age that are really the product differences in ability between Rodriguez and Gonzalez. In a sense, accounting for career performance gives each player an aging curve for his own talent—Gonzalez will improve and decline similar to Rodriquez, but Rodriguez will always be performing at a higher level. I also used league-season identifier variables to control for league-wide changes in performance in any given year. Changes in performance that were felt league-wide—possibly due to new rules, parks, weather patterns, etc.—will be picked up by these indicators.[32]

Identifying Peak Performance

One way to gauge the impact of age on performance is to identify when players tend to reach their peaks. An advantage of using a quadratic function is that its peak is simple to calculate.[33] Table 3-1 lists the estimated peak ages for two over-all performance measures each for hitters and pitchers, and both player groups appear to peak around age 29. This is consistent with estimates of peak age in other activities that find highly athletic sports generating peaks in the early-20s while less-athletic sports that tend to have peaks in the late-20s/early-30s.

Performance Metric	Peak Age
Linear Weights	29.41
OPS	29.13
ERA	29.16
Runs Allowed	29.05

TABLE 3-1   Peak-Age Performance Estimates

The historical nature of the sample also permits analyzing changes in peak age over time. With advances in health and wealth, it would not be surprising to see modern players peaking later than their predecessors. However, one interesting finding among researchers studying aging in sports is that even though athletes continue to break performance records, the age at which athletes break these records has remained stable over time. Rather than pushing peak age higher, medical and training advances have simply allowed the athletes at their peak to outperform their predecessors. While there is little doubt that today's athletes are superior to past athletes, *when* athletes are the best they can be in their life cycles has not changed.[34]

Table 3-2 lists peak ages by decade of birth using linear weights for hitters and ERA for pitchers. At first glance, there appears to be some evidence for increasing peaks: the oldest cohorts of hitters and pitchers have the lowest peaks, and the most recent cohorts have the highest peak age for hitters. However, there is not a continuous rise in peak age from decade to decade. Hitters born in the 1910s have a higher peak than hitters born in the 1930s and 1950s. The highest peak age among the pitchers occurs among pitchers born in the 1920s; and, four of the peak age estimates are not statistically significant.

	Peak Age	
Decade	Hitters	Pitchers
1900s	28.05*	27.61
1910s	29.17	28.71
1920s	29.45*	31.61
1930s	28.45*	29.28*
1940s	29.48*	30.22
1950s	28.59*	28.42*
1960s	30.53*	29.31*

TABLE 3-2   Peak-Age Estimates by Birth Decade
*Statistical significance at 5% level

It is unclear whether the stable-peak-age phenomenon exists among baseball players. Baseball players may be peaking a little later than they used to, but it is difficult to determine if this is a product of random variation or a change in aging. If peak ages for hitters and pitchers have risen, they have done so only by a small margin—say, from 29 to 30.

The data can also be used to investigate the different components of player performance, because certain skills may peak earlier than others. For batters, hitting requires swinging at pitches followed by running around the bases. As players age, declines in bat- and foot-speed may cause power numbers to drop, especially as players have trouble legging out doubles and triples. In terms of walking, acquired knowledge of the strike zone, opposing pitchers' tendencies, and friendships with umpires are possible attributes likely to be acquired with age. In addition, players may compensate for diminished hitting ability by trying to draw more walks, because they know they can't get around on fastballs. It is similar to a strategy used by golfers who chose to compensate for diminished driving distance by hitting more fairways.[35]

Table 3-3 lists the peak-age estimates for several performance categories. The peaks are consistent with previous findings regarding aging in different skills. On-base percentage peaks at age 30, slightly later than the overall peak; however, its main components, the walk rate and batting average peak five years apart. It is no surprise that walks peak much later considering that walking involves little athletic skill, while hitting requires hand–eye coordination and strength. Players may also adjust their plate strategy to include more walks in order to compensate for the loss of hitting ability.

Performance Metric	Peak Age
On-Base Percentage	30.04
Slugging Average	28.58
Batting Average	28.35
Walk Rate	32.30
Double-Plus-Triples Rate	28.26
Home Run Rate	29.89

TABLE 3-3   Peak-Age Estimates by Performance Categories (Hitters)

Slugging average peaks close to batting average, but breaking the extra-base hitting down into its components reveals another interesting finding. The doubles-plus-triples rate peaks approximately a year and a half earlier than the home run rate; thus, it appears that the loss of hitting power may have more to do with foot-speed as opposed to hitting strength. Home run hitting also may involve better pitch recognition that is acquired with age. Even though batting average and slugging average begin to fall in a player's late-20s, the improved walk rate is sufficient to offset the overall decline for about a year.

The differences among the components of overall performance for pitchers are striking. Table 3-4 lists the peak-age estimates for strikeouts, walks, and home runs per nine innings pitched. The peak of the aging function for striking out batters is at 23.56 years, which is close to the average rookie age of 24. This means that pitchers' strikeout ability appears to be near its peak almost as soon as they enter the league. The good news is that pitchers seem to be able to compensate for the loss of strikeouts by improving in other areas. Walks peak nine years later at around 32, and home run prevention peaks at 27. Even as the abilities to strike out and prevent home runs wane, pitchers continue to improve enough at preventing walks to improve their overall performances into their late-20s.

Performance Metric	Peak Age
Strikeout Rate	23.56
Walk Rate	32.47
Home Run Rate	27.39

TABLE 3-4   Estimates of the Impact of Age on Performance Categories (Pitchers)

It is interesting that the late peak in walk prevention for pitchers corresponds with the walk production peak for hitters. Based on hitters alone, it would be difficult to determine whether the late peak was a product of veteran knowledge or a strategic response to compensate for declining skills in other areas. Pitchers cannot improve their walk rates by not pitching, unlike hitters who can earn more walks by simply swinging the bat less—also the preferred strategy of nine-year-old little-leaguers. Pitchers must exert effort with every pitch, and for pitches placed in the strike zone, the effort must be of high quality or it will result in hits by the opposing batters. Veteran know-how appears to be a significant contributor to walk rates improving with age.

Of the three pitching components examined here, it is not surprising that strikeout ability is the first skill to deteriorate. Strikeouts typically come from high-velocity power pitchers who must rely on arm strength and elbow ligament integrity. With age, strength begins to dissipate, and the ligament begins to stretch with repeated use like underwear elastic. This is why many pitchers have ligament-replacement surgery, more commonly known as "Tommy John" surgery, named for the first pitcher to undergo this procedure and return successfully to the majors.

Mapping Aging Functions

Identifying performance peaks is useful, but the estimates also map aging functions of players that can be used to project performance changes over time. What will that young prospect become, and when will the veteran All-Star become a bench player? These are practical questions that are important to real and fantasy general managers. The aging functions can be used to project how players will perform over the course of a career cycle. Tables 3-5 and 3-6 report the change in performance as a percentage of peak performance.[36] The peak ages are shaded dark gray, and the ages where performances are less than 2 percent of the peak are shaded light gray. The overall measures show that though players experience a pattern of improvement and decline, the change is not dramatic.

For hitters, the impact of age on on-base percentage is a little steeper than it is for slugging average, and thus the aging slopes for OPS lie in-between its components. Batting average is quite stable over time with player performance declining less than two percent from its peak from age 24 to 33. Home run hitting has the tightest peak with only three years within two percent of the peak. The

Age	OPS (%)	OBP (%)	SLG (%)	AVG (%)	BB (%)	DPT (%)	HR (%)
22	−7.09	−9.65	−6.94	−3.50	−25.87	−12.52	−56.42
23	−5.24	−7.40	−4.98	−2.49	−21.09	−8.83	−43.02
24	−3.67	−5.45	−3.35	−1.64	−16.79	−5.78	−31.43
25	−2.38	−3.79	−2.03	−0.97	−12.98	−3.38	−21.66
26	−1.37	−2.44	−1.04	−0.47	−9.66	−1.61	−13.70
27	−0.63	−1.38	−0.37	−0.15	−6.83	−0.48	−7.55
28	−0.18	−0.62	−0.03	0.00	−4.49	0.00	−3.22
29	0.00	−0.16	0.00	−0.03	−2.64	−0.16	−0.70
30	−0.10	0.00	−0.30	−0.23	−1.27	−0.95	0.00
31	−0.48	−0.14	−0.91	−0.60	−0.39	−2.39	−1.11
32	−1.14	−0.57	−1.85	−1.15	0.00	−4.47	−4.04
33	−2.08	−1.30	−3.12	−1.87	−0.10	−7.19	−8.78
34	−3.30	−2.33	−4.70	−2.77	−0.68	−10.56	−15.33
35	−4.80	−3.66	−6.61	−3.84	−1.76	−14.56	−23.70
36	−6.57	−5.29	−8.83	−5.08	−3.32	−19.20	−33.88
37	−8.62	−7.21	−11.38	−6.50	−5.37	−24.49	−45.88
38	−10.96	−9.44	−14.25	−8.09	−7.91	−30.42	−59.69

TABLE 3-5   Percent Difference in Performance from Peak (Hitters)

Based on sample mean at estimated peak age

Age	ERA (%)	K9 (%)	BB9 (%)	HR9 (%)
22	11.33	−0.19	29.81	6.87
23	8.39	−0.01	24.37	4.54
24	5.88	0.00	19.48	2.69
25	3.82	−0.16	15.14	1.32
26	2.21	−0.49	11.34	0.42
27	1.03	−1.00	8.09	0.00
28	0.29	−1.68	5.38	0.05
29	0.00	−2.52	3.22	0.58
30	0.15	−3.55	1.60	1.59
31	0.74	−4.74	0.53	3.06
32	1.77	−6.10	0.00	5.02
33	3.24	−7.64	0.02	7.45
34	5.16	−9.35	0.58	10.35
35	7.52	−11.23	1.69	13.74
36	10.31	−13.28	3.34	17.59
37	13.56	−15.51	5.53	21.92
38	17.24	−17.90	8.27	26.73

TABLE 3-6   Percent Difference in Performance from Peak (Pitchers)

Based on sample mean at estimated peak age

other individual performance areas have steeper slopes, which counter-balance one another in the overall measures.

Pitchers show a similar pattern, with ERA gradually rising and falling. Though strikeout ability peaks earlier than the other skills, it deteriorates at a slower rate than walk and home run prevention. A pitcher who strikes out five batters per nine innings at 24 will be striking out 4.5 per nine innings at 34. Even though pitchers are losing their ability to strikeout batters the moment they enter the league, good strikeout pitchers tend to remain good strikeout pitchers.

The aging functions also reveal the gradual impact of aging. I often hear commentators refer to aging as if it were an Egyptian pyramid, steep with a pointed peak. However, the performance improvement and decline of baseball players are quite gradual, such that it's probably best to compare aging curves of baseball players to the roof of the Arizona Diamondbacks' Chase Field, slightly rounded and almost flat at the peak. For example, take a player who will peak with an .800 OPS at 29. From age 25 to 33 his expected OPS will lie above .780. Yes, some players do "fall off a cliff" at the end of their careers—sometimes in their early-30s—but such occurrences are unlikely to be the natural product of aging. An abrupt performance decline is normally the product of a major injury or another significant event. General managers who sign players in their 30s should expect a decline; but, the decline is so gradual that an excellent player will continue to be a good player for many years beyond his peak.

The estimates reveal the aging functions for hitting and pitching; however, an important facet of the game that I have not addressed is fielding. At this time, I do not believe that any suitable defensive metrics exist over a long enough period to evaluate aging. Maybe in a few years sufficient plus/minus data will be available to track aging in fielding ability, but until that time, I suggest relying on the body of academic studies that show athletic contests requiring quick bursts of speed tend to peak earlier than other skills. Defensive ability likely peaks slightly earlier than hitting ability because of its higher athletic requirements; therefore, the total value of a player may peak slightly earlier than the hitting estimates. Given that the bulk of position players' value is tied up in hitting—about five times more valuable according to the estimates of average performance in Chapter 4—I think the correct course is to use the batting estimates to project the aging patterns of position players. I'll leave it to readers to subtract a quarter year, year, multiple years, etc. if they see fit to do so.

Is the Sample Biased?

The aging function estimates the impact of age on players within a fairly restricted sample of players, which invites the question as to how applicable the estimates are to all baseball players. A sample of players with sufficiently long careers means that the players analyzed are likely to be above-average performers. An ideal sample would be composed by players of different quality who took the same number of plate appearances over a set number of years. This sample doesn't exist because managers and fans want to see the best players play, and no one really cares about ruining a social science experiment.

Good or bad, baseball players are all human beings with similar physiology. Aging occurs in all humans whether they play baseball or not; thus it is likely that aging affects all players similarly. Still, the possibility exists that the attributes that make some players better than others allow good players to age more gracefully. After all, if physical gifts differentiate the players from one another, it is not too far a stretch to imagine the gifts that generate superior performance also slow the aging process. Though it is impossible to observe inferior players excluded from the sample, it is possible to see if the best players in the sample age differently than the entire sample. Table 3-7 reports the peak ages of Hall-of-Fame players in the metrics listed above and reports the differences from the full-sample estimates.

	Peak Age		Difference	
Performance Metric	HOF	Full Sample	Raw	%
Hitters				
Linear Weights	28.51	29.41	−0.90	−3.06
OPS	28.52	29.13	−0.61	−2.09
On-Base Percentage	29.80	30.04	−0.24	−0.80
Slugging Average	27.81	28.58	−0.77	−2.69
Batting Average	27.92	28.35	−0.43	−1.52
Walk Rate	32.44	32.30	0.14	0.43
Doubles-Plus-Triples Rate	32.72	28.26	4.46	15.78
Home-Run Rate	28.54	29.89	−1.35	−4.52
Pitchers				
ERA	29.08	29.16	−0.08	−0.27
Runs Allowed	28.89	29.05	−0.16	−0.55
Strikeout Rate	—	23.56	—	—
Walk Rate	33.45	32.47	0.98	3.02
Home-Run Rate	25.94	27.39	−1.45	−5.29

TABLE 3-7   Peak Age Estimates of Hall-of-Fame Players

For the most part, the estimates are similar to the estimates using the full sample. If anything, Hall-of-Fame players peak earlier, rather than later, than the full sample of players, with a few notable exceptions. For hitters, the doubles-plus-triples rate peaks four-and-a-half years later for Hall-of-Famers than for the full sample. One possible explanation for this is that exceptional players improve and maintain their foot-speed longer than most players, possibly due to continued practice and fitness training to maintain health.

The other odd result is for strikeouts, for which the regression estimates strikeout performance declines and improves with age—a counterintuitive result that we should probably ignore. Of the estimates for Hall-of-Fame pitchers, only walks generated statistically significant estimates. The small sample of pitchers—26, compared to 75 hitters—does not generate estimates in which we should have strong confidence. Even in the case of hitters, I am not sure how much should be drawn from the estimates, as the reduced sample allows a few players to affect the estimates. Overall, the excellent players did not appear to age much differently than good players.

Another avenue for determining if the abilities of players in the sample age differently from excluded players is to see how ability is correlated with another aspect of aging: mortality. Sociologists Jarron Saint Onge, Richard Rogers, and Patrick Krueger examined the life expectancies of major-league baseball players and found that though major-league baseball players tended to live five years longer than average US males, performance on the field was not associated with longevity. Thus, in a second area where it is possible to observe the impact of performance on another aspect of aging, researchers do not find performance to be correlated with aging.

As a final test, I also lowered the requirements for being included in the sample to 1,000 career plate appearances, eliminating the number of seasons requirement, and including players of all ages. Figure 3-4 compares the restrictive-sample aging estimates reported in my study to the less-restrictive sample and compares them at their peaks for linear weights. The functions peak at nearly the same time and the slopes are similar. While I prefer the more-restrictive sample to avoid some of the problems discussed above, this comparison indicates that the sample doesn't appear to be biasing the estimates.

Between the Hall-of-Fame estimates, the mortality study, and the robustness of the estimates in a much larger sample, I think it is best to assume that the estimates of aging reported here are applicable for projecting aging effects for all players, not just good players. Yes, some players will age different than others for reasons that are difficult to identify, but the estimates provide a general aging function to use as a benchmark.

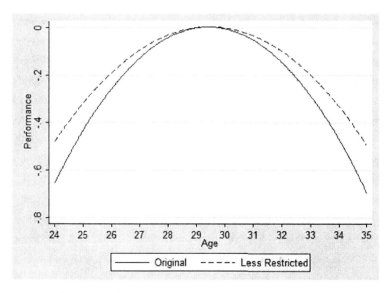

FIGURE 3-4   Estimated Aging of Hitters (LWTS)

Financial Implications

A curious aspect of baseball's service-class system is that players tend to finish up their last arbitration year just as they peak. The average age of baseball rookies is 24, which means after six years of providing below-market services to his team a typical player is just reaching his peak as he hits the free-agent market. Peaking at this moment has potentially positive and negative consequences. On the positive side, the player is most likely playing the best baseball of his career right at the time that many clubs are bidding on his services. By putting his best foot forward, a free agent may be able to get a bigger contract than if he had been granted his free agency earlier. However, this requires quite a bit of ignorance on the part of front-office personnel. While there may be some question of when exactly baseball players reach their peak performance level, I suspect that most general managers understand that 30-year-old free agents are entering the decline phase of their careers. Thus, as players enter the free-agent market their most valuable years may be behind them.

The impact of age on performance means that the service-time rules governing player compensation disproportionately harm less-talented players than more-talented players. Superstars usually begin their major-league service time earlier than marginal players; thus, they enter free agency at a younger age, with possibly several good years of improving performance ahead of them. For example, Ken Griffey, Jr. entered the league at 19, and became eligible for free agency when average players typically begin their reserved indenture. Some poor players may never see the benefits of free agency, as they are only good enough to play in the league for a few years around their peak, and thus have already aged out of the league before their service-time requirement is fulfilled.

* * *

This brings us back to the saga of Carlos Lugo. The .906 OPS and MVP award he produced in 2008 may have seemed impressive, but as ESPN's Keith Law would write, "the age change all but ends Gonzalez's status as a prospect; a 23-year-old prospect should be in Double-A, not the Gulf Coast League, and his performance as a 23-year-old GCL repeater is completely unimpressive."[37] Rather than being a decade away from his peak playing against players of similar physical maturity, Lugo was four years closer to his peak, playing against boys far less mature than he was. In the unlikely event that he does make it to the big leagues, his career will be brief and he will be more remembered for his off-field deception than his on-field performance.

Summing Up

The rise and decline of performance with age has considerable impact not only on how major-league performance changes over time, but also who chooses to become baseball players. Age cutoffs that put children into age categories have the unintentional effect of pitting children with large gaps against one another. This allows the older children in each category to excel because of a maturity advantage, which results in players with favorable birthdays (post-July in baseball) having an advantage that leads to an increased likelihood of success in the future.

After reaching the big leagues, players typically improve through their twenties, peak just before their 30th birthdays, and then decline. The rise and decline differs with player skills, with speed and strength peaking earlier, while endurance and knowledge peak later. The performance changes over the course of a player's career are gradual, and when players reach their peak has not changed much over baseball's history.

Now that we know how players contribute to winning and how that contribution is expected to change over time, we can progress toward assigning dollar values to players based on their performance. In the next chapter, I explain how winning affects teams' bottom lines to convert on-field performance into dollars.

Hot Stove Myth: Players Peak at 27

If you follow discussions of aging among sabermetricians, then the results presented in the preceding chapter may seem surprising. For many years there has been a strong consensus among this community that baseball players peak at age 27, and this belief is supported by several studies. I want to use this aside to address some of the weaknesses of these studies.

The origin of the age-27 peak stems from a 1982 chapter from *The Bill James Baseball Abstract* in which James wrote:

> There is no set of questions in the game which, as a practical need, are any more crucial to a team than those of aging . . . .
> And yet, incongruously, incredibly, baseball's accumulated wisdom on the subject for many years consisted of little more than a pat, one-size-fits-all truism about the prime of a player's career being 28 to 32, and that one truism is blatantly false.[38]

In the chapter, James casually explored several methods for evaluating the aging patterns of baseball players. The central empirical study of his analysis looked at the total value generated by all players at each age level. Using his "Value Approximation Method" (VAM), James converted the performance of individual players into a single number and then summed the total value produced by all players born in the 1930s by age. Age-27 produced more total value than any other age.

But, there are a few problems with interpreting the data as demonstrating 27 is the age at which players play their best baseball. First, the sum of VAM values by age group is influenced by more than just the quality of players in the sample, the *quantity* of players is also important. Most players will get their first shot at baseball earlier rather than later. The league is constantly replenishing itself with younger talent, much of which is marginal and will not remain in the league for long. These borderline players will be at their best as they approach their late-20s, and, therefore, this is when they will enter the league.

The sum of VAM is highest in the age-27 category not because every player is at his peak at this age, but simply because there are many 27-year olds in the league. Twenty-seven is close enough to the peak for players to generate good VAMs, but still young enough to capture the time when teams still consider holding on to players who may not pan out as prospects. All good players play baseball at 27; but most bad ones do too, and they don't play much beyond that age. The sheer number of 27-year olds in the league raises the total value produced by the age group; thus, the sum of value produced by age tells us very little about the aging process.

A second problem with James's analysis is that the VAM metric he relied is suspect. James would eventually abandon VAM because it was, in his own words, "ultimately undermined by the lack of logic behind it."[39]

But James is not the only person to identify peak age to be around 27. Two other methods have been employed by sabermetricians to identify when players peak.[40] While there is useful information contained in these studies, I believe they suffer from biases that my analysis avoids.

One approach, commonly known as the "delta" method, identifies players who played in consecutive seasons and observes how their performances changed from season to season. The data contains significant noise—some players improve, others decline—but averaging all players' changes generates a general aging trend. Unfortunately, this method is subject to a bias in sample selection from who gets to play that pushes the estimated peak below its true peak.

Playing time is a function of present performance and past performance. A good performance in the past will keep you in the lineup even if you slump through the short term. Bad performance in the past will prevent playing in the future. To have a two-year sample you have to reach the playing-time minimum in consecutive seasons, and this creates the problem. For simplicity, let's assume that players can have two types of seasons (good or bad), generating the following combinations of seasons in a two-year sample: good–good, good–bad, bad–good, and bad–bad. We'll get plenty of the first two types of seasons, but the latter two won't get the opportunity to occur. The draws from year 1 to year 2 talent pools are not random, because the lucky-good can go from good to bad, but the lucky-bad don't get the opportunity to go from bad to good. I call this phenomena the survivor effect.

The survivor effect can be seen in the following example. Imagine we have two players who are both true .750 OPS hitters. In year 1, Gary Goodseason hits .775 and Bill Badseason hits .725. Both players' actual performances deviate from their true abilities as a result of random fluctuations, but it's difficult to know that Gary and Bill are equally talented players from this one-year sample. How can a general manager know that Bill is a true .750 OPS player who had bad luck rather than a .700 OPS player who had some good luck? In most cases, Gary is going to be considered better than Bill. Bill likely won't get the opportunity to play in year 2 to have a corresponding upward rebound, while Gary likely will play in year 2 when his performance is apt to fall. Thus, when we average in the changes for many Garys, but not a lot of Bills, we will see more declines than improvements. The delta method is going to capture declines that have nothing to do with aging and thus underestimate when players peak.

If the survivor effect biases average performance changes downwards, then why do we see any positive improvement up to the mid-20s at all? The survivor effect is less relevant when players are younger, because the aging function is steeper at this point (meaning improvements are larger and likely to overcome bad luck) and managers expect improvement and will be more tolerant of one bad year ("Tough year, kid. Hang in there."). For older players the effect is the opposite. Having a hard-luck year at 36 may cause teams to disallow a bounce-back year because they believe the decline is a sign that his career is over. In summary, the delta method estimates of peak age will underestimate peaks and overestimate declines in performance because its sample-inclusion requirements favor players who are likely to decline for reasons other than age.

Another method for identifying peak age is to find the most common (or "mode") age at which players typically have their best season. The mode method is also likely to estimate peak age to be younger than the true peak.

The reason for the downward bias is that there are two main factors that cause players to decline: aging and random non-aging-related injuries. An example of the former is when a player's reflexes slow and he can't get around on a fastball. An example of the latter is when a player blows out his knee sliding hard into a base and he never heals to reach his original potential. Players decline and leave the sport for both reasons, but the latter is definitely not aging. When we look at the mode, we are not differentiating from the cause of deterioration. Because of non-aging attrition, more players will have an opportunity to have their best season earlier than later. The thing is, it isn't predictable who will suffer these injuries (though some injuries are associated with age). The attrition isn't aging, and players who avoid injuries should improve beyond the mode best season. The mode method is also not very helpful for measuring aging rates: we can find peaks, but can't track the path to and from them. If we want to know if a 27-year-old free agent will decline or improve, knowing that the most common age for peaks is 27 doesn't answer the important question we're asking.

In conclusion, though several sabermetricians have investigated when baseball players peak, I believe that the methods employed suffer from biases that result in an estimate that is too low. Though Bill James may have been responsible for introducing the notion that players peak at 27, in his essay he acknowledges the weaknesses in his own study and offers many keen insights on what future studies of aging need to address. He concludes the chapter in a tone that is demonstrably softer than its introduction and puts forth a general dictum on aging with which I wholeheartedly agree.

> Good hitters stay around, weak hitters don't. Most players are declining by age 30; all players are declining by age 33. There are difference in rates of decline, but those differences are far less significant for the assessment of future value than are the differing levels of ability.[41]

Part II
Translating Performance Into Dollars

Chapter 4
Putting A Dollar Sign On The Muscle: Valuing Players

Valuing baseball players is something that professional baseball teams have been doing since their inception. Enterprising businessmen founded teams because they saw a profit opportunity: fans liked baseball and were willing to pay to see it. This caused owners to build fields, erect stands, and hire players to play games in order to attract paying customers. Owners soon learned that fans preferred winners to losers, which meant stocking rosters with better players to generate more revenue at the gate.

As new teams popped up around the country, players began to find competition for their services. To get a jump on the competition, owners dispersed armies of scouts to scour the land for the best talent. Some players were signed after organized amateur games, with the top talent going to the highest bidder. Or an unknown gem might be plucked off a rural farm for virtually nothing after a scout witnessed him plunking crows with rocks with deadly accuracy. Other times, a major-league club would pay a minor-league owner a fee to purchase a player from his roster. In every case, owners were all business when signing players, making money by putting a "dollar sign on the muscle," as Brach Rickey famously described the rational business calculation. Kevin Kerrane would use Rickey's description as the title of his classic book on scouting, because it described what the scouts he interviewed were doing. In baseball's early days, estimates of player worth may have been more educated guesses than explicit calculations, but roster management has always been a business decision.

In his seminal 1974 paper in *American Economic Review*, economist Gerald Scully published his method for estimating player revenue contributions from on-field performance. The paper garnered much attention, not just because it

J.C. Bradbury, *Hot Stove Economics*, DOI 10.1007/978-1-4419-6269-0_4,
© Springer Science+Business Media, LLC 2011

shed light on baseball's unique business, but because performance data provided an opportunity to apply economic theory to an area that is difficult to measure in practice. The contributions of everyday workers are not as visible as they are among baseball players. Though admittedly crude, his method represented the first attempt to place a dollar value on baseball players outside of a baseball front office. His technique was quite simple: estimate the value of wins, determine how much individual performances contribute to winning, and use this information to impute the values of players.

Scully's estimates helped settle an argument between players and owners regarding player salaries. At the time, players claimed that they were vastly underpaid, while owners pleaded that their operations were skirting financial ruin. Prior to introduction of free agency in 1976, the reserve clause bound all players to play for the team that owned their rights. After initially signing with a team, a player who didn't like his team's future contract offers could either accept the terms or walk away. Considering that there were few other opportunities for professional baseball players, Major League Baseball teams held considerable bargaining power over their employees. Scully's estimates indicated that players earned salaries far less than the revenue they generated, and thus team owners were extracting a large fraction of the revenue generated by players. His findings would soon be tested with the advent of free agency, and free-agent salaries jumped as he predicted they would. And updated estimates in the mid-1980s showed that owner collusion was suppressing the wages of free agents below their estimated worth.[42]

Scully's approach was grounded in labor economics, estimating a player's value in terms of his *marginal revenue product* (MRP). Marginal revenue product is an economics term that refers to the added dollar value of output provided by an additional unit of an input. It is calculated by counting up the output generated from an input and then multiplied by the revenue that the additional unit produces. For example, if hiring an additional worker in a baseball factory produced ten extra baseballs a day that can be sold for $5 a piece, then the worker's estimated marginal revenue product for the day is $50. The output from baseball's labor market can be measured similarly. Players are inputs that produce wins for their teams, which teams translate into revenue. A player who generates a win for his team in a market where an additional win is worth $5 million will have a marginal revenue product of $5 million.

In a perfectly competitive labor market many employers bid against each other for employees who generate value to the hiring firm. An employer ought to be willing to pay employees a salary that is less than or equal to his marginal revenue product. For example, a team would gladly pay $10 million for a player who generates $15 million in revenue to the team. Though a player might be willing to play baseball for less—for most of baseball's history players were willing to work for wages far below their revenue-generating value—economic theory suggests that the final wage should approach $15 million. The reason for this is that as long as the projected revenue produced by the player exceeds the contract offer, other teams ought to be willing to offer higher salaries until the wage approximates his marginal revenue product.

More recently, another economist developed an alternative method for estimating player marginal revenue products, which he called the "free market returns" approach. DePaul economist Anthony Krautmann used market prices for free agents—something that didn't exist when Scully first estimated player marginal revenue products—to value players' on-field contributions. The use of market prices to impute the value of assets based on its components is known as hedonic pricing. It's the method employed by loan officers for estimating the value of a mortgaged house to ensure the home's value serves as sufficient collateral for the loan. By looking at how home prices vary according to differences in location, age, square-footage, etc., the appraiser estimates a dollar value for the property.

In a similar vein, Krautmann compared the characteristics of free agents to the salaries they received to generate hedonic estimates of players.[43] Following the same logic that Scully used to suggest that players ought to earn wages approximating their marginal revenue products, Krautmann turned the notion around by looking at player salaries set by the free-agent market to place a dollar value on performance. These estimates, which should reflect the value of the different talents of free agents, are then used to value all players based on their performances. If teams in the free-agent market are rational and knowledgeable, then wages that teams offer players ought to reflect player marginal revenue products. For example, if a free agent everyday shortstop with a slugging average of .600 receives an annual salary of $10 million, then other everyday shortstops who slug .600 are likely to generate $10 million in revenue to the team.

A major drawback of the Scully method is that it requires knowledge of team revenue streams, which are not released to the public. Before broadcast rights and sponsorship became major sources of revenue, reasonable approximations of earnings could be computed with widely available attendance figures. In baseball's current business structure, which relies heavily on outside revenue sources in addition to stadium attendance, such estimates would grossly underestimate the value of players. The Krautmann method avoids needing this information by relying on market participants who are aware of this secret information. Because teams have an interest in hiring the best players, its front-office personnel have strong incentives to learn what breeds success on the field. The free-agent market sheds light on the hidden information that teams use to value players. Thus, even without important information about team revenue, it is possible to estimate player value using the market.

However, there are several reasons why free-agent salaries may not approximate marginal revenue products—the key assumption that justifies free market returns estimation strategy. First, assuming market-determined salaries equal marginal revenue products is tautological; and thus, it is difficult to use these estimates to comment on the correctness of salaries when working off the assumption that salaries properly value players. What if market participants are systematically making mistakes and incorrectly price aspects of player performance? Prior to the 2007 season, former Oakland Athletics pitcher Barry Zito signed a seven-year, $126 million deal with the San Francisco Giants. In his first three seasons (2007 through 2009) he received $43 million while pitching 569 innings of mediocre baseball. Though it is fair to argue that Zito's post-contract performance has not lived up to expectations, his expected-worth projections would have to have been excessively optimistic to justify the contract. Using the salary-projection method that I introduce in Chapter 7, I estimate Zito's performance to be worth about $53 million over the term of his contract at the signing of the contract—60 percent less than his actual deal. Estimating marginal revenue products of other pitchers based on numbers that include Zito's pay and performance will overestimate value of all pitchers.

Pricing mistakes are bound to happen, but Barry Zito's contract isn't a rare exception. Michael Lewis's bestseller *Moneyball* chronicles how the Oakland A's took advantage of other teams' mis-measurement of player value to build a winning franchise on a small budget. Pricing mistakes are a product of market inefficiency, which the A's exploited. Economists Jahn Hakes and Skip Sauer confirmed with statistical analysis what Lewis articulated: during the time *Moneyball* was written, the labor market for players undervalued on-base percentage relative to slugging percentage. In basketball's labor market, economists David Berri, Martin Schmidt, and Stacey Brook found strong evidence of persistent mispricing of basketball talent, as NBA teams overpaid players who score points relative to players who rebound and have higher shooting percentages. Pricing mistakes in competitive markets typically do not persist for long—in the case of on-base percentage, the inefficiency evaporated before the publication of *Moneyball*—however, the fact that economists have documented sports labor markets making mistakes means that free-agent salaries may not properly value talent.

Another reason that that salaries may not equal marginal revenue products is that players are sometimes willing to accept contracts below their expected financial value in return for in-kind compensation. For example, assume that three excellent free-agent power-hitters all choose to play for their hometown teams at discounts of $5 million per year. For athletes who have already earned tens of millions of dollars, it is not unexpected that they might be willing to make such sacrifices. Thus, attempting to value all players according their slugging ability will estimate marginal revenue products to be lower than their true revenue contributions.

Exacerbating the factors that may cause salaries to not approximate marginal revenue products is that the conditions needed to generate competitive outcomes may be lacking in baseball's labor market. Most competitive labor markets have many more employers competing to hire many more employees. For example, the market for waiters is composed of hundreds of thousands of restaurants hiring many millions of servers. Employers can hire and fire waiters with ease, and waiters can move from restaurant to restaurant just as easily. Baseball's labor market is more complex. The free-agent market in baseball usually involves a few teams with specific needs chasing a few uniquely skilled free agents. In 2007, 91 free-agent players signed major-league contracts with teams—42 pitchers and 49 position players. Thirty teams competed for the right to sign these players to a variety of roles that include everyday position players at eight positions, designated hitters, utility fielders, pinch-hitters, starting pitchers, and relievers. Even within these numerous delineations of responsibility, players are valued for different roles that are difficult to capture with a few performance measures. When estimating marginal revenue products from salary-performance comparisons, the statistical methods employed are sensitive to pricing mistakes. The small sample of free agents and the many explanatory factors used to estimate salaries increase the sensitivity of estimates to a few odd occurrences in the data; in this case, a few bad contracts may generate biased estimates pay from performance.[44]

Economists may debate the superiority of the Scully and Krautmann methods, but both techniques have merit. Because the baseball labor market is complex, has few participants, and has produced market inefficiencies, I believe the best approach is to use a revenue-based Scully approach to estimate player marginal revenue products. However, the key assumption of the Krautmann free market returns approach—that free-agent salaries ought equal marginal revenue products—should not be forgotten when evaluating estimates generated using Scully's technique. Significant deviations between salaries and revenue-based estimates may indicate mistakes in the estimates and ought to be investigated.

A Revised Model for Estimating Player Worth

What follows explains the translation of on-field performance to dollars. Off-field factors such fan popularity may affect returns to individual players, but I do not address such factors here, because knowing how much Derek Jeter's hitting and fielding are worth is complicated enough without investigating the value of his smile. Even though I do not explicitly analyze the potential impact community affections and disdain that are unrelated to performance, they are factors that may improve or deflate a player's worth. It is acceptable to make rough adjustments around the general estimates to account for these factors, and I believe that only in rare cases do off-field characteristics significantly affect player value.

Though Scully's model is the basis for my method, it needs updating. Scully's original model valued player contributions toward winning by estimating the impact of team slugging percentage (to account for the impact of hitters) and team strikeout-to-walk ratio (to account for the impact of pitchers) on team winning percentage.[45] A problem with measuring the impact of individual performance benchmarks on winning is that winning is determined by the difference between runs scored and runs allowed. It is possible for a team to be good on one side of the ball, while still being very bad on the other side. If a few teams had excellent pitching and terrible hitting, or vice versa, then improving on one side of the ball might not yield any additional wins to those teams, when such improvements would likely produce additional wins on more-balanced teams. Evaluating team performance using the difference between runs scored and runs allowed avoids this problem. Figure 2-1 shows that winning and run differential are highly correlated: as runs scored outnumber runs allowed, a team gains in the standings and on its balance sheet as more fans follow the team. Furthermore, it is simple to measure individual performances in terms of run contribution and convert to monetary terms. Therefore, I use team run differentials to measure team performances as opposed to wins.

What Are Runs Worth?

The main drawback to a revenue-based estimation method is that it requires knowing how much revenue each team takes in; a step complicated by the fact that teams don't like to open their books to the public, and on the few occasions that they have, the books have not been all that informative. As former Major League Baseball president and Toronto Blue Jays executive Paul Beeston once said, "I can turn a $4 million profit into a $2 million loss and get every national accounting firm to agree with me."

That financial data can be manipulated doesn't mean approximating team revenue streams is impossible. Every year *Forbes* publishes "The Business of Baseball" report, which provides estimates of the financial positions of each baseball franchise. *Forbes* has a strong reputation as an evaluator of financial matters, and the authors of the report go to great lengths to estimate team revenue. I believe that the *Forbes* estimates provide a reasonable estimate of team revenue, and they can be used to approximate the financial impact of winning on club revenue.[46]

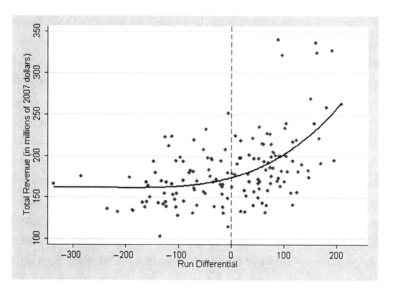

FIGURE 4-1   Total Revenue and Run Differential of MLB Teams (2003–2007)

Figure 4-1 graphs the relationship between *Forbes* total revenue estimates and run differentials for all teams from 2003 to 2007. The diamonds are actual observations, and the dark curve maps the relationship between the run differential on team revenue.[47] The left side of the revenue function is flat, which indicates that winning has little impact on revenue for bad teams. On the right side, the function becomes positive and is increasing, which means that every run scored or prevented adds more revenue than the preceding run.

Why are the returns to runs increasing? An obvious contributor is that the better a team becomes, the more fans come to the games and tune in to broadcasts, which generates higher revenue. Moving from a 75-win team to an 80-win team increases fan interest, but it doesn't have the same effect as going from an 85-win team to a 90-win team. The former team has gone from being a laughable entertainment option to a moderately respectable baseball franchise—it's difficult to get excited about not being as bad as the Kansas City Royals. However, adding five more victories to get to 90 wins is the difference between being a possible contender in a weak division to a team that has a decent shot of making the playoffs. Additional wins signal an even better team that has a higher probability of going to the post-season, where the team will receive a share of post-season revenue. Using a linear relationship to measure the impact of wins on revenue—every win yields the same additional revenue no matter the team's record—misvalues the impact of winning by overestimating the returns to winning for losing squads and underestimating the returns for winners.

Quantifying the financial impact of wins requires knowing more than the general relationship between winning and revenue. Several factors other than wins influence the revenue that teams take in during the season. Differentiating the impact of wins on revenue from these factors requires using multiple regression analysis, which holds individual factors constant among a group of many causal factors to isolate the impact of each individual factor (see Appendix A for further explanation). Other factors that might affect revenue include market size, stadium quality, the wealth of fans, the loyalty of the fanbase, and the existence of another team in the area (five metropolitan areas host two teams: Chicago, Los Angeles, New York, San Francisco–Oakland, and Washington–Baltimore). As a preliminary step, I investigated many potential influences on team revenue, and I found only market size and stadium quality appeared to have a significant impact on revenue. It is no surprise that these variables affect team revenue. Larger markets tend to generate more revenue than smaller markets by virtue of simply having a larger population from which to draw fans. Whether or not a team puts a winner on the field, a big market should expect revenue that has nothing to do with the product on the field.

Economists have found strong evidence that new stadiums generate more revenue than old stadiums, a phenomenon known as the "honeymoon effect." In the 1990s, baseball teams began to replace utilitarian large multi-purpose stadiums with deluxe smaller baseball-only stadiums, such as Jacobs Field in Cleveland and Camden Yards in Baltimore. Fans found the intimate setting more appealing and increased their attendance and purchases accordingly. Economists Christopher Clapp and Jahn Hakes found that the honeymoon effect lasts for about eight years after the stadium is opened, and the effect is unrelated to team performance. This latter finding is disheartening to fans expecting owners to use honeymoon revenues to build a winning team. It turns out that fans are coming to the stadium to experience the new stadium rather than to see better baseball, and, therefore, owners have little reason to reinvest these additional dollars back into the club. The good news for taxpayers is that economists Marc Poitras and Lawrence Hadley found that the honeymoon effect generates sufficient revenue to outweigh the cost of building a new stadium, which means public subsidies are not needed to build new stadiums.

I estimated the impact of team quality, market size, and stadium quality on team revenue for all Major League Baseball teams from 2003 to 2007 using the following equation:

$$
\begin{aligned}
\text{Team revenue} = {} & (W_1 \times \text{Run differential}) + (W_2 \times \text{Run differential}^2) \\
& + (W_3 \times \text{ Run differntial}^3) + (W_4 \times \text{Population}) \qquad (4.1) \\
& + (W_5 \times \text{Honeymoon}) + \text{Constant}
\end{aligned}
$$

Team revenue is the revenue each team collected in each year, with yearly revenues converted to 2007 values to keep dollar terms equivalent over time. Major League Baseball teams earn revenue from many things that players do for their teams locally, mainly through ticket sales, concessions sales, and local broadcast rights. In addition, teams receive a portion of revenues generated by the league that are shared equally across all teams. Most of this revenue comes from national television contracts with Fox, ESPN, and TBS, but some revenue comes from other joint league ventures.[48] In 2007, MLB disbursed $37 million to each team from these revenues; thus, I subtracted this amount from the reported *Forbes* estimates.[49] Player contributions do not affect the amount of revenue a team receives from this source, and, therefore, should not be considered as marginal revenue derived from player performance.

W_1, W_2, and W_3 weight each run's linear, squared, and cubed impact on total revenue. Adding squared and cubed terms gives more weight to additional runs, which captures the increasing returns to wins. W_4 is the weight that each additional person in a city's metropolitan statistical area adds to total revenue, and W_5 is the additional revenue to be expected by a franchise in its honeymoon stage of revenue generation from a new stadium.[50] The constant factor is required to capture the average impact of factors not included in the model. Multiple regression analysis uses a mathematical procedure to "pick" weights that minimize the deviation from actual observations from outcomes generated by the function. Substituting actual values for each variable generates predicted total revenue using these weights to predict how much revenue that additional runs generate.

Equation 4.2 lists the regression-estimated weights for each factor included in the model of team revenue. This is the final model I settled on for valuing performance, but I considered many other models and estimation techniques, several of which are discussed in Appendix B.

$$\text{Team revenue} = (0.0641 \times \text{Run differential}) + (0.000979 \times \text{Run differential}^2)$$
$$+ (0.00000312 \times \text{Run differential}^3) + (0.0000061 \times \text{Population})$$
$$+ (19.55 \times \text{Honeymoon}) + 95.5$$

$$(4.2)$$

The weights report the impact of each unit of each explanatory variable had on revenue, while holding other factors constant. For population and the honeymoon effect, the interpretation is simple: the addition of one person to the city increased revenue by around $6, and a stadium in its honeymoon period generated just under $20 million. For valuing players, these estimates are not relevant because they are outside players' control. The factors are included in the regression equation so that their impacts do not cloud the impact of runs on revenue. The weights on run differentials predict the financial impact of each run as it affects the run differential, run differential squared, and run differential cubed.

Using the Run-Value Estimates to Value Players

Position Players

For valuing position players, park-adjusted linear weights and plus/minus estimates of run contributions for each player were input into the equation.[51] The above-average contributions on offense and defense must be summed before converting runs to revenue, because the impact of runs is increasing at an increasing rate. In some cases, defense will significantly dampen the impact of a hitter. For example, nearly half of Pat Burrell's above-average hitting contribution was erased by his poor defense in 2007. In the same manner, good defenders like Albert Pujols enhance their value by contributing additional runs that are increasingly valuable. While offense makes up far more of a position player's contribution to run production than defense, defense contributes significant value to players that should not be ignored.

In order to demonstrate how runs affect revenue through these weights, I use Albert Pujols's 2007 as an example. In total, Pujols produced 82.5 runs more than the average player in 2007. Adding the products of each weight multiplied times the runs contributed, transformed to the relevant polynomial power, generates an estimate of the player's financial impact in producing runs above average. Table 4-1 lists the calculations for the revenue contributions using Pujols's runs above average, multiplying each weight times runs contributed.

Estimating separate weights for each polynomial power allows us to measure the non-linearity in the returns to wins, revealed by Figure 4-1. Model 1 uses the weights in Equation 2, but Model 2 reveals what would have happened if the relationship was estimated linearly—every run scored or saved above average adds $118,800 in revenue to the team. Pujols's estimated value is considerably less when the increasing returns to winning are not properly taken into account. This demonstrates why adding higher polynomials to the model is a necessary complexity.

The sum of the weights times runs above average does not provide complete information regarding Pujols's worth. To estimate his total value we must add on what an average player is worth, which is actually quite tricky. The constant term in the regression term provides a potential solution. The constant is the intercept of the function, which reports how much revenue an average team would receive if all the other values were zero. By design, the constant is set to equal average revenue minus the impacts of the weights times the average

Model	Power	Runs	Coefficients	Runs × Coefficients
1	1	82.50	0.0641	$5.29
	2	6,806.25	9.79E-004	$6.66
	3	561,515.63	3.12E-006	$1.75
	Sum			$13.70
2	1	82.5	0.1188	$9.80
	Sum			$9.80

TABLE 4-1   Albert Pujols's 2007 Estimated Value of Runs Above Average
Dollars in millions

values of the variables they impact. In most cases, researchers pay little attention to a constant term, because it serves to pick up unobserved random factors
so that the estimated weights are not biased; but it is useful in this instance. On
average a team's run differential will be zero and its winning percentage will be
0.500. Thus, holding constant population and the honeymoon effect, the constant
in Model 1 estimates that an average generates approximately $96 million in
revenue.

If we assume that each player contributes a portion of the average value to
his team's success, then we can add each player's average contribution to his
above- or below-average value to generate his estimated worth. Dividing up the
constant value among its team's players according to playing time adds the necessary component to complete each player's marginal revenue product estimate.
Splitting the total value into $48 million halves provides the average value of
run production and run prevention.

On offense, multiplying the percentage of the team's plate appearances that
the player takes times $48 million apportions a share of the average value con-
tributed by every player, according to his share of plate appearances. Pujols
took 10.93 percent of the St. Louis Cardinals plate appearances in 2007, and
the value of an average player with this playing time is $5.25 million (0.1093 $\times$
$48 million). Position players also deserve credit for average performance at pre-
venting runs on defense. Because pitchers and fielders jointly prevent runs, it
is necessary to allocate a portion of the average run-prevention value to both.
Determining the value of average fielding contributions requires identifying the
responsibility of pitchers and fielders in preventing runs.

The instability in performance on hits on balls in play reveals that pitchers do
not have much influence in this area. Therefore, when evaluating pitchers I used
defense-independent pitching statistics—walks, strikeouts, and home runs—to
gauge pitching quality. It might seem appropriate to apportion the defensive
responsibility between pitchers and fielders according to the percentage of balls
that are hit into play, with pitchers only getting credit for defense-independent
outcomes. Given that 70 percent of plate appearances result with a ball hit into
play this would mean that pitchers would be responsible for only 30 percent
of run prevention. However, to divide defensive responsibility in this manner
would be incorrect for two reasons. First, defense-independent performance is
correlated with pitcher performance on balls in play; therefore, pitchers with

better defense-independent pitching statistics tend to generate more outs on hits on balls in play than pitchers with poor defense-independent performance.[52] Second, a pitcher's ability to prevent runs with defense-independent pitching statistics occurs even when balls are hit into play, because striking out batters, preventing walks, and giving up fewer homers means that he can limit the damage when batters reach base. Thus, even when the ball is put into play, the pitcher exerts important control over run scoring.

In an attempt to disentangle the joint production of run prevention I previously studied the impact of pitchers on run prevention by comparing models of run prevention when information on fielders was included and excluded. The difference indicated that fielding explains 27 percent of runs allowed, and fielding explains 73 percent.[53] Thus, I assigned $13 million (approximately 27 percent) of the $48 million devoted to run prevention to fielders, with the remaining $35 million going to pitchers.

How should the $13 million be allocated among fielders? Shortstops, second basemen, and center fielders are considered important defensive positions to be manned by the best fielders. Often, teams will tolerate poor hitting from players at these positions because of their excellent defensive contributions. On the other hand, first base and corner outfield positions are commonly manned by weak-fielding sluggers in order to minimize their damage on defense. The reason for putting the best defenders up the middle is that these positions see more action than corner positions. As the opposing team hits the ball around the field, managers are going to allocate defenders to positions according to their ability—good players going to positions that field many balls and bad players to positions that field few balls. Therefore, I allocated the $13 million to each position according to its average fielding opportunities.

Baseball Info Solutions tracks the frequency with which defenders have balls hit to their zone of responsibility, which I use to generate average values for each position listed in Table 4-2.[54] Each player is credited with a percentage of this value according to percentage of his team's playing time at that position. For example, Albert Pujols played 92.26 percent of the St. Louis Cardinals innings at first base in 2007, and thus his average defensive value was $0.99 million (0.9226 × $1.07 million). Players who play multiple positions receive credit for each position played according the percentage of his team's innings in the field that he manned the position. Catchers are valued for keeping runners from stealing bases, which is their main defensive contribution.[55]

Position	Average Value ($)
First Base	1.07
Second Base	1.93
Third Base	1.74
Shortstop	2.15
Left Field	1.49
Center Field	1.99
Right Field	1.58
Catcher	2.93

TABLE 4-2   Value of Average Fielder by Position

For each player, the average fielding value is summed with the average hitting value and the value generated from his runs contributed above average to produce a marginal revenue product estimate. Appendix D reports the marginal revenue product estimates of all players in baseball in 2008 and 2009 by team. Table 4-3 lists the top-30 most valuable position players in baseball in 2007 by their estimated marginal revenue products. The table also reports the percentage of plate appearances taken, the dollar value of an average player with identical playing time (hitting and fielding), and the additional dollar value above average contributed by each player. The sum of the three columns preceding the last column is equal to the marginal revenue product.

According to the estimates, Albert Pujols was the most valuable position player (as well as the most-valuable player overall) in baseball in 2007, generating approximately $20 million in value. Yet, Pujols did not win the NL MVP award, which typically goes to the best position player in the league. That honor went to Philadelphia's Jimmy Rollins, who was the 13th most valuable position player in the majors, worth approximately $11 million. $11 million is quite valuable, but it is a whopping 45 percent less than Pujols's value. The baseball writers erred badly in awarding the MVP to Rollins, as seven other NL players were more valuable than Rollins, including his middle-infield teammate Chase Utley who was worth $14.5 million. Jimmy Rollins is an excellent player whom I admire, but he wasn't the most-valuable player in the NL in 2007, and it wasn't even close. To be fair to the writers who vote on the award, the exact MVP criteria

Rank	Player	Team	PA%	Average Value		Value Above Average ($)	MRP ($)
				Hitting ($)	Fielding ($)		
1	Albert Pujols	St. Louis Cardinals	10.93	5.25	0.99	13.70	19.93
2	Alex Rodriguez	New York Yankees	10.85	5.21	1.60	11.75	18.55
3	David Wright	New York Mets	11.21	5.38	1.70	9.98	17.06
4	Magglio Ordonez	Detroit Tigers	10.66	5.11	1.33	9.04	15.49
5	Chase Utley	Philadelphia Phillies	9.38	4.50	1.55	8.40	14.45
6	David Ortiz	Boston Red Sox	10.38	4.98	0.04	9.11	14.13
7	Matt Holliday	Colorado Rockies	10.97	5.27	1.40	7.40	14.07
8	Chipper Jones	Atlanta Braves	9.41	4.52	1.30	7.92	13.74
9	Carlos Pena	Tampa Bay Devil Rays	9.75	4.68	0.91	7.85	13.44
10	Curtis Granderson	Detroit Tigers	10.62	5.10	1.77	5.20	12.07
11	Todd Helton	Colorado Rockies	10.50	5.04	0.97	5.36	11.37
12	Carlos Beltran	New York Mets	10.03	4.81	1.70	4.86	11.37
13	Jimmy Rollins	Philadelphia Phillies	11.90	5.71	2.12	3.38	11.22
14	Prince Fielder	Milwaukee Brewers	10.92	5.24	0.99	4.84	11.07
15	Troy Tulowitzki	Colorado Rockies	10.50	5.04	2.01	3.96	11.01
16	Ichiro Suzuki	Seattle Mariners	11.86	5.69	1.86	2.93	10.48
17	Grady Sizemore	Cleveland Indians	11.75	5.64	1.92	2.83	10.39
18	Vladimir Guerrero	L.A. Angels of Anaheim	10.65	5.11	1.02	4.18	10.32
19	Jose Reyes	New York Mets	12.06	5.79	2.12	2.36	10.27
20	Jorge Posada	New York Yankees	9.02	4.33	0.00	3.46	10.04
21	Eric Byrnes	Arizona Diamondbacks	11.44	5.49	1.51	2.94	9.95
22	Alexis Rios	Toronto Blue Jays	11.47	5.51	1.59	2.80	9.89
23	Ryan Zimmerman	Washington Nationals	11.64	5.59	1.72	2.57	9.89
24	Miguel Cabrera	Florida Marlins	10.72	5.15	1.58	3.11	9.83
25	Ryan Howard	Philadelphia Phillies	9.91	4.76	0.91	4.10	9.77
26	Carlos Lee	Houston Astros	11.02	5.29	1.39	2.82	9.50
27	Robinson Cano	New York Yankees	10.25	4.92	1.87	2.68	9.47
28	Nick Swisher	Oakland Athletics	10.36	4.97	1.37	3.13	9.47
29	Hanley Ramirez	Florida Marlins	11.13	5.34	1.94	2.18	9.46
30	Barry Bonds	San Francisco Giants	7.68	3.69	0.86	4.83	9.38

TABLE 4-3   Top-30 Most Valuable Position Players (2007)
Dollars in millions

are somewhat subjective, so a "most valuable" vote could be defended on other grounds. In the AL, the writers were correct to award the MVP to Alex Rodriguez, who was only slightly less valuable than Pujols, with a value of just under $19 million.

Valuing Pitchers

For pitchers, I estimated pitchers' run-prevention ability based on DIPS performance using multiple regression analysis, estimating the expected runs pitchers ought to allow based on strikeouts, walks, and home runs. I adjusted the numbers for home park influence using park factors to dampen the impact of run-friendly and run-unfriendly parks then subtracted the expected runs allowed from the league average so that pitchers are evaluated according to runs allowed above/below average, just as linear weights does for hitters.[56]

The total runs prevented were generated from team data and were adjusted to measure individual performance by multiplying the percent of team's batters faced that the pitcher faced times the predicted runs prevented. The calculation produced the total runs prevented above and below average for each pitcher, which were then converted into dollar values using the run-value estimates reported in Equation 4.1. As I explained above, pitchers contribute approximately 73 percent of run prevention; thus the average pitcher will contribute his percentage of batters faced times $35 million (0.73 × $48 million), which must be added to the value of runs prevented above average.

Table 4-4 lists the top-30 most valuable pitchers in 2007 based on a straight runs-to-revenue conversion. The pitchers on the list have one quality in common: they are all starters. It should not be surprising that C.C. Sabathia, Brandon Webb, and Josh Beckett are at the top of the list; but, Mariano Rivera—arguably the best closer in the history of baseball—takes the last spot in the top-100. Rivera's estimated worth is a measly $3.4 million—about a third of what the top

Rank	Player	Team	BFP%	MRP (raw) ($)
1	C.C. Sabathia	Cleveland Indians	15.71	11.66
2	Brandon Webb	Arizona Diamondbacks	15.69	10.79
3	Josh Beckett	Boston Red Sox	13.54	10.07
4	Jake Peavy	San Diego Padres	14.36	9.67
5	John Lackey	L.A. Angels of Anaheim	15.08	8.95
6	John Smoltz	Atlanta Braves	13.62	8.68
7	Tim Hudson	Atlanta Braves	14.77	8.60
8	Roy Halladay	Toronto Blue Jays	15.18	8.45
9	Aaron Harang	Cincinnati Reds	14.92	8.42
10	Joe Blanton	Oakland Athletics	15.21	8.34
11	Roy Oswalt	Houston Astros	14.18	7.75
12	Javier Vazquez	Chicago White Sox	14.02	7.45
13	Scott Kazmir	Tampa Bay Devil Rays	13.85	7.40
14	Kelvim Escobar	L.A. Angels of Anaheim	13.18	7.32
15	Erik Bedard	Baltimore Orioles	11.42	7.13
16	Danny Haren	Oakland Athletics	14.97	7.10
17	James Shields	Tampa Bay Devil Rays	13.65	7.06
18	Brad Penny	Los Angeles Dodgers	13.96	7.05
19	Jeff Francis	Colorado Rockies	14.65	6.90
20	Greg Maddux	San Diego Padres	13.27	6.85
21	Fausto Carmona	Cleveland Indians	14.16	6.68
22	Justin Verlander	Detroit Tigers	13.65	6.68
23	Andy Pettitte	New York Yankees	14.52	6.62
24	Adam Wainwright	St. Louis Cardinals	14.04	6.51
25	Johan Santana	Minnesota Twins	14.32	6.47
26	Gil Meche	Kansas City Royals	14.49	6.43
27	Chien-Ming Wang	New York Yankees	13.05	6.41
28	Daisuke Matsuzaka	Boston Red Sox	14.40	6.32
29	Matt Cain	San Francisco Giants	13.21	6.16
30	Felix Hernandez	Seattle Mariners	12.80	6.05

TABLE 4-4   Top-30 Pitchers (Raw MRP Estimates, 2007)
Dollars in millions

starters are worth. In fact, he's valued less than mediocre starter Jason Marquis, whose estimated 2007 marginal revenue product was $4.67 million. How can this be?

Though Marquis isn't considered one of baseball's better starting pitchers, his contribution is valuable. In 2007, he was a league-average pitcher who was good enough to throw nearly 14 percent of his team's innings. He's not excellent, but he's better than who would be pitching if he wasn't in his role. Pitchers of Marquis's caliber keep games close enough to give their teams a chance to win. A team will frequently lose games when its pitcher gives up four runs, but the team will win more games than if it had a pitcher who routinely spotted the other team five runs. Marquis is also capable of pitching many innings; this also increases his value, because his team doesn't have to use inferior arms as often as it would than if he pitched fewer innings.

Rivera, on the other hand, doesn't pitch nearly as often as Marquis. He pitched just under five percent of his team's innings, compared to Marquis's 13.68 percent. While Rivera pitches much better than Marquis when he pitches, he pitches far fewer innings as a one-inning-at-a-time reliever; which requires his team, the Yankees, to fill the remaining innings with inferior pitchers.

The free-agent market, however, tends to disagree with the raw marginal revenue product estimates of the pitchers. Prior to the 2008 season, Rivera agreed to a three-year, $45 million contract to re-sign with the Yankees. The year before, Marquis signed a three-year, $21 million contract with the Cubs. The above estimates suggest that Marquis is 40 percent more valuable than Rivera, while the free-agent market feels that Rivera is more than twice as valuable as Marquis. In *Moneyball*, Michael Lewis contended that Billy Beane used the overvaluing of saves—the benchmark of excellent closers—to pawn off mediocre pitching talent for more valuable players. Is Rivera an example of this inefficiency?

Rivera may be a bit overpaid but his contract is not an isolated case. In recent years, Francisco Rodriguez, Francisco Cordero, Joe Nathan, and Billy Wagner are examples of closers who were awarded contracts with annual salaries exceeding $10 million per season. While I used a Scully-based method to estimate player marginal revenue products, I believe that the Krautmann method should inform our analysis. In the case of closers, the Krautmann method indicates that something is awry. General managers may make mistakes from time to time, but such a persistent mistake of overvaluing closers is unlikely. Where could the estimates be going wrong?

The most likely explanation for the disparity in values between starters and relievers is that the runs that the two classes of pitchers prevent are not equal. At the start of the game, the score is tied. As a team scores and allows runs over the course of a game, the likelihood that an additional run will affect the outcome changes. When relievers enter the game, the situation is different than what it is for starters. Starters normally begin the game with a close score, with the approximate end of the game nine innings away, while relievers take over when much of the game has already been played. When the game is close and nearing completion, runs allowed can dramatically change the probability of a team winning the game in a way they did not in the early innings. One run given up in the first inning can easily be overcome during the eight innings that follow, but one run given up in the ninth has a much higher probability of costing a team the game.

Operations research analyst George Lindsey calculated the probability of winning any game based on the state of the game.[57] His win probabilities offer a reasonable approximation of the likelihood that a team wins the game based on the run differential at different points in the game. Giving up one run at the start of the second inning of a tie game lowers a team's win probability from 50 to 38.9 percent, while, in the ninth inning, a pitcher who gives up a run lowers his team's probability of winning to 15.3 percent—a drastic difference. All runs are not equal in terms of how they affect winning.

The differing importance of runs over the course of a game may seem odd considering that one run scored in the second inning counts the same as a walk-off solo home run. On the scoreboard the runs count the same, but this doesn't conflict with the fact that some runs are more valuable than others when it comes to assessing the value of pitchers. If pitchers were assigned to pitch to batters randomly throughout the game, or rotated in a pitching order like batters, the differing value of runs by game situation wouldn't be an issue. What changes the analysis is that pitching assignments are not random. Managers chose the best relievers to pitch in spots where the outcome of the game hangs in the balance, while weak pitchers typically pitch with big leads or deficits, when their sub-average performance is less likely affect the outcome of the game. Late innings, when the game is close, are the most valuable innings in the game; therefore, managers tend to withhold their best relief pitchers until that time. Top closers like Mariano Rivera almost always pitch at the end of close games when runs have more value. Setup men who typically handle the seventh and eighth innings also deserve some credit for pitching when runs are more valuable. Pitchers capable of pitching in tight spots need to be valued for their ability to prevent runs when they matter most.

Table 4-5 lists the additional improvement in win probability from scoring a run by inning groups based on Lindsey's calculations. For the first five innings, when starters typically pitch, the mean impact of a one-run change is approximately 13.4 percentage points. Beyond the sixth inning, when setup men enter and occasionally finish the game, the mean impact of a single run is 27.6 percentage points—approximately double the value of a run when starters pitch. In the ninth, which is exclusively reserved for closers, a run is approximately 2.5 times more valuable than starter innings. This information can be used to adjust the raw marginal revenue product estimates of pitchers to reflect their value in pitching at times when runs are valuable.

Innings	Impact of Run on Win Probability	Ratio to Innings 1–5
1–5	0.134	–
7–9	0.276	2
9	0.346	2.5

TABLE 4-5   Change in Win Probability by Inning Conclusion

One way we might want to adjust pitchers' value according to the importance of the situations that they faced. For example, a pitcher who got out of several bases-loaded jams could be credited for the improvement in win probability associated with his performances, using a metric like win probability added (WPA).[58] But, WPA suffers from the same context-dependence problem that plagues RBI. A pitcher pitches how he pitches, and while some pitchers may fade or shine in the moment, there doesn't appear to be a lot of evidence for this (see the Hot Stove Myth following Chapter 2). WPA is largely a product of when pitchers get to pitch, which is determined by managers. And in some years good pitchers will have more opportunities than others through random chance. While WPA ought to be correlated with ability—managers want to pitch their best pitchers when the greatest swings in win probability are on the line—the metric is polluted by outside factors.

When we value players, we want to do so according to their expected contributions based on their capabilities. What about relievers who are good enough to pitch in tight spots, but don't get the opportunity to do so, because of a logjam of good relievers or managerial stupidity? These pitchers would otherwise be producing value in important situations and should be rewarded for doing so. Similarly, pitchers who pitch at valuable moments should not have their run prevention valued more, simply because of when they pitch. Elite relief pitchers should be valued as closers, according to their expected production in that spot, whether they pitch in the closer role or not, because this role is the most valuable use of their skills.

To adjust for the added value of pitching in more valuable game spots, I ranked relievers according to their run-prevention rates. The top-30 relievers, defined as pitchers who never started a game during the season and averaged less than four outs or less per appearance, were designated as "closers." That is one pitcher per team to handle the tight situations that teams may find themselves in over the course of the season. They may not always pitch the ninth inning when the game is on the line—they might be deployed to handle a bases-loaded jam in the seventh or they might occasionally handle the ninth inning during a blowout just to get some work in—but, on average the runs they prevent will normally be more valuable. Because the runs prevented in the ninth inning are, on average, worth 2.5 times more than runs during the starter's innings, I adjusted the value of designated closers by multiplying their raw marginal revenue product by 2.5. The next 60 relief pitchers are designated as "setup men."[59] I doubled their raw marginal revenue products, because these pitchers typically handle the seventh, eighth, and ninth (occasionally) innings, which are twice as valuable as the first six innings.

Relievers are not the only pitchers who need to be rewarded for pitching when runs are more valuable. Many starting pitchers frequently pitch into the late innings and should be credited for preventing runs when they are typically more valuable. Not only do they directly prevent those important runs from scoring, but also do they reduce the need for the team to rely on a setup man. For every out that a starting pitcher averages per game beyond six innings, I double the value of the runs prevented, but only for this additional output. Pitchers who regularly pitch beyond the sixth inning receive a bonus for their durable excellence.

Table 4-6 lists the top-30 most valuable pitchers in 2007 according to revised marginal revenue products that adjust for pitching roles. The raw marginal revenue product and its rank among all pitchers are also included, in order to demonstrate the effect of the adjustment. Raw marginal revenue products are provided in Appendix D as well so that the reader can compare and possibly adjust the value of performance if he/she wants to adjust for pitching roles with alternate multipliers (consider the multipliers to be rough but informed estimates). Though the list is still dominated by starters, several relievers also appear in the top-30. The list includes prominent closers Mariano Rivera,

Rank (adjusted)	Rank (raw)	Player	Team	BFP%	MRP (raw) ($)	MRP (adjusted) ($)
1	1	C.C. Sabathia	Cleveland Indians	15.71	11.66	13.45
2	2	Brandon Webb	Arizona Diamondbacks	15.69	10.79	12.27
3	3	Josh Beckett	Boston Red Sox	13.54	10.07	11.11
4	4	Jake Peavy	San Diego Padres	14.36	9.67	10.51
5	5	John Lackey	L.A. Angels of Anaheim	15.08	8.95	9.99
6	8	Roy Halladay	Toronto Blue Jays	15.18	8.45	9.92
7	88	Heath Bell	San Diego Padres	5.80	3.84	9.61
8	90	Rafael Betancourt	Cleveland Indians	4.66	3.78	9.46
9	9	Aaron Harang	Cincinnati Reds	14.92	8.42	9.43
10	7	Tim Hudson	Atlanta Braves	14.77	8.60	9.38
11	10	Joe Blanton	Oakland Athletics	15.21	8.34	9.29
12	6	John Smoltz	Atlanta Braves	13.62	8.68	9.25
13	99	Jonathan Broxton	Los Angeles Dodgers	5.39	3.49	8.72
14	100	Mariano Rivera	New York Yankees	4.68	3.42	8.55
15	12	Javier Vazquez	Chicago White Sox	14.02	7.45	8.30
16	11	Roy Oswalt	Houston Astros	14.18	7.75	8.26
17	17	James Shields	Tampa Bay Devil Rays	13.65	7.06	8.01
18	14	Kelvim Escobar	L.A. Angels of Anaheim	13.18	7.32	7.91
19	16	Danny Haren	Oakland Athletics	14.97	7.10	7.70
20	15	Erik Bedard	Baltimore Orioles	11.42	7.13	7.68
21	110	Francisco Cordero	Milwaukee Brewers	4.15	3.04	7.59
22	13	Scott Kazmir	Tampa Bay Devil Rays	13.85	7.40	7.50
23	113	Joakim Soria	Kansas City Royals	4.32	2.99	7.48
24	114	Joaquin Benoit	Texas Rangers	5.27	2.97	7.42
25	21	Fausto Carmona	Cleveland Indians	14.16	6.68	7.40
26	115	Joe Nathan	Minnesota Twins	4.60	2.96	7.39
27	18	Brad Penny	Los Angeles Dodgers	13.96	7.05	7.39
28	118	Bobby Howry	Chicago Cubs	5.43	2.93	7.33
29	119	Carlos Marmol	Chicago Cubs	4.61	2.91	7.26
30	19	Jeff Francis	Colorado Rockies	14.65	6.90	7.26

TABLE 4-6   The Top-35 Most Valuable Pitchers (2007)
Dollars in millions

Francisco Cordero, and Joe Nathan as well as noted setup men such as Heath Bell, Rafael Betancourt, and Jonathan Broxton. Starters also show a significant boost in their value, with several increasing their worth by over $1 million.

Though pitchers are sometimes awarded MVPs, it is more common for position players to receive the award, and the best position players do tend to be more valuable than pitchers. The best pitcher in each league typically receives the Cy Young Award. In 2007, C.C. Sabathia, the most valuable pitcher in both leagues generating $13.45 million, won the AL Cy Young. Brandon Webb, the second most valuable pitcher ($12.27 million) and who won the NL award in 2006, was beaten out by Jake Peavy, number four on the list at $10.51 million. Though the most-valuable player did not take home the top prize in the NL, just as happened with position players, there is not as big a disparity between the award winners and the most-valuable pitchers as there was with position players. The differences between Webb and Peavy were slight. And while I imagine Webb wouldn't mind a second trophy, I suspect he's not all broken up that Jake Peavy, clearly a worthy recipient, won the award.

Summing Up

Baseball team owners are rational professionals who seek to hire players because players generate revenue from their on-field performance. This chapter details a method for valuing players based on past economic analyses of baseball's labor market. Revenue and performance data generate a runs-to-revenue function that can be used to translate performance into dollars. Applied to individual player performances, the function estimates players values in terms of their revenue contribution.

But estimates are just estimates. No matter how confident we may be in the method, the numbers deserve further scrutiny. In the next chapter, I take a closer look at the numbers to better understand the information they convey. I compare the estimates to actual salaries to see how well the model predicts and identifies market mistakes. I also point out where the estimates can lead to erroneous interpretations of player value, and discuss how to avoid making such mistakes.

Hot Stove Myth: Replacement Players are Cheap and Abundant

Over the past few years, "replacement-level" metrics such as value over replacement player (VORP) and wins above replacement (WAR) have become popular advanced yardsticks for gauging players. These metrics measure every player's performance relative to a "replacement player." In this instance, a replacement player isn't a scab worker who crosses the picket line, but a hypothetical player who hovers on the edge between the minor and major leagues. Should a major-leaguer go down, this Platonic form would fill his slot in the lineup.

Replacement-level metrics differ slightly from each other (e.g., VORP uses runs and WAR uses wins for denominating value), and they measure on-field performance similar to the metrics I use in this book for evaluating on-field play. The difference is the baseline to which players are compared. I use the league average, replacement-based metrics express value relative to what a replacement player would produce. Where exactly the replacement cutoff is generates plenty of disagreement among their adherents.

A supposed advantage of replacement-level metrics is that they offer quick insight into the financial value of players. A player who is near replacement level can theoretically be replaced by a player from a large talent pool of players who are no worse than each other. Therefore, teams ought to be able to acquire this level of talent cheaply, paying no more than the league minimum (currently $400,000 per season) to low-service-time substitutes. There is no need to keep a veteran on the payroll who won't play for less than $1 million, when you can pull up a similarly-skilled youngster from Triple-A who will make the league minimum. Paying a replacement-level player more than the league minimum, even when his expected marginal revenue product exceeds his salary, generates less profit than if a team just employed a league-minimum player. Or, so it seems.

The assumption that minimally competent major-league caliber play-ers are available at near minimum wages rests on the notion that there is little scarcity among replacement-level talent. And this lack of scarcity is derived from the distribution of baseball talent. Keith Woolner, saberme-trician and Manager of Baseball Research and Analytics for the Cleveland Indians, explains

> A commodity which is easily available to all teams at no or low cost confers no competitive advantage, and therefore is of minimal value. Thus, baseball value comes from scarcity.
>   The talent distribution in baseball can be summed up as follows: there are very few "superstar" level players, a somewhat larger number of "average" producers, and a practically unlimited number of "scrubs". This is usually represented as the tail end of a bell curve or normal distribution, with the vast majority of the overall population already weeded out through other factors prior to reaching professional ball.[60]

And so, it would appear that when any player is bumped from the league, there is a dearth of similarly-skilled replacements ready to take his place. If baseball talent isn't particularly scarce at the base level, then teams ought to be able to fill their final roster spots with the cheapest play-ers in this group—young players with little service time earning the league minimum. However, the assumption of abundant equivalent talent at the edge of the majors is mistaken.

The figures below plot the frequency of major-league hitters and pitchers by OPS and ERA in 2009, respectively.[61] The histograms peak around the league average and the frequency diminishes gradually in both directions—the solid line marks the league average and the dashed lines reflect the standard deviation. There are many average players and few elite players, but a glut of replacements is not reflected.

Rather than observing the far tail of a normal distribution of base-ball talent among the general population as replacement-level theory posits, the talent among major leaguers appears to be normally distributed around its mean. What does this mean regarding the value of replacement-level players? Baseball talent at the bottom of the league is, in fact, quite scarce. Dropping down to the minors to pick up replacements means bringing up inferior talent, which will generate less revenue. Signing a relatively bad major-league player may be a better alternative to calling up a low-salaried minor-leaguer.

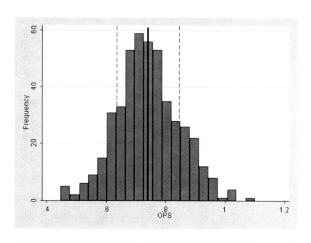

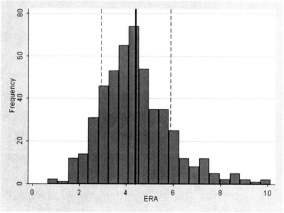

This doesn't mean that teams won't sometimes prefer the cheaper less-talented player over a more-expensive superior veteran. As economist Simon Rottenberg noted, competition from less-skilled players may drive salaries down somewhat for more-skilled players, because teams don't want to pay the premium for a slightly superior player.[62] But the more important implication is that the distribution of talent indicates that it's often worthwhile to pay more than the league minimum to purchase marginal major-league talent because they generate more revenue than available replacement players.

But this invites the following question: if major-league teams draw from the far tail of the general population's baseball talent distribution, then why isn't the frequency distributed from many marginal players to a few stars? Baseball players make up approximately 0.003 percent of American males between the ages of 20 and 40.[63] The population of players capable of playing in the major leagues is so far out on the extreme tail that it's not surprising that we don't see an increase in frequency of players as we move from more- to less-talented players. The normal-like distributions above may be generated by a lump in a long-thin tail of the distribution of the general population. But, no matter what the reason is for the shape, within the range of major-league caliber players there does not appear to be a dramatic increase in frequency of players as they diminish in quality as postulated by the replacement-level theory.

It should also be pointed out that just because a capable player can be paid the league minimum doesn't mean that promoting him is the best use of resources. Bringing up marginal prospects has the consequence of using service time when a player has plenty of improvement left. An early call-up means he will become increasingly more expensive before he reaches his peak. Therefore, it may be cheaper to pay a veteran a higher salary to keep the position warm so that the team gets higher return from his best years in the long run.

The problems with replacement-level metrics for valuing players are evident in the popular method of converting these metrics into real dollars.[64] These dollar-value estimates are derived from new free-agent contracts according to the overall wins the free-agent class is expected to generate and the salaries they receive. This is similar to the Krautmann method, but uses a more rudimentary estimator: total salary dollars divided by estimated added wins. Estimates of financial worth are then based on the notion that replacement-level players should be valued at no more than the league minimum; therefore, only value contributed above this threshold is counted. This method suffers from several problems—for example, the estimates assume that all wins are equally valuable, which goes against the evidence that there are increasing returns to wins (see Figure 4-1)—but here I want to focus on the implications of assuming replacement players are worth the league minimum.

If only above-replacement performance produces positive value, then players who are deemed to be below replacement level produce negative values—they allegedly cost their employers revenue because they can be easily replaced by young marginal players willing to work for minimum wage. Theoretically, no team should be willing to employ below-replacement players. However, the league is well-stocked with talent that falls well below standard replacement-level thresholds.

Value estimates posted on the popular website Fangraphs, based on WAR, report that 32 percent of major-league players were below replacement level in 2009. That would mean that nearly one-third of the league's players cost their clubs money, because they employed players who were inferior to a large population of players available for the league minimum. And this isn't just from a few players hanging around the replacement-level benchmark: 16 percent of players cost their teams $1 million or more. If there is a large group of equally capable players willing to work for the league minimum, then employing eight players per team who cost their teams money is quite a failure of management. General managers make mistakes, but not this broadly or consistently.

The histograms above indicate that the replacement-level assumption about the scarcity of baseball talent is flawed. The reality is that even among the league's marginal players, there are real talent disparities between them. The notion of a large pool of equally-qualified replacements isn't supported by the data. And estimates based on this assumption do not appear to properly value this talent. While it may bother you as a fan to see a player at the bottom of the league making several million dollars, just remember that it could be worse.

Chapter 5
Deals, Duds, And Caveats: What Do The Estimates Reveal?

The estimates presented in the previous chapter are based on a theoretical approach to valuing players. Though the method is intuitive and has a strong economic foundation, the model requires further testing. The measure of any model is its predictive power: good models generate predictions similar to actual outcomes, while bad models have poor predictive accuracy. Comparing the estimates to actual player salaries provides information regarding the model's efficacy and may shed some light on how well baseball's labor market values talent.

The obvious starting point for comparing marginal revenue product estimates to player salaries is free agents. The free-agent market supposedly represents an unconstrained market where teams bid against each other for player services. The teams are run by informed front-office personnel who have the incentive to properly value player services. If marginal revenue product estimates are similar to free-agent salaries, then we can have some confidence in the estimates. If the values diverge, we need to investigate further to understand the cause.

Figures 5-1 and 5-2 map the relationships between free-agent player salaries and marginal revenue product estimates for position players and pitchers from 2006 to 2009.[65] The graphs reveal a positive correlation, with the observations loosely clustered around the 45° line that marks the points where salaries and estimates are identical. For hitters, the observations fall above and below the line with almost equal frequency, which indicates minimal bias from the estimates. In contrast, pitchers have more observations falling above the line than below it, which indicates that free-agent pitchers' salaries are more frequently above their estimated marginal revenue products than below them. This asymmetry may indicate bias in the estimates or an inefficiency in the pitching market. Though

J.C. Bradbury, *Hot Stove Economics*, DOI 10.1007/978-1-4419-6269-0_5,
© Springer Science+Business Media, LLC 2011

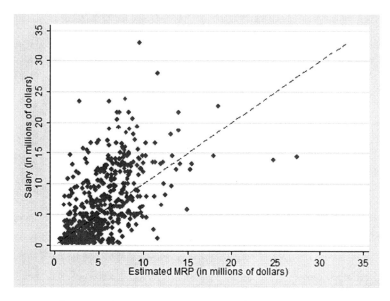

FIGURE 5-1   Free-Agent Salary and Estimated MRP (Hitters, 2006–2009)

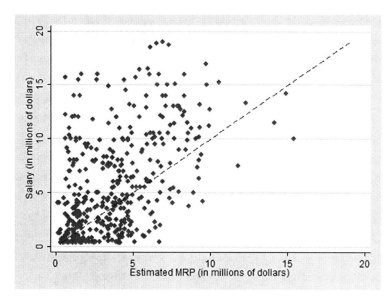

FIGURE 5-2   Free-Agent Salary and Estimated MRP (Pitchers, 2006–2009)

the imbalance is small, the pitching estimates receive further investigation later in this chapter.

A comparison between salaries and the marginal revenue product estimates indicates that the estimates explain 33 percent of the difference in salaries across hitters, and 27 percent across pitchers.[66] While a perfect correlation would be nice—meaning the variation of marginal revenue products explains 100 percent of the differences in salaries across players—the explained variation is about as good as could have been expected given the normal variation in player performances over time. Even if salaries were directly tied to past performance (e.g., ERA in the previous year results in a salary commensurate with the value of that ERA in the following year) the correlation would be far from perfect. The reason for the imperfect correlation is that, from season to season, individual performances fluctuate quite a bit.

While good players tend to perform well, and bad players tend to perform poorly, over their careers, there exists considerable variation over time. Tables 2-1 and 2-2 in Chapter 2 report imperfect correlations from year to year for all players in several areas of performances. The squared correlations in the tables—often referred to as R^2—reveal the percent differences in performances across players than can be explained by differences in performance in the preceding year. According to the tables, linear weights explain approximately 40 percent of the season-to-season difference in performance $(0.63^2 = 0.40)$ and the DIPS ERA explains approximately 30 percent of the difference $(0.54^2 = 0.29)$. This lack of stability means that it is difficult for teams to estimate precisely what a player will produce over the term of a multi-year contract. It turns out that the deviation in player salaries from marginal revenue product estimates is consistent with the variation in player performance; and, it should be noted that hitting performance is more stable than pitching performance.[67] Overall, the model predicts free agents' salaries about as well as could be expected given the natural variance in player performance.

What about comparing the estimate to non-free-agent salaries? The collective bargaining agreement rules dictate that players with less than seven years of service should earn significantly less than their revenue-generating ability. Table 5-1 breaks down compensation differences by service class using the

Service Class	Median % Difference from MRP	
	Hitters	*Pitchers*
Reserved	−89	−80
Arbitration Eligible	−78	−74
Fourth Year	*−90*	*−84*
Fifth Year	*−75*	*−66*
Sixth Year	*−56*	*−60*
Free Agent	−13	18
Total	*−68*	*−66*

TABLE 5-1   Player Compensation Relative to Estimated MRP (%)
Service time estimated; sample includes players with more than 2% team's plate appearances

median percent differences in salaries from players' estimated marginal revenue products.[68]

As expected, players earn a greater percentage of their marginal revenue products as their service time rises. For purely-reserved players in their first three years of service, hitters earn approximately 89 percent less than their marginal revenue products, and pitchers earn 80 percent less. Arbitration-eligible hitters and pitchers earn 78 and 74 percent less than their marginal revenue products, respectively. For an arbitration hearing, the rules permit comparisons to players with at most one more year of service, which causes salaries to differ by service year in a predictable manner. As service time increases, arbitration-eligible players garner a larger share of their marginal revenue products. Sixth-year players can compare themselves to free agents, but they are also hampered by being compared to other arbitration-eligible players. In turn, the higher salaries benefit fifth-year players who can compare themselves to higher-salaried sixth-year players, but still have their salaries limited by comparisons with lower-service players; and, the effect trickles down to fourth-year players.[69]

Free-agent hitters earn approximately 13 percent less than their marginal revenue products, which is not surprising. In a competitive market, teams ought to be willing to spend up to a player's marginal revenue product to employ the player. While salary is the main component of this cost, it is not the only component. The estimates are based on gross revenue generated without accounting for other employment costs associated with hiring players such as coaching, medical care, travel, etc. To be precise, a player's salary ought to approximate his net marginal revenue product, which subtracts out non-salary employment costs. It is not surprising that the estimates exceed salaries because of other employment costs, which are difficult to know.

| | Difference from MRP | | | |
| | Starters | | Relievers | |
Service Class	Absolute ($)	%	Absolute ($)	%
Reserved	−2.49	−86	−1.36	−77
Arbitration Eligible	−3.55	−72	−1.61	−75
Free Agent	2.74	52	−0.31	−20
Total	−1.13	−58	−0.95	−65

TABLE 5-2   Player Compensation Relative to Estimated MRP (Pitchers)
Dollars in millions

However, free-agent pitchers earn an average of 18 percent more than their marginal revenue products. While pitchers receive more of their estimated worth at all levels, the chasm is wider among free agents.[70] Players should not be receiving more than their marginal revenue products from rational owners. Breaking down salary differences by starters and relievers, it turns out that starters are responsible for most of the "overpayment" of pitchers. Table 5-2 lists the median differences in salaries and marginal revenue products according to pitcher roles. Free-agent starters earn 52 percent more than their estimated marginal revenue products, while free-agent relievers earn about 20 percent less than their estimated marginal revenue products.

Free-agent salaries exceeding and falling below marginal revenue product estimates may indicate some over- and under-estimation of player worth; however, the absolute dollar differences in Table 5-3 reveals that the divergences in real dollars are less than $500,000, which is especially small considering the normal variation in player performance from year to year. Thus, free-agents' salaries are close to marginal revenue product estimates, while non-free agents earn considerably less, which is consistent with the restrictions on low-service players.

| | Median Difference from MRP | |
Service Class	Hitters ($)	Pitchers ($)
Reserved	−3.41	−1.55
Arbitration Eligible	−3.57	−1.82
Free Agent	−0.48	0.49
Total	−1.97	−1.00

TABLE 5-3   Player Compensation Relative to Estimated MRP
Dollars in millions

Though inefficiencies in the baseball labor market may exist—particularly, for starting pitchers—if the inefficiency is real, it is small. Therefore, it is probably best to say that free-agent salaries approximate player marginal revenue products, and if any inefficiency exists it occurs among starting pitchers, who appear to be overpaid by a small margin. The estimates are not perfect and should be interpreted with caution. The following section reveals the pitfalls of drawing too literal inferences from these estimates.

Baseball's Worst and Best Contracts

Probably the most debated topic of the hot stove league is whether or not players are "worth" their salaries. What worth means varies among fans. To some, simply earning the league minimum is too much: "it's a child's game, and I'd play for free." By this standard, there is no pleasing anyone. Major League Baseball is a lucrative business, generating billions of dollars annually. Baseball players earn large salaries because teams earn substantial revenue from their players' on-field contributions. If the league was able to cap player salaries, baseball would still continue to generate billions of dollars and would cause more revenue to flow to owners—a cohort vastly more wealthy than players. Mandating lower player salaries transfers income from millionaires to billionaires, and don't think that owners don't know this when they openly complain about player salaries.

Viewing baseball as a business means evaluating whether player compensation is too high or too low according to how much revenue each player generates for his team. When a player earns more than what he generates in revenue, the team receives a negative return; and when a player generates more revenue than he earns in salary, the team receives a positive return. Comparing marginal revenue product estimates and salaries of individual players provides a way to evaluate individual contracts to identify white elephants and bargains.

Table 5-4 lists the top-40 worst contracts from 2006 to 2009 based on actual compensation paid out that year.[71] These players cost their teams between $11 and $23 million per year, for total losses of close to $500 million. One team and a few players dominate the list: the New York Yankees had eleven player-seasons of the top-40 worst contracts during this period. These contracts are

Rank	Pos/Pit	Player	Team	Year	PT (%)	Salary ($)	MRP ($)	Difference ($)
1	1	Alex Rodriguez	New York Yankees	2009	8.30	33.00	9.55	−23.45
2	2	Jason Giambi	New York Yankees	2007	4.64	23.43	2.78	−20.64
3	3	Jason Giambi	New York Yankees	2008	9.03	23.43	6.06	−17.37
4	4	Alex Rodriguez	New York Yankees	2008	9.49	28.00	11.60	−16.40
5	5	Manny Ramirez	Los Angeles Dodgers	2009	6.75	23.85	7.97	−15.88
6	1	Jason Schmidt	Los Angeles Dodgers	2007	2.02	15.70	0.56	−15.14
7	2	Jason Schmidt	Los Angeles Dodgers	2009	1.34	15.22	0.35	−14.86
8	6	Derek Jeter	New York Yankees	2007	10.94	21.60	6.97	−14.63
9	7	Derek Jeter	New York Yankees	2008	10.68	21.60	7.23	−14.37
10	3	Mike Hampton	Atlanta Braves	2008	5.30	15.98	1.62	−14.35
11	4	Tim Hudson	Atlanta Braves	2009	2.90	15.50	1.44	−14.06
12	8	Jason Giambi	New York Yankees	2006	8.97	20.43	6.93	−13.49
13	9	Alex Rodriguez	New York Yankees	2006	10.44	21.68	8.37	−13.31
14	5	Bartolo Colon	L.A. Angels of Anaheim	2007	7.35	16.00	2.69	−13.31
15	10	Andruw Jones	Los Angeles Dodgers	2008	3.84	14.73	1.70	−13.03
16	11	Magglio Ordonez	Detroit Tigers	2009	8.31	18.97	6.08	−12.89
17	6	Bartolo Colon	L.A. Angels of Anaheim	2006	4.08	14.00	1.11	−12.89
18	7	Chan Ho Park	San Diego Padres	2006	9.81	15.51	2.63	−12.87
19	8	John Smoltz	Atlanta Braves	2008	1.87	14.00	1.29	−12.71
20	9	Jeremy Bonderman	Detroit Tigers	2009	0.85	12.50	−0.11	−12.61
21	12	Rafael Furcal	Los Angeles Dodgers	2008	2.65	15.73	3.22	−12.51
22	10	Pedro Martinez	New York Mets	2007	2.03	14.00	1.52	−12.48
23	13	Todd Helton	Colorado Rockies	2008	5.72	16.60	4.12	−12.48
24	11	Barry Zito	San Francisco Giants	2009	13.40	18.50	6.06	−12.44
25	12	Johan Santana	New York Mets	2009	11.16	18.88	6.46	−12.42
26	13	Mike Mussina	New York Yankees	2006	12.94	19.00	6.88	−12.12
27	14	Carlos Beltran	New York Mets	2009	5.80	19.24	7.16	−12.08
28	15	Alfonso Soriano	Chicago Cubs	2009	8.36	17.00	4.97	−12.03
29	14	B.J. Ryan	Toronto Blue Jays	2009	1.51	12.00	−0.03	−12.03
30	16	Troy Glaus	St. Louis Cardinals	2009	0.52	12.14	0.16	−11.98
31	17	Richie Sexson	Seattle Mariners	2007	7.91	15.50	3.61	−11.89
32	18	Aramis Ramirez	Chicago Cubs	2009	5.48	16.65	4.81	−11.84
33	15	Kerry Wood	Chicago Cubs	2006	1.35	12.00	0.19	−11.81
34	19	Derek Jeter	New York Yankees	2006	11.08	20.60	8.85	−11.75
35	16	Carlos Silva	Seattle Mariners	2009	2.31	12.25	0.59	−11.66
36	20	Eric Chavez	Oakland Athletics	2009	0.50	11.50	−0.06	−11.56
37	17	Pedro Martinez	New York Mets	2006	8.81	14.88	3.40	−11.47
38	18	Carlos Zambrano	Chicago Cubs	2009	11.87	18.75	7.29	−11.46
39	21	Vladimir Guerrero	L.A. Angels of Anaheim	2009	6.46	15.00	3.81	−11.19
40	22	Jorge Posada	New York Yankees	2008	3.12	13.10	1.96	−11.14

TABLE 5-4   Top-40 Worst Annual Contracts (2006–2009)

Dollars in millions. PT = Playing time as percent of team's plate appearances or batters faced

spread among five players, with Jason Giambi, Derek Jeter, and Alex Rodriguez all appearing on the list three times. Before condemning the Yankees for reckless spending it is important to acknowledge that the Yankees were a good team during this time period—averaging 96 wins and winning the 2009 World Series—and thus their players' production was more valuable than the estimates based on a 0.500 ballclub. Still, this difference is not sufficient to justify fully the exorbitant salaries paid to these players, and I will discuss this further in Chapter 6. The Yankees built possibly the best team in baseball during this time period partially because of their willingness to spend high dollars on free agents. Also, several players on the list received very little playing time as a result of injuries.

Rank	Pit/Pos	Player	Team	Year	PT (%)	Salary ($)	MRP ($)	Difference ($)
1	1	Tim Lincecum	San Francisco Giants	2009	14.83	0.65	19.01	18.36
2	1	Ben Zobrist	Tampa Bay Rays	2009	9.63	0.42	18.33	17.91
3	2	David Wright	New York Mets	2007	11.21	1.25	17.06	15.81
4	3	Adrian Gonzalez	San Diego Padres	2009	11.02	3.13	18.67	15.55
5	2	Zack Greinke	Kansas City Royals	2009	14.60	3.75	18.48	14.73
6	4	Evan Longoria	Tampa Bay Rays	2009	10.78	0.55	14.40	13.85
7	3	Tim Lincecum	San Francisco Giants	2008	14.63	0.41	13.96	13.56
8	5	Hanley Ramirez	Florida Marlins	2008	11.17	0.44	13.98	13.54
9	6	Shin-Soo Choo	Cleveland Indians	2009	10.84	0.42	13.69	13.27
10	7	Ryan Howard	Philadelphia Phillies	2006	10.82	0.36	13.43	13.08
11	8	Albert Pujols	St. Louis Cardinals	2009	11.35	14.43	27.43	13.00
12	4	Justin Verlander	Detroit Tigers	2009	15.74	3.68	16.43	12.75
13	9	Carlos Pena	Tampa Bay Devil Rays	2007	9.75	0.80	13.44	12.64
14	10	Chase Utley	Philadelphia Phillies	2008	11.27	7.79	20.32	12.53
15	11	Ryan Zimmerman	Washington Nationals	2009	11.05	3.33	15.82	12.49
16	12	Nick Markakis	Baltimore Orioles	2008	11.23	0.46	12.62	12.16
17	13	Dustin Pedroia	Boston Red Sox	2008	11.34	0.46	12.24	11.78
18	14	Miguel Cabrera	Florida Marlins	2006	10.92	0.47	12.20	11.73
19	15	Curtis Granderson	Detroit Tigers	2007	10.62	0.41	12.07	11.66
20	16	Troy Tulowitzki	Colorado Rockies	2009	10.06	1.00	12.52	11.52
21	17	Chase Utley	Philadelphia Phillies	2006	11.35	0.50	11.49	10.99
22	5	Ubaldo Jimenez	Colorado Rockies	2009	14.81	0.75	11.70	10.95
23	18	Franklin Gutierrez	Seattle Mariners	2009	10.29	0.46	11.39	10.93
24	6	Ervin Santana	L.A. Angels of Anaheim	2008	14.56	0.42	11.35	10.93
25	19	Albert Pujols	St. Louis Cardinals	2008	10.06	13.87	24.72	10.85
26	20	Grady Sizemore	Cleveland Indians	2006	11.92	0.50	11.35	10.85
27	21	Joey Votto	Cincinnati Reds	2009	8.79	0.44	11.21	10.77
28	22	Jason Bay	Pittsburgh Pirates	2006	11.08	1.00	11.77	10.77
29	23	Denard Span	Minnesota Twins	2009	10.65	0.44	11.17	10.73
30	24	Prince Fielder	Milwaukee Brewers	2007	10.92	0.42	11.07	10.66
31	25	Troy Tulowitzki	Colorado Rockies	2007	10.50	0.38	11.01	10.63
32	26	Marco Scutaro	Toronto Blue Jays	2009	10.69	1.10	11.64	10.54
33	27	Prince Fielder	Milwaukee Brewers	2009	11.42	7.00	17.52	10.52
34	28	Joe Mauer	Minnesota Twins	2006	9.76	0.40	10.76	10.36
35	29	Garrett Atkins	Colorado Rockies	2006	10.95	0.34	10.66	10.32
36	30	Pablo Sandoval	San Francisco Giants	2009	10.45	0.40	10.68	10.28
37	31	Ryan Braun	Milwaukee Brewers	2009	11.25	1.03	11.31	10.27
38	7	Adam Wainwright	St. Louis Cardinals	2009	15.94	2.79	13.06	10.27
39	8	Cliff Lee	Cleveland Indians	2008	14.45	$4.00	14.22	10.22
40	32	Ryan Ludwick	St. Louis Cardinals	2008	9.69	0.41	10.58	10.17

TABLE 5-5   Top-40 Best Annual Contracts (2006–2009)

Dollars in millions. PT = Playing time as percent of team's plate appearances or batters faced

Table 5-5 lists baseball's top-40 best annual contracts from 2006 to 2009. The players with the best contracts in baseball tend to have one thing in common: they are all players with very few years of service. Only one player on the list had a salary of over $10 million, Albert Pujols in 2007 and 2009. While excellent players tend to be worth big bucks, they don't necessarily generate the consistent returns that low-service players can. Low-service stars are the best player-assets to own, and merely good young players can be valuable players assets if they are found early.

I want to highlight a few players on the list who exemplify different methods that teams can use to find bargains. The following players are just three examples of teams purchasing players for less than what they generate in revenue and represent strategies that clubs can use to win games without breaking the bank.

The San Francisco Giants received two top-ten seasons from Tim Lincecum in 2008 and 2009. Lincecum won back-to-back Cy Young Awards, generating nearly $33 million in value for a total salary of just over $1 million. The Giants acquired Lincecum by drafting him with the tenth pick in the 2006 draft. The front office used its bargaining power of being the only major-league team allowed to employ Lincecum to sign him for a $2 million bonus. After signing his contract, Lincecum's salary became subject to the collectively bargained salary rules, and the team benefited from its rights under the agreement that allowed the team to pay him a salary far below his worth.

The Tampa Bay Rays received the 13th highest return by picking up Carlos Pena off the scrap heap. In the years prior to his signing, Pena had bounced between minor-league and major-league clubs in several organizations. Though he was considered to have promise and posted a respectable career OPS of .790, he was released by the Tigers, Yankees, and Red Sox before the Rays picked him up in 2007 for a measly $800,000. Pena is your prototypical *Moneyball*-type player, who tends to hit for a low average with many strikeouts, but walks frequently and hits with power. He is an example of the type of player that Michael Lewis argued that baseball's labor market tended to undervalue. In Pena's case, it appears that the Rays benefited from many other teams ignoring his valuable skill set, which included Gold-Glove-caliber defense in addition to his productive bat.

Ervin Santana produced the 24th highest return in 2008 for the Los Angeles Angels of Anaheim, and he wasn't drafted or picked up off the scrap heap. Finding Santana required scouting a different talent pool. Santana was signed by the Angels as an amateur free agent in the Dominican Republic for $700,000. Unlike players born in the United States and Canada, players outside the United States are not subject to the draft. The poverty-stricken Dominican Republic has been a hot-bed for finding talent, where players will readily sign deals that vastly increase their wealth. In the amateur free-agent market teams don't have to wait their turn to sign a player. To facilitate finding talent, Dominican agents known as *buscones* scout the island for talent in return for receiving a portion of a players' future earnings. By scouring the globe for hidden talent, the Angels were able to find a bargain missed by other teams.

Table 5-5 also reveals that 32 of the top-40 best contracts belonged to hitters, which indicates that teams have been able to find better deals on hitting than pitching, which is consistent with the finding that pitchers have been receiving a greater share of the marginal revenue products than hitters in recent years. However, the anomalous high salaries to pitchers have occurred among free agents while most of the player bargains are among non-free agents.

Caveats: Further Interpretation of Marginal Revenue Product Estimates

Just because we have a number that says a player generated $X does not necessarily mean that a player ought to be valued at $X, because the estimates reflect some simplifying assumptions that may not hold true in all situations. The exact impact that a player has on any specific team will vary by the unique circumstances of the team. How good is the team? What specific revenue sources does the team have, and how do they respond to team performance? How much playing time will the manger give the player? These are idiosyncratic calculations that can only be made by front-office personnel with access to this private information.

Albert Pujols did not increase the St. Louis Cardinals's revenue by exactly $19.93 million in 2007, nor did he generate a specified dollar amount each and every time he produced or prevented a run for his team for which he could bill his manager after each game. That number is an estimate based on what an overall performance like Pujols's typically generates for the typical major-league baseball team. The marginal revenue product estimates reflect the expected added value of any player to an average team in an average market. The following factors are not included in the general estimates presented in Appendix D but should be considered when valuing player performance in specific instances.

Differences in Team Quality

The first reason that players may be worth more or less than their marginal revenue product estimates is that performance value varies with team quality. Because the impact of wins is non-linear—revenue increases with each win—the value of the marginal contribution of any player depends on the performance of his teammates. A good team that adds a player is farther along the revenue curve than a losing club. This fact is often seen in mid-season trades when bad teams tend to trade their best players to good teams. The output provided by the player has more value in a winning market; therefore, it is not surprising to see good teams seek to acquire such players in the summer rather than in the winter, when both clubs were less certain of where they would be on the revenue curve.

A player on a winning team may be "more valuable" in the sense that he generates more money than a superior player in another market; however, if they were to swap teams, the other player would be more valuable. For the purpose of identifying the league's best player, I think it is best to value players so that their performance comparisons across teams are on equal footing—in most cases, players don't have much control over where they play or how good their teammates are—but as a practical matter, teams must consider expected returns that are unique to each franchise. In Chapter 7, I illustrate how to account for team quality when estimating the worth of C.C. Sabathia to the New York Yankees.

Differences Across Markets

Another potential external impact on player value is that wins may differ across markets for reasons other than team quality. Though I have not been able to isolate and estimate differences in the value of wins across markets—and I employed several strategies to generate estimates unsuccessfully (see Appendix B)—I believe that wins impact revenue differently across major-league markets. The difficulty in identifying the effect stems from the fact that several factors, such as population, wealth, weather, infrastructure, and fan loyalty all contribute in unique ways that complicate estimating the effect. There are just not enough observations across 30 teams over a recent period of time to tease out the effects; but, I don't think the effect should be dismissed. If a particular team is spending more on free agents than the estimates project, market factors may explain the divergence, and that possibility should be acknowledged.

Are Resources Being Properly Allocated?

How managers allocate playing time affects the marginal revenue product estimates because of the way players are credited for playing time. Suboptimal roster management may cause the estimates to deviate from true marginal revenue products. A player who is estimated to produce a certain amount of revenue may do so at the expense of a superior player who would generate higher returns. And a good player who spends too much time on the bench may be worth more than his estimated marginal revenue product. Large mistakes in resource allocation may not happen often, but when they occur, the marginal revenue product estimates can be misleading.

An example of how poor roster management can generate incorrect estimates occurred on the 2007 Atlanta Braves. On that team, Jeff Francoeur's estimated marginal revenue product was $7.81 million, but this does not mean that a team ought to be willing to pay nearly $8 million for his services. Further analysis reveals that the Braves' use of Francoeur actually cost the team revenue in terms of the way he played on the field.

The principle error in declaring Francoeur to be a $8 million player comes from assuming that his manager properly allocated his roster talent to generate the maximum output for his team. In the Braves' case, it is clear that the lineup choice was suboptimal, and that Francoeur's played far more than he should have. In 2007, the Braves had three principle outfielders playing the left and right outfield positions: Matt Diaz, Jeff Francoeur, and Willy Harris. The Braves employed a two-man platoon in left field, with the righty Diaz playing against left-handed pitchers and the lefty Harris playing against right-handed pitchers. In right field, Francouer played all but 15 innings of the team's games at the position. Quite a bit of Francoeur's estimated worth is derived from the fact that he played so much. What might have happened if the Braves had played Diaz full-time and platooned Francoeur with Harris?

Francoeur produced 13 more runs than the average hitter who played right field, while taking eleven percent of the Braves' plate appearances and playing

99 percent of the defensive innings at the position. Diaz produced 22 more runs than the average hitter playing the corner outfield slots while taking six percent of the Braves plate appearances and playing 47 percent of the Braves' corner outfield innings—nearly all of it in left field.

Diaz was a much better hitter than Francoeur, generating twice as many runs above average in about half as many opportunities. While Diaz's performance may be a bit biased because he faced more left-handed pitching than Francoeur did—batters tend to hit better against pitchers of the opposite handedness, a phenomenon known as the "platoon effect"—this is not enough to erode Diaz's sizable hitting advantage. Clearly, the Braves would have been better off giving some, if not all, of Francoeur's playing time to Matt Diaz.

Harris was not better than Francoeur with the bat, but he was a superior defensive player. However, the fact that Harris bats left-handed means that if he was to take some of Francoeur's at-bats against right-handers, the Braves' overall run production would likely have increased. A Francoeur–Harris platoon arrangement would have been a superior use of resources, by reducing the quantity of Francoeur's plate appearances and improving their total productiveness by matching Francoeur against left-handers.

Reassigning playing time from Francoeur to Diaz would have been superior to the allocation employed by the 2007 Braves. The opportunity cost of playing Francoeur was not playing a player who would have generated a greater output. The team could have generated more than $7.81 million in revenue from its right field position if manager Bobby Cox had given a portion of his plate appearances to Matt Diaz. Table 5-6 projects hypothetical revenue generated by swapping the playing time of Francoeur and Diaz, assuming each player performed at the same rate over reduced or expanded playing time.

	Playing Time	
	Actual ($)	Switched ($)
Jeff Francoeur	7.81	4.11
Matt Diaz	5.51	11.08
Sum	13.32	15.19

TABLE 5-6   The Reallocation of Playing Time from Jeff Francoeur to Matt Diaz
Dollars in millions

The obvious change is that Diaz's value increases and Francoeur's value shrinks, which is not surprising given the change in playing time. However, when comparing the players' performances with equal playing time (compare the columns diagonally) Diaz has a higher value at both levels of playing time. By reallocating the labor inputs in this manner, the Braves would have received $3.27 million more from Diaz taking Francoeur's playing time ($11.08 − $7.81), and $1.4 million less from Francoeur taking Diaz's playing time ($4.11 − $5.51). The net gain is a $1.87 million increase from using the exact same inputs in inverse proportions. That is additional output that the Braves could have acquired without spending a dime on free agents or in traded prospects to other teams—*the Braves wasted nearly $2 million by not properly allocating the talent they already owned.*

Though Francoeur may look to be more valuable than Diaz from their marginal revenue product estimates, the Braves or any other team could generate more revenue with Diaz than Francoeur; thus, the $7.81 million value of Jeff Francoeur is deceptive.

The failure of the teams to play superior players over inferior ones is normally the fault of the manager for not getting the most out of his 25-man "budget." But, general managers can misallocate resources as well by overspending, acquiring/promoting inferior talent, or using players whose skills are more valued on another club. Take, for example, slugger Adam Dunn. Dunn is a controversial figure among baseball pundits for his high totals in three specific areas: hitting home runs, drawing walks, and striking out. From 2004 to 2009, Dunn averaged 41 home runs and 112 walks per season; however, he also averaged 177 strikeouts per season. While everyone agrees that homers are good and strikeouts are bad, after balancing the bad with the good Dunn remains a good offensive player. According to linear weights, Dunn's 2007 offensive performance was in the top 25 in the league. But that's not the end of the controversy, as strikeouts are not Dunn's only nemesis.

Dunn's nickname "Big Donkey" stems not just from his size and power, but from his lumbering gait, which costs his team runs on defense. While his poor fielding isn't enough to completely cancel out his stellar performance at the plate, it reduces Dunn from an excellent player to a good player.

Table 5-7 lists Dunn's value in several circumstances. In 2007, Dunn's estimated marginal revenue product was $7.67 million. If he was an average defender, he would have been worth $9.62 million—a difference of nearly $2 million. To ignore Dunn's defensive failings, and assume he is not much worse than an average first basemen is as unforgivable as playing Jeff Francoeur over Matt Diaz. However, Dunn is still a valuable player whose offensive capabilities more than offset his defensive liability. If there are no superior alternatives on the team then it makes sense to keep him on the field. But the fact that Adam Dunn has primarily played outfield and first base for his entire career is a travesty, because there exists a league where a team can benefit from Dunn's offense without bearing the cost of his defense.

Type of Player	Value ($)
Actual Performance	7.67
Average Defender	9.62
Designated Hitter	8.40

TABLE 5-7   Adam Dunn's Estimated Value (2007)
Dollars in millions

The last row of Table 5-7 reports that if Dunn had played in the American League as a designated hitter, his estimated marginal revenue product would have been $8.4 million—three-quarters of a million dollars more valuable than he was as an outfielder. Yet, despite this, Dunn has spent his entire career in the National League, playing for Cincinnati, Arizona, and Washington.

Though poor roster management can skew estimates of player worth, the good news is that managers on the field and in the front office have strong incentives to employ their players optimally. Managers want to win because winning provides job security and begets higher compensation. Therefore, managers ought to allocate playing time in order to put their labor inputs to their most highly valued uses, which, in turn, facilitates optimal revenue generation for the franchise. The end result is that in most cases the marginal revenue product estimates should reflect expected player contributions to revenue. Deviations from the optimum are going to happen, but they ought to be the exception. In Jeff Francoeur's case, it may be that his top-prospect reputation, hometown-player popularity, or good looks meant that the Braves were willing to tolerate inferior play. For Adam Dunn, his defensive shortcomings may have been difficult to quantify. With better defensive metrics like plus/minus becoming available to teams, such misallocations should happen less often.

Summing Up

The marginal revenue product estimates generated by the model presented in the previous chapter are correlated to the salaries of major-league free agents, and the salaries of non-free agents are correspondingly dampened according to the league's labor restrictions. There may be some overpricing of pitchers, especially starting pitchers, in baseball's labor market; however, the average deviation of salaries from marginal revenue product estimates is small.

Even though the estimates perform reasonably well, there exist several factors that may cause the estimates to under- or over-state player contributions to teams. Team quality, market size, and improperly allocating playing talent are factors that must be considered when evaluating the estimates. And while roster management may skew estimates of player true worth, the incentives of decision-makers tend to promote the optimal use of players.

Identifying bargain and albatross contracts among individual players may be fun, but occasional good and bad deals are bound to happen to any franchise by chance. Good teams make mistakes and bad teams benefit from good fortune. It would be nice to know how teams perform as a whole. A good organization should be able to string many good deals together to overcome its bad deals, while a poorly run club may not be able to scrape together the remaining pieces to complement a few bargains that fall into its lap. In the next chapter, I evaluate clubs according to how they have constructed their rosters over the past few years to identify the best and worst managed organizations in baseball.

Hot Stove Myth: The Size of the Free-Agent Pool Affects Player Salaries

Image you're an agent for a prominent baseball client whose contract has an out-clause after the season. He can continue to play for his current club for an additional year at a wage close to his marginal revenue product, or he can declare himself to be a free agent and shop his services to the highest bidder. Of course, you should consider factors such as your client's fit with his current club, risk preference, and injury history, but what about the number of comparable free agents expected to be on the market this year and next? If there are many players in the market, this could generate competition and drive down his expected wage. Maybe it's best to enter the market when the free-agent market is thin in order to maximize your expected salary.

The idea that the size of the free-agent pool affects player salaries seems to follow from the interaction of supply and demand. The greater the supply of free agents, the more options teams have. Similar free agents serve as substitutes to one another, and thus a courting team can pit the players against one another by threatening to sign the other free agents. The end result is that salaries for all players in this market will be less than if the free-agent market included fewer participants. Indeed, union leader Marvin Miller believed flooding the market with free agents would depress free-agent salaries. However, the situation is a bit more complicated than just dumping excess players into the labor market.

The size of the free-agent pool fluctuates with another important factor that determines wages in the supply-and-demand framework. The number of players available affects not just the supply side of the market, but the demand side as well. Free agents have come from somewhere, and that somewhere is major-league rosters. The number of free agents and number of open slots are directly connected: a great number of players looking for new teams means that there is a corresponding number of vacated slots that teams need to fill. For example, if there are four good shortstops on the market this means that there are also four openings on major-league teams. The increased supply of players is counteracted by the increased demand by teams needing replacements. To further demonstrate that this is the case, we can look at the other side of the market. Would you prefer to prefer to hit a market with many or few teams needing your client's services? I think the instinctive response would be the one with many openings; however, the openings have the side effect of creating competition from the players who vacated the slots.

But it is also the case that teams which lose players to free agency do not have to replace them with free agents. Instead, they may use in-house substitutes—from the minors or shuffling the major-league roster—thus, removing available landing spots for free agents on the market. This is true, but promoting a player from within is just one of many options that teams have to fill a vacant roster spot, and all of these options affect the price of free agents. Cheaper substitutes affect the wages that teams are willing to pay their players even before they became free agents.

The wages that free agents command are affected by scarcity in the entire baseball labor market, not just other free agents. For example, the 2008–2009 off-season had one of the more-plentiful free-agent classes of top starting pitchers in recent years. In any given year C.C. Sabathia, Derek Lowe, or A.J. Burnett could have been the top starter on the market, but they all hit free agency at once—Burnett actually opted out of contract guaranteeing him $24 million over the next two seasons to join the market. If you followed this market you know that the pitchers faced competition not just from each other, but from non-free agents as well. The Atlanta Braves wanted two of the three and made offers to Burnett and Lowe, landing only the latter. But this wasn't the Braves' only outlet: they tried hard to acquire Jake Peavy and eventually landed Javier Vazquez through a trade. Peavy would eventually land with the Chicago White Sox at mid-season to fill Vazquez's departed rotation slot. This example reveals that though Peavy and Vazquez were not free agents, they served as substitutes who were just as important for generating competition for free agents as actual free agents like Sabathia, Burnett, and Lowe—so were many other starting pitchers who were discussed behind closed doors but never switched teams.

The free-agent market does not exist on its own, rather it is one sector of the labor market where teams purchase player services from many available substitutes. Top prospects and controlled veterans are just as relevant—though maybe less liquid—to the wages that free agents can command as the number of competitors offering their services through free agency. An offseason with many similar free agents will not necessarily yield lower wages any more than a market with few free agents will yield high wages. And because baseball talent is quite scarce, it doesn't take much competition to drive players' wages toward their marginal revenue products.

It is always possible to quibble with theory, so let's examine the recent history of free-agent signings to see how the number of free agents affected the salaries that free agents received. I used the marginal revenue product estimates of players and the number of free agents available by position among free agents to predict the salaries received by free agents from the three off-seasons preceding the 2007, 2008, and 2009 seasons.[72] The results are presented in the following equation:

$$\text{Annual salary} = (1.24 \times \text{MRP}) - (0.075 \times \text{Free agents at a position}) + (1.5 \times 2007 \text{ indicator}) + (2.05 \times 2008 \text{ indicator}) - 1.04$$

The results indicate that, after controlling for the quality of the free-agent players, an additional free agent on the market costs a player about $75,000—peanuts in baseball salary terms. Given that there are an average of nine free agents available per position, it's unlikely that the size of the free-agent pool has a large effect on player salaries. Furthermore, unlike all the other variables included in the regression estimate, the estimated impact of the number of free agents on annual salary is not statistically different from zero (t statistic: 0.64, p value: 0.52), meaning the effect is not different from what would be expected because of random chance. There does not appear to be a strong link between the size of the free-agent pool and free-agent salaries.

In the end, the size of the free-agent pool gives us very little information about the money a free agent can expect to receive. Both sides of the market are linked, and non-free agents serve as competition to free agents.

Chapter 6
Winning On A Dime: The Best- And Worst-Managed Franchises Of The Decade

Identifying good and bad contracts is useful, but individual instances of over- and under-payment don't necessarily provide an accurate picture of how good a general manager is at his craft. Bench players hit grand slam home runs, and Hall-of-Fame sluggers strike out with the game on the line. Just as these isolated events tell us very little about the quality of players, a single contract doesn't tell us much about how well a front office manages its ballclub. Certainly, a general manager who signs a player to a good(bad) contract deserves some credit(blame); however, the sum of the good and the bad decisions provides a clearer picture of his business acumen.

Baseball is a business, where even the least-valuable teams sell for hundreds of millions of dollars. As much a team owners talk a good game about their desire to win at all costs, it's hard to take such claims seriously. After all, look who typically owns baseball teams: successful business executives. The good news for fans is that winning normally begets revenue, so the motives of fans and owners are somewhat congruent. That means investing in the things that produce wins, and hiring the right personnel to ensure the proper baseball decisions are being made.

In *The Baseball Economist*, I proposed two simple criteria for evaluating the management of baseball franchises: how they perform on the baseball field and how much performance they get out of every dollar spent. In summary, good organizations are those that win and win efficiently. I rate organizations for the 2000s according to these criteria using the salaries paid to players and the expected revenue generated by performance. As I detail below, it is possible to have a team

J.C. Bradbury, *Hot Stove Economics*, DOI 10.1007/978-1-4419-6269-0_6,
© Springer Science+Business Media, LLC 2011

that earns profits without winning or to win while paying a steep price for it, but the best organizations win while earning profits.

Valuing Performance: From the Loss Trap to Increasing Returns

Estimating performance value for teams instead of individual players is simpler in some respects, but it also has some additional complications. On the simple side, generating individual player values requires using the assumption that each player's performance is added to the average team. This assumption is needed to make cross-player comparisons based on quality of performance; but for teams, this assumption is unnecessary and may even lead to misguided estimates of team performance value. In particular, the increasing returns to winning means that it is perfectly rational for winning teams to value their players more than teams with fewer wins, and thus offer their players higher salaries. The players themselves may not be any better—though winning teams will likely target the best players as they capture higher returns that weaker teams cannot—their performances are more valuable on winning teams, which justifies paying higher salaries.

The revenue function from Chapter 4 can be used to estimate the marginal impact of runs on team revenue, and Figure 6-1 plots the relationship between the run differential and team revenue. The function differs slightly from Figure 4-1, which maps a relationship between winning and total revenue using a different estimation method. Though the shapes of the relationships are similar, the revenue function in Figure 6-1 excludes external factors that are not impacted by play on the field: centrally shared revenue, population, and the honeymoon effect.

The right side of the function shows the increasing run differential being associated with higher revenues at an increasing rate: each run scored or prevented generates more revenue than the preceding run. But, as a team begins to allow more runs than it scores (moving from right to left on the graph), performance matters less, until it eventually levels off for a period. The degree to which it levels off is debatable and merits further discussion.

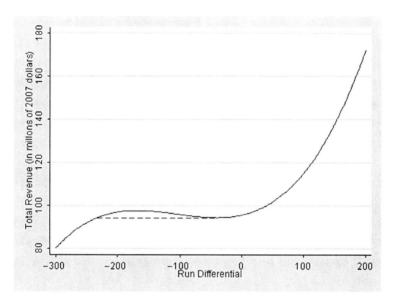

FIGURE 6-1   The Impact of Run Differential on Revenue

The cubic revenue function does something funny as the run differential reaches −41 runs: revenue begins to increase as the run differential grows more negative. Though the increase is gradual, revenue continues to increase until the run differential reaches −170 runs and then declines. At −232 runs the revenue is equivalent to the −41-run revenue level, after which revenue continues to fall at an increasing rate. The bump in the function is troublesome because it means that within this range losing teams can increase revenue by losing more games, and improving by a few games can actually cost a team revenue. I refer to this range as "the loss trap," because at this low level of wins the financial incentives actually discourage winning. Converting the runs to wins, the loss trap occurs approximately between 63 and 77 wins in a season.[73] A team on the high end of this range would benefit from improving, but teams in the low-to-middle range only wish to avoid falling off into the sub-60-win abyss.

There are two possible explanations for why the estimated function identifies a loss trap. The first explanation is that winning increases local revenue which results in decreased revenue-sharing disbursements. This allocation of funds differs from the share of revenue distributed equally to clubs from national television contracts, and other league revenue sources. Local revenue sharing collects a portion of local revenue from all clubs—currently at a rate of 31 percent—pools it, and redistributes it to clubs. The end result being that some revenue is transferred from high-revenue clubs to low-revenue clubs. Revenue sharing creates a financial incentive to lose games, because decreased revenue brought on by losing may be offset by a revenue transfer from high-revenue clubs. Why spend resources on winning when the returns are negative? The loss trap may reflect the disincentive effects created by revenue sharing.

The second explanation is more benign: simply, the bump from losing is an artifact of the waviness of the cubic function. Losing doesn't really beget higher revenue, it just happens that the functional form that best fits the data generates a meaningless bump. Such ill behavior of polynomial functions is common. I suspect that both factors are contributing to the counterintuitive relationship.

There is no need to be concerned about the effect of the loss trap on the already-presented player estimates. The loss trap anomaly does not affect individual player valuations, because a player capable of costing his team 40 runs a year won't get the opportunity to do so, as he'll be demoted or released. −170 runs? That guy is having enough trouble managing a large beer and two hot dogs in the bleachers. The loss trap occurs far below what even an atrocious player could contribute to his team, but teams can easily fall into the loss trap as the losses pile up.

Though I think it is possible for a loss trap to exist as a result of revenue sharing, I do not think that most teams attempt to exploit it. The size of the gains from losing is small: dropping from 77 wins to 63 wins generates about $3 million, a small percentage of expected revenue. Some owners may be satisfied with losing because their poor performance is subsidized by winning clubs, but I suspect the gains are too small for owners to actively discourage winning. I believe it is best to assume that the revenue loss from losing has a floor that begins to kick in around −41 runs, remains flat until −232 runs, and then drops off along the path of the original function. The dotted horizontal line shows this adjustment on the graph. Thus, teams are not rewarded for losing even when the function suggests losing may be a sound financial strategy for a team in this range.

After accounting for the loss trap, the shape of the revenue function reveals an important lesson for ballclubs. If you are going to lose, don't worry about losing a few more games; and, if you're going to win, then try to win more. A club in the midst of a losing season may fear that trading away its few good players will cost it revenue, because what few fans you have will stop turning out for games. However, the revenue function indicates that once losses drop into the low-70s, there doesn't appear to be an additional negative impact on revenue until a team falls below 60 wins, which is difficult to do.[74] A struggling team loses little from trading away its good players for prospects in the hope of generating large gains in the future that can offset current losses.

Correspondingly, winning teams shouldn't feel guilty about adding more wins, because winning increases revenue through two channels. First, winning brings additional attention from fans during the regular season, generating more ticket and concessions sales as well as boosting sponsorship revenue from the added eyes. Second, winning improves the likelihood of earning post-season revenue—which includes approximately 40 percent of the gate revenue for mandatory games plus 100 percent of "if necessary" games. In the future, a team may miss a traded prospect who significantly outperforms his salary for another club, but that financial loss may be overcome by the high returns to winning in the present. For example, in 1987 the Detroit Tigers traded struggling minor-league prospect John Smoltz to the Atlanta Braves in return for veteran starter Doyle Alexander. John Smoltz would mature in the Braves' minor-league system to become a Hall-of-Fame pitcher. While the loss of Smoltz was regrettable, let's not forget that Alexander proved to be quite valuable to the Tigers, posting a 1.38 ERA down the stretch, which helped the Tigers win their division.

The Most- and Least-Valuable Teams of the 2000s

Table 6-1 lists Major League Baseball organizations according to the revenue generated from play on the field. The teams are ordered according to their average rank of total performance value produced by season.[75]

Rank	Franchise	Average Performance Rank	Average Performance ($)	Average Wins	Playoff Appearances	World Series Wins
1	New York Yankees	4.9	131.58	96.50	9	2
2	Boston Red Sox	6.2	132.43	92.00	6	2
3	Atlanta Braves	7.4	116.37	89.20	6	0
4	St. Louis Cardinals	8.4	121.34	91.30	7	1
5	L.A. Angels of Anaheim	9.6	114.00	90.00	6	1
6	Oakland Athletics	9.8	120.56	89.00	5	0
7	Philadelphia Phillies	10.2	106.14	85.00	3	1
8	Los Angeles Dodgers	11.2	106.00	86.20	4	0
9	Cleveland Indians	11.3	108.03	81.60	2	0
10	Chicago White Sox	11.5	105.56	85.70	3	1
11	Minnesota Twins	11.7	102.42	86.30	5	0
12	San Francisco Giants	12.2	111.32	85.50	3	0
13	Chicago Cubs	12.5	107.26	80.70	3	0
14	Toronto Blue Jays	12.9	101.03	80.50	0	0
15	Houston Astros	13.1	103.77	83.20	3	0
16	Seattle Mariners	13.5	124.20	83.70	2	0
17	New York Mets	13.8	101.24	81.50	2	0
18	Colorado Rockies	14.8	99.68	76.90	2	0
19	Arizona Diamondbacks	16.0	102.51	80.50	3	1
20	Texas Rangers	16.5	96.90	77.60	0	0
21	San Diego Padres	16.6	97.36	76.90	2	0
22	Florida Marlins	17.1	95.98	81.10	1	1
23	Detroit Tigers	17.7	96.48	72.90	1	0
24	Milwaukee Brewers	17.7	95.99	74.10	1	0
25	Tampa Bay Rays	18.6	97.01	69.40	1	0
26	Washington Nationals	19.1	94.65	71.10	0	0
27	Cincinnati Reds	19.4	95.23	75.10	0	0
28	Baltimore Orioles	19.8	94.51	69.80	0	0
29	Pittsburgh Pirates	20.1	94.30	68.10	0	0
30	Kansas City Royals	21.0	94.29	67.20	0	0

TABLE 6-1   Average Revenue from Player Performance by MLB Team (2000–2009)
Dollars in millions

It should be no surprise that the New York Yankees had the highest average output over the decade, with an average performance-value rank of fifth. The Red Sox come in a close second with an average performance-value rank of sixth. Both teams produced around $132 million per season, and between them they won four World Series titles.

As expected, winning teams produced the highest revenue; however, it's interesting that good performance didn't necessarily guarantee a championship, nor does poor performance necessarily prevent one. Six of the ten World Series winners came from the top-five performing franchises, but the third-ranked Braves didn't even make an appearance in the fall classic (much to my dismay). Two teams in the bottom half of the league in performance value—the Arizona Diamondbacks (19th) and the Florida Marlins (22nd)—each captured a title. Good regular-season teams may have a better chance of winning a championship than weaker teams, but they are by no means guaranteed a World Series title.

While it is common to judge teams by their post-season success, the performance over five-game and two seven-game series tells us less about the quality of a team than a 162-game season. The laws of probability allow plenty of room for the best not to rise to the top in the current playoff format. For example, assume there is a series between two unevenly-talented teams, and the superior team has a 55-percent probability of winning any game against the inferior opponent. In a best-of-seven contest the inferior team would still be expected to emerge as the champion 40 percent of the time. It would take 23 games for the inferior team to have less than a 5-percent chance of winning more games than the superior team.[76] Statisticians Jim Albert and Jay Bennett estimate that the best team in the league has a 75-percent chance of making the playoffs, but only a 21-percent chance of wining the World Series.[77]

The short-series playoff format is an institution that fuels the uncertainty of competition, which breeds interest and excitement in the sport. High-payroll clubs like the Yankees do have an advantage over those with low budgets, but the disparity is one that is frequently overcome with the help of good management and chance. You have to be good enough to get to the playoffs, but once you get there, the playoff format gives every team a decent chance of winning. Even though the Yankees can build the best team in baseball, it does not guarantee a World Series victory. Despite wining an average of 96.5 games per season from 2000 to 2010, the team captured only two World Series.

As a side note, the post-season performance column of Table 6-1 reveals another fact about the recent competitiveness in the league. Twenty-three different teams made the playoffs during these seasons—that's three-fourths of the league! That so many teams have played beyond the regular season over such a short period of time indicates that the league is meeting the competitive balance standard laid out by Commissioner Bud Selig's Blue Ribbon Panel: "every well-run club has a regularly recurring reasonable hope of reaching postseason play."[78]

The Blue Ribbon Panel on Baseball Economics was organized to evaluate the impact of the league's economic structure on the competitive balance of the league. At the time the report was issued, there was a fear among many baseball officials that the disparity between team revenues across clubs was making the game less competitive. If winning is nothing more than a product of financial determinism, then fans might lose interest in the game. The report was published in 2000 and made several recommendations to improve league structure. Though, most recommendations were not adopted fully, it could be argued that the report did influence league policy toward competitive balance. But it turns out that there may not have been any need for changes anyway.

Figure 6-2 maps the change in competitive balance among Major League Baseball teams in the modern era, using the Noll-Scully measure of competitive balance, which is commonly used by sports economists for quantifying competitiveness.[79] The dotted curve plots a smoothed average of the trend over time (using a Lowess fit), and the trend is clearly improving competitive balance—optimal competitive balance improves as the Noll-Scully metric approaches one—though the improvement appears to have leveled off. Competitive balance today is about what it was in the 1980s, and it is the best it's been in the league's entire history. Recent attempts to improve competitive balance with policies such as revenue sharing and a luxury tax don't appear to have had much effect. In recent times, baseball attendance has been reaching

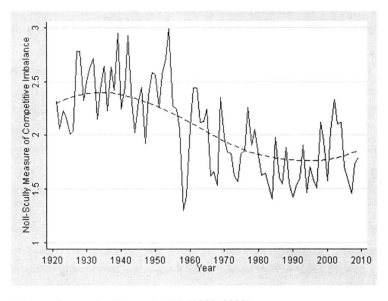

FIGURE 6-2   Competitive Balance in MLB (1921–2009)

new highs, indicating that fans don't appear to be deterred by any perceived lack of competitive balance.

The next section identifies the teams who got the most bang for their buck from their rosters. They're not all big-money teams, and they employ strategies that other perennial losers can adopt to get back on top. There is no doubt that teams in larger and more-intense markets have revenue-generating advantages over teams in smaller and less-intense markets; however, the fact that several teams have found ways to win despite their disadvantages means that perennial losers' complaints about financial determinism may be overstated. I don't believe that the seven teams who missed the playoffs in the 2000s are doomed by the system.

Efficiency: Building a Contender on a Budget

The second standard for judging the quality of team management is how efficiently each club constructs its roster. Better-managed teams ought to get more performance out of every dollar spent than poorly-managed teams. Most teams get back more in performance value than they spend in salaries, because the league's salary rules allow teams to pay players less than their market values during their first six years of league service.

It is my view that the biggest equalizer of talent across teams is not revenue sharing, the luxury tax, or any other policies traditionally thought to aid competitiveness. The allocation of property rights to low-service players whom teams can pay below-market wages is Major League Baseball's most important institution for supporting competitive balance. Though low-revenue clubs may not be able to snap up the top free agents like the New York Yankees or the Boston Red Sox, they are given a valuable commodity that they can use to generate revenue.

A nice feature of this in-kind subsidy is that it does not generate the perverse incentives that revenue sharing does. Revenue sharing directly transfers wealth from high- to low-revenue clubs with the expectation that recipients will use the transferred wealth to become more competitive. But good intentions are not sufficient to guarantee the desired result. With revenue sharing, bad teams have less motivation to win—if not an incentive to lose in the loss trap region—because they are subsidized for their losing ways. Teams that receive revenue sharing have little incentive to use the redistributed funds to improve their clubs. If they are disadvantaged by a poor market, pouring money into payroll is not a smart decision because it does not increase revenue.

Giving teams the rights to player-assets that only become valuable if properly chosen and allocated encourages low-revenue clubs to build good teams, because an organization owns the rights to any valuable players it discovers and develops. A club that fails to do so will not reap the rewards of employing players at reduced wages. The developed players can play for the developing club, or they can be traded for other pieces that the club can use to build a better team. Even when the best talent migrates to other teams via trades, the developing organization at least collects some profit. You can't reap the rewards of cheap talent unless your club is properly managed to find and properly allocate it.

The draft gives every team an opportunity to acquire talent cheaply by awarding teams the sole right to the players it drafts. Before the implementation of the amateur draft, teams were required to flood the country with armies of scouts who would bid on talent that may or may not yield returns at the major-league level. This system gave an advantage to wealthier clubs who could afford a vast scouting network and payed out high bonuses to net the best prospects. In 1965, the year Major League Baseball implemented the draft, Branch Rickey argued that the equalization of access to talent was important for improving competitive balance in baseball.

> The Yankee success story is not due to the play of luck or fortune at all. It is the result of excellence primarily in the front office . . . . Now, the wealth of the world could be redistributed among all mankind today . . . and tomorrow you would have paupers and millionaires all over again. You cannot equalize the ingenuity and effort of the individual, and no one wants to. There will never be a way to equalize individual ability such as the Yankees have had. But there must be **legislation to establish equal opportunity for all clubs in the field of young talent**. (Emphasis original)[80]

The draft's contribution to competitive balance is often discussed only in relation to its reverse-order process that allows the best players to be drafted by the worst teams. But the depth of talent available to clubs allows them to sign talent at below-market rates no matter where they draft. The key feature of the draft for improving competitive balance is that all teams get rights to low-cost talent. Prior to the draft, the average Noll-Scully measure of competitive balance was 2.34, and since that time it has improved to 1.77. While the change was gradual and certainly the introduction of the draft does not deserve all the credit for the improvement, there is more evidence that allocating low-wage talent equally to all clubs improved competitive balance than there is for recently-adopted revenue-sharing policies.

So, which clubs got the most out of their rosters? Table 6-2 reports the average difference between the amount each team spent on salaries from the total revenue generated from player performance.[81] The teams are listed according to their average annual rank over the decade. All but one of the top-five most efficient clubs made the playoffs during the decade, with the Athletics and Twins making the playoffs five times each. The success of these low-spending clubs demonstrates that just because you don't spend a lot of player salaries

Rank	Franchise	Average Difference Rank	Average Difference ($)	Average Wins	Playoff Appearances	World Series Wins
1	Tampa Bay Rays	4.2	40.93	69.4	1	0
2	Florida Marlins	5.5	39.35	81.1	1	1
3	Pittsburgh Pirates	5.6	34.35	68.1	0	0
4	Oakland Athletics	6.5	40.16	89.0	5	0
5	Minnesota Twins	7.2	32.08	86.3	5	0
6	Washington Nationals	8.3	29.11	71.1	0	0
7	Kansas City Royals	9.2	26.57	67.2	0	0
8	Milwaukee Brewers	10.5	24.83	74.1	1	0
9	Cleveland Indians	11.0	24.58	81.6	2	0
10	San Diego Padres	11.2	23.10	76.9	2	0
11	Colorado Rockies	13.6	20.25	76.9	2	0
12	Cincinnati Reds	13.7	17.42	75.1	0	0
13	Toronto Blue Jays	14.3	15.75	80.5	0	0
14	Baltimore Orioles	16.5	10.67	69.8	0	0
15	Texas Rangers	16.8	6.48	77.6	0	0
16	St. Louis Cardinals	17.5	8.11	91.3	7	1
17	San Francisco Giants	17.6	8.28	85.5	3	0
18	Chicago White Sox	17.9	4.71	85.7	3	1
19	Philadelphia Phillies	17.9	7.79	85.0	3	1
20	Arizona Diamondbacks	18.2	7.81	80.5	3	1
21	L.A. Angels of Anaheim	18.3	6.56	90.0	6	1
22	Houston Astros	18.3	6.14	83.2	3	0
23	Detroit Tigers	18.7	2.53	72.9	1	0
24	Seattle Mariners	20.0	6.19	83.7	2	0
25	Atlanta Braves	20.5	0.75	89.2	6	0
26	Chicago Cubs	22.5	−4.88	80.7	3	0
27	Boston Red Sox	22.9	−8.51	92.0	6	2
28	Los Angeles Dodgers	23.8	−12.36	86.2	4	0
29	New York Mets	27.2	−24.93	81.5	2	0
30	New York Yankees	29.6	−62.70	96.5	9	2

TABLE 6-2   Spending Efficiency by MLB Team (2000–2009)

Dollars in millions

doesn't mean you are doomed to failure. These clubs excelled in scouting and management in order to acquire players who were cheap due to player salary constraints or by identifying mispriced talent in the players market.

While the Yankees were at the top in terms of performance, they take the bottom slot in winning efficiency by a large margin. The Yankees actually spent more than their talent generated, and they were not the only team to do so. Four other teams doled out more in salaries than they received in terms of estimated revenue: Cubs, Red Sox, Dodgers, and Mets. However, this does not imply necessarily that these clubs lost money. The losses are generated from an estimated revenue function based on the average of all teams. It's possible that these clubs have unique, but difficult-to-identify, qualities that yield higher returns from player performance. In addition, teams can use money from other parts of their operations to subsidize the hypothetical losses from player costs; thus, the negative values do not denote fiscal insolvency. But still, a team that is spending more than, or close to, its performance value in salaries isn't taking proper advantage of its right to pay a large group of players below-market wages.

These numbers also can be used to compare teams according to how well they allocate resources to player talent relative to one another. For example, the Red Sox received performance value similar to the Yankees, spending $54 million less per year—an amount that could purchase two C.C. Sabathia's a year and still have money left over. While the rival clubs may have put equally-talented teams on the field over the decade, the Red Sox were clearly the better-managed club.

The teams earning the highest returns are all spending relatively little on talent; however, we can see two distinct groups at the top. Eight teams in the top-half made the playoffs during the decade, turning a profit while also putting competitive team on the field. The other seven teams generated profits without reaching the playoffs.[82] Some of these teams hovered in the heart of the loss trap region—potentially boosting their revenues beyond my estimates—consuming the benefits of being a Major League Baseball club and collecting revenue sharing. This may be a rational business strategy, but it is not one that I believe ought to be heavily rewarded when gauging the managerial wisdom across clubs.

Winning Efficiently

According to the management criteria above, a well-managed organization should succeed in the areas of performance and efficiency. Table 6-3 ranks Major League Baseball clubs according to both criteria. The final ranking is generated by summing the ranks of the two categories, weighting both equally. Teams with lower sums receive superior ranks to those with higher sums. Teams at the top performed well on the field, and did so while devoting less money to player salaries than other teams. Teams at the bottom performed poorly and spent relatively more than other teams.

The best-managed organization in baseball during the 2000s was the Oakland Athletics, and this might explain why Michael Lewis chose the Athletics as his subject for *Moneyball*. The A's entrepreneurial spirit pushed them to use new methods to win more games while spending relatively less than other franchises. But, the Twins, Indians, Marlins, and Rays were also successful on the field and in terms of getting the most out of their player-budgets over the decade—with the

Rank	Franchise	Summed Ranks	Average Difference Rank	Average MRP Rank	Average Wins	Playoff Appearances	World Series Wins
1	Oakland Athletics	16.3	6.5	9.8	89.0	5	0
2	Minnesota Twins	18.9	7.2	11.7	86.3	5	0
3	Cleveland Indians	22.3	11.0	11.3	81.6	2	0
4	Florida Marlins	22.6	5.5	17.1	81.1	1	1
5	Tampa Bay Rays	22.8	4.2	18.6	69.4	1	0
6	Pittsburgh Pirates	25.7	5.6	20.1	68.1	0	0
7	St. Louis Cardinals	25.9	17.5	8.4	91.3	7	1
8	Toronto Blue Jays	27.2	14.3	12.9	80.5	0	0
9	Washington Nationals	27.4	8.3	19.1	71.1	0	0
10	San Diego Padres	27.8	11.2	16.6	76.9	2	0
11	L.A. Angels of Anaheim	27.9	18.3	9.6	90.0	6	1
12	Atlanta Braves	27.9	20.5	7.4	89.2	6	0
13	Philadelphia Phillies	28.1	17.9	10.2	85.0	3	1
14	Milwaukee Brewers	28.2	10.5	17.7	74.1	1	0
15	Colorado Rockies	28.4	13.6	14.8	76.9	2	0
16	Boston Red Sox	29.1	22.9	6.2	92.0	6	2
17	Chicago White Sox	29.4	17.9	11.5	85.7	3	1
18	San Francisco Giants	29.8	17.6	12.2	85.5	3	0
19	Kansas City Royals	30.2	9.2	21.0	67.2	0	0
20	Houston Astros	31.4	18.3	13.1	83.2	3	0
21	Cincinnati Reds	33.1	13.7	19.4	75.1	0	0
22	Texas Rangers	33.3	16.8	16.5	77.6	0	0
23	Seattle Mariners	33.5	20.0	13.5	83.7	2	0
24	Arizona Diamondbacks	34.2	18.2	16.0	80.5	3	1
25	New York Yankees	34.5	29.6	4.9	96.5	9	2
26	Chicago Cubs	35.0	22.5	12.5	80.7	3	0
27	Los Angeles Dodgers	35.0	23.8	11.2	86.2	4	0
28	Baltimore Orioles	36.3	16.5	19.8	69.8	0	0
29	Detroit Tigers	36.4	18.7	17.7	72.9	1	0
30	New York Mets	41.0	27.2	13.8	81.5	2	0

TABLE 6-3   Ranking the Management of MLB Teams (2000–2009)

latter team only recently rising from its dismal beginnings to become a legitimate contender at the end of the decade. The top-five managed teams in baseball made 14 playoff appearances over this span, which is four more than the bottom-five big-spending duds at the bottom of the table.

Different rankings on the list may elicit protests from readers. "How can that team be ranked so high (low)?" Setting up objective criteria for ranking management allows helps avoid personal biases that may be based on mis-perceptions. If the results are unsatisfying then it is necessary to either alter beliefs or question the method. I believe the criteria I set out and the methods I used to gauge them are non-controversial; therefore, I think it provides information as to how well teams manage their resources. While some teams may be better or worse than the ranking conveys useful information regarding managerial tendencies.

Summing Up

Franchises engage in an exercise of constrained maximization, where front-office personnel must seek out the best possible players at the lowest possible cost. The player-value estimates and actual player salaries provide a benchmark for evaluating how well Major League Baseball organizations win and win efficiently.

The key to finding success on the field is identifying low-cost players, which mainly include young players who have not reached free agency. Good organizations use player compensation rules to their advantage to hire good, but inexpensive, talent.

The next chapters focus on valuing two pools from which teams can draw their talent: aging veterans and young prospects. Teams that can value talent properly in these areas will have an edge over teams that can't.

Hot Stove Myth: General Managers can Buy Low and Sell High

Hypothetical trade suggestions are a staple of conversation in the hot stove league. One type of trade that is frequently proposed is to move a player who recently performed much better or worse from his career norm. For example, "I think we should trade Gary Goodyear for Bill Badseason. Bill's a much better player than he showed this season and Gary's coming off the best season of his career. We should dump Gary while his value is high and pick up Bill while his value is low." The logic seems sound. Player performance does fluctuate from year to year, and players with bad years are likely to improve while players with good years are likely to decline—a statistics concept known as regression. But the error in this kind of argument is that it requires the general manager on the other team to be more than a little naïve. He would have to be oblivious to a concept that is widely known to millions of message-board posters and talk-radio junkies.

My contention is not that general managers are infallible, just that we should not expect them predictably to make mistakes that are obvious to everyone else. Several years ago, I asked Oakland A's Director of Baseball Operations Farhan Zaidi if there are any sucker general managers in baseball, and his response was telling:

> Absolutely not. Working in baseball has given me a newfound respect for GM's in baseball. It takes a lot to rise through the ranks of the industry to one of those 30 positions. Fans and media like to deride some GM's as being clueless, but from what I've seen, being a clueless GM is an oxymoron of the highest order.[83]

Before you think he's just defending his brethren, I think it's important to note that Zaidi is no lifetime insider. I conducted this interview a few months after the A's hired him out of the University of California's economics doctoral program, and his advisor was world-renowned behavioral economist Matthew Rabin. In the interview, he did acknowledge that front-office personnel may be subject to some types of biases that affect all humans, but that's not the type of mistake we're talking about here. Remember, message-board posters are getting this right, while general managers continue to make mistakes.

In addition, even if some general managers could be so easily fooled, the key knowledge of when players peak or trough doesn't exist. When teaching investment concepts in class, I often begin with a hypothetical graph of a stock's price changing over time. I ask students to predict whether the stock will move up or down in the following period. One student suggests it will go up, "the stock was down last period, so I think it's going to rise." Another student disagrees, "I think the stock will eventually go up, but not next period. The stock has previously shown a tendency to decline for several periods before rebounding. I say it's going to fall." I then pull a quarter out of my pocket and say, "heads equals up and tails equals down," flip the coin and then record the outcome on the board. The prices on the graph were generated by coin flips that were random; yet, when looking back on the data, it seemed easy to identify a predictable and exploitable pattern from random events. The lesson is that seemingly meaningful and predictable patterns can be generated from randomness; such patterns are not predictable and, therefore, cannot be exploited.

Baseball player performance isn't as random as coin flips, but identifying exactly how a player will perform in the future is difficult from the limited observations we normally see from players. If a player with two seasons of experience, one good and one bad, does one season better reflect his performance ability than the other, or should his projection fall somewhere in between? Fluctuations in performance do create uncertainty, which affect the price that general managers are willing to pay for players. But when it comes to identifying ups and downs, it's difficult to know whether a performance change represents random noise that will disappear or whether it reflects a real change in performance capability. Therefore, when attempting to buy low or sell high, it's just as easy to buy when a player has farther to fall or sell before a player rises to new heights.

In a similar vein, fans sometimes like to point out differences in parks, or focus on advanced metrics to demonstrate that players are better or worse than what some unwitting general manager might think he's worth. I think such suggestions are also unlikely to yield fruit, because baseball front offices personnel are likely familiar with concepts widely understood by devoted baseball fans.

In this book, I identify several instances where general mangers have made mistakes; however, this does not mean that general managers are incompetent. Though some men who have held this title haven't fared well, I believe that most general managers are highly capable agents who generally make good decisions. All humans make mistakes, so it is unfair to pick on individual cases where something went awry. Teams are constantly looking for errors by other clubs and do take advantage of them when they find them; however, selling (buying) high (low) isn't one of those areas where inefficiencies persist unless general managers are colossal morons.

I think it is unlikely that business-savvy owners trust franchises valued at hundreds of millions of dollars to individuals who don't understand the many variables that go into projecting performance as well as the people who sit in the bleachers. General managers are not above criticism—after all, that would take all the fun out of the hot stove league—but I think it's wrong to assume they are so myopic that they make such simple mistakes.

Part III
Projecting Performance

Chapter 7
Is C.C. Sabathia Worth $161 Million? Valuing Long-Run Contracts

In December 2008, the hot stove league received its biggest jolt in years when the New York Yankees signed ace C.C. Sabathia to a contract that would pay him $161 million over the seven following seasons. There was little debate that Sabathia was the best pitcher among the available free agents; but, to many observers, an average salary of $23 million a year was just too much, especially in the climate of a recession. Mike Cramer, a former Texas Rangers president turned Sport Management Professor commented, "I think it's crazy and I think the numbers are out of whack." During a radio interview, Florida Marlins President David Sampson commented that the Sabathia signing was irresponsible and compared the Yankees to "drunken sailors."

But Yankees president Randy Levine dismissed the critics and responded: "[We are] very, very methodical, analytical and careful in what we do ... so these are big numbers, but you have to invest .... We understand these are difficult times for a lot of people. We're sensitive to it. All the more reason if we can reinvest now, reinvest in the team, rather than holding it back for ourselves." In other words, signing Sabathia was a smart business move that would ultimately pay for itself.

The estimates of players' revenue-generating potential derived in the preceding chapters are obviously applicable for determining whether or not the Yankees' offer was sober. If the contract far exceeds a reasonable estimate of Sabathia's worth, then the claims of overzealous spending are justified. But, if the expected revenue generated approaches the contract payout, then the Yankees likely made a sound business decision.

J.C. Bradbury, *Hot Stove Economics*, DOI 10.1007/978-1-4419-6269-0_7,
© Springer Science+Business Media, LLC 2011

Year	Team	Runs > Average	2007 Dollars ($)	Current Dollars ($)
2006	CLE	31.91	8.66	7.94
2007	CLE	50.64	13.45	13.45
2008	*CLE*	*16.63*	*4.95*	*5.40*
2008	*MIL*	*35.46*	*7.66*	*8.35*
2008	Total	52.09	14.27	15.55
Two-year mean		51.37	13.86	14.50
Three-year mean		44.88	12.13	12.31

TABLE 7-1   Performance and Estimated MRP of C.C. Sabathia (2006–2008)

Dollars in millions

Let's begin by looking at Sabathia's performance just prior to his signing the contract. Sabathia had been one of the league's better pitchers, winning his third Cy Young Award in 2007. Table 7-1 lists the marginal revenue product estimates of Sabathia's performance from the three seasons that preceded his contract.[84] During this span, Sabathia averaged about 45 more runs prevented than the average pitcher, generating average annual revenue between $12 and $15 million—well below that average annual salary of his new contract. At first glance, the intoxication theory looks like it may have some support; however, it would be naïve to compare his future salary with the past estimates of his worth. Raw estimates from the past must be adjusted before we determine if he is worth the salary owed to him over the life of the contract.

Projecting Future Performance

Sabathia isn't being paid for what he has done, but for what the Yankees expect him to do. This doesn't mean the past is irrelevant—in fact the past is a good source of information about future performance—but it would be wrong to assume that any baseball player will continue to perform exactly as he has in the past. The estimated aging function for pitchers introduced in Chapter 3 can be used to project how a player with Sabathia's talent ought to progress over the term of his contract.

Sabathia would be 28 for most of the first season of his new Yankees contract, and thus ought to have been expected to improve and decline over the contract's term. Table 3-6 in Chapter 3 reports the expected performance changes relative to peak performance for a large sample of pitchers. While that table can be used

Age	ERA (%)	K9 (%)	BB9 (%)	HR9 (%)
22	−2.95	0.36	−4.40	−2.55
23	−2.64	0.18	−4.19	−2.17
24	−2.31	0.01	−3.93	−1.77
25	−1.95	−0.16	−3.63	−1.34
26	−1.56	−0.33	−3.30	−0.89
27	−1.15	−0.51	−2.92	−0.42
28	−0.73	−0.68	−2.51	0.05
29	−0.29	−0.86	−2.05	0.53
30	0.15	−1.05	−1.57	1.00
31	0.59	−1.24	−1.06	1.46
32	1.02	−1.43	−0.53	1.90
33	1.45	−1.64	0.02	2.31
34	1.86	−1.85	0.56	2.70
35	2.24	−2.07	1.10	3.06
36	2.60	−2.31	1.62	3.39
37	2.94	−2.56	2.13	3.68
38	3.24	−2.84	2.60	3.94

TABLE 7-2   Predicted Annual Change in Performance by Age (Pitchers)

for projecting performance, it is simpler to project aging estimates that refer to changes from year to year. This eases projecting performance for players at any point in their careers. Tables 7-2 and 7-3 list the annual changes in performance by age for pitchers and hitters, respectively. While I use only ERA and OPS to project aging effects over time, I include the changes in the other measures as well. The dark bars mark peak performance in each area.

Age	OPS (%)	OBP (%)	SLG (%)	AVG (%)	BB (%)	DPT (%)	HR (%)
22	2.34	2.90	2.51	1.25	7.66	5.21	53.66
23	1.99	2.49	2.10	1.06	6.45	4.22	30.76
24	1.66	2.11	1.72	0.87	5.44	3.34	20.34
25	1.34	1.75	1.36	0.68	4.58	2.56	14.25
26	1.04	1.41	1.01	0.50	3.81	1.83	10.16
27	0.74	1.08	0.68	0.32	3.13	1.14	7.12
28	0.46	0.77	0.35	0.15	2.51	0.49	4.69
29	0.18	0.46	0.03	−0.03	1.94	−0.16	2.60
30	−0.10	0.16	−0.30	−0.20	1.40	−0.80	0.71
31	−0.38	−0.14	−0.62	−0.37	0.89	−1.45	−1.11
32	−0.66	−0.43	−0.95	−0.55	0.39	−2.13	−2.96
33	−0.95	−0.74	−1.29	−0.73	−0.10	−2.85	−4.94
34	−1.24	−1.04	−1.63	−0.91	−0.59	−3.62	−7.19
35	−1.55	−1.36	−2.00	−1.10	−1.08	−4.48	−9.88
36	−1.86	−1.69	−2.38	−1.29	−1.59	−5.44	−13.35
37	−2.20	−2.03	−2.80	−1.50	−2.12	−6.54	−18.15
38	−2.55	−2.40	−3.24	−1.70	−2.68	−7.85	−25.52

TABLE 7-3   Predicted Annual Change in Performance by Age (Hitters)

Based on Sabathia's age, any team signing him to a long-run contract ought to expect the already-dominant Sabathia to improve over the next two years, before beginning a performance descent. Thus, in the final year of his contract at age 34, Sabathia can be expected to perform about five-percent worse than his peak level, which would be four-percent worse than his 2008 performance at age 27. To put this in perspective, in 2008, Sabathia posted a 2.70 ERA; a four-percent worse performance is a 2.81 ERA. That sounds too good to be true, because it is. Though Sabathia was good in 2008, he wasn't *that* good.

Sabathia probably pitched of a quality somewhere close to the observed outcome with luck pushing the outcome a little above or below his ability. In 2008, Sabathia had some good luck aiding his excellent performance, and it would be incorrect to give him extra credit for being the beneficiary of good fortune.

Using past performance to project the future requires filtering out luck from ability. One way to dampen the impact of luck is to focus on the most stable statistics over time to identify retained ability that is the strongest determinant of future performance. For pitchers, strikeouts, walks, and home runs are some convenient stable measures for evaluating pitchers. The valued performance from 2006 to 2008 in Table 7-1 is based on Sabathia's performance in these areas, but even these stable measures fluctuate over time. Pitcher performances in strikeouts, walks, and home runs still include luck, just less luck than other metrics.

Another filter to proxy ability is to take an average of several seasons of performance in order to smooth out odd deviations in performance that may crop up in individual years. However, averaging performances from past years also has a weakness: going too far back in time picks up information that is less relevant to the present. What if a pitcher learned a new pitch or has finally found a workout regimen that makes him a more effective pitcher than he was previously? Conversely, he might develop a drug problem or suffer an injury that will plague him for the rest of his career. The older the information is, the more likely it is that performance estimates will be biased by erroneous information. There is no best solution as to how far one should go back when gauging a player's ability for projecting performance. I generally look at the three previous seasons, but samples of two, four, or some sort of weighted average of years may produce satisfactory estimates of player talent. In some cases where unique information regarding no-longer relevant factors affected a player's past performance are well-known (e.g., an injury that has healed); it may be best to choose particular seasons but ignore others to proxy ability. To keep things simple for this example, I focus on Sabathia's three- and two-year averages for projecting performance.

Age	Aging (%)	Three Years ($)	Two Years ($)
28	0.73	12.22	13.96
29	0.29	12.17	13.90
30	−0.15	12.11	13.84
31	−0.59	12.06	13.78
32	−1.02	12.01	13.72
33	−1.45	11.95	13.66
34	−1.86	11.90	13.60
Total		84.42	96.46
Average		12.06	13.78

TABLE 7-4   Projected MRP of C.C. Sabathia Based on Aging (2009–2015)
Dollars in millions

From 2006 to 2008, Sabathia's average estimated marginal revenue product was just over $12 million, but a closer look at his performance indicates that 2006 was an odd year. While Sabathia's performance per innings pitched was quite similar over all three years, he enhanced his value by increasing his innings pitched from 193 in 2006 to 241 and 253 in 2007 and 2008, respectively. Thus, the Yankees, and other bidders, may have expected Sabathia to pitch his more-recent workload and valued him as such.

Table 7-4 reports how age ought to affect his performance value using the previous three- and two-year averages of performance value. Even when using the most-recent two years of performance to estimate his talent and subsequent ascension and decline with age, his projected value is nowhere close to the $23 million a year that he would collect for the duration of his contract. But Sabathia's age isn't the only factor affecting his future worth. In particular, the expected growth in league revenue will increase his value over time.

League Revenue Growth and Player Salaries

When Sabathia agreed to a long-term contract with the Yankees, he guaranteed that he would receive a large sum of money for his performance over the following seven seasons. But, he also gave up something: his right to sign a contract with other clubs. After a few more seasons of excellent performance, other teams ought to be willing to employ Sabathia for more than his current deal. Accepting the Yankees' contract offer means that he is prohibited from agreeing to better deals that might come along in the future.[85] Therefore, as compensation for forgoing his free-agency right in future years, he must be assured that his compensation will be in line with what he expects to receive in the future. And given the excellent growth of Major League Baseball revenue in the recent past, his performance will likely to be valued considerably more in the future.

Table 7-5 lists *Forbes*'s Major League Baseball revenue estimates from 2003 to 2008, and the average revenue growth rate is around nine percent per year.[86] Continued growth is typical for most sports industry products, because sports are *normal goods*. A normal good is a product whose consumption moves with the wealth of its consumers. As wealth rises, people consume more normal goods; and, as wealth declines, they consume less. The long-run trend of the US economy is steady positive growth, and despite occasional business cycle fluctuations we expect this trend to continue.

Year	Revenue ($)	Annual Change (%)
2003	3,878	---
2004	4,263	9.9
2005	4,733	11.0
2006	5,111	8.0
2007	5,489	7.4
2008	5,819	6.0
Mean revenue growth		8.5

TABLE 7-5   Change in MLB Revenue (2003–2008)
Dollars in millions
Source: Forbes *Business of Baseball*

There is no doubt that recessions hamper financial returns in baseball; however, sports tend to be quite resilient to recessions, because fans are resistant to give up a relatively cheap entertainment option to which they are deeply devoted. Individuals are more likely to cut back in other areas when times get tough, before cutting back on sports. In the midst of a major recession, the 2008 baseball season saw only a 1.1 percent decline in attendance from 2007 when attendance was at an all-time high. 2008 attendance was actually 3.4 percent higher than it was in 2006. During the Great Depression, not a single Major League Baseball team folded.[87] So, even as the economy was slumping when Sabathia inked his deal, it is probably best to focus on the long-run trend of growing revenues continuing while acknowledging that revenues may suffer some during economic downturns. Furthermore, for a contract as long as Sabathia's, the slowing of revenue growth in the short run may be offset by higher-than-normal growth in the future.

As baseball generates more revenue with each passing season, the performances of its players become more valuable in terms of nominal dollars; thus, the things that C.C. Sabathia does now will be even more valuable in the future, even as age saps some of his ability. When a player and a team agree to a long-run contract, both parties must make some calculation about what that player's services will be worth in the future.

Using a nine-percent annual growth rate for salaries as a rule of thumb, Table 7-6 converts the performance values in 2007 dollars in Table 7-4 into current dollars, and this adjustment significantly boosts Sabathia's expected worth.[88] In the final years of his contract, Sabathia approaches and eventually surpasses his average annual salary of $23 million; however, for the entire contract, Sabathia is still earning $1 to $4 million per year more than he is expected to generate in revenue. Thus, the league revenue growth adjustment is still not enough to justify the contract. But there is still one more factor that may increase his value, Sabathia may be worth more to the Yankees than to the average team.

Year	Three Years ($)	Two Years ($)
2009	14.52	16.59
2010	15.75	18.00
2011	17.10	19.54
2012	18.55	21.20
2013	20.13	23.01
2014	21.85	24.97
2015	23.72	27.10
Total	131.63	150.40
Per year	18.80	21.49

TABLE 7-6   Projected Average Revenue Generation of C.C. Sabathia in Current Dollars
Dollars in millions

Team Performance Impact

The general marginal revenue product estimates presented in Appendix D are designed to compare players on equal footing, and thus assume that each player is added to a team with a .500 record. This assumption is employed for simplicity, but as the run differential between runs scored and runs allowed expands, each additional run adds more revenue than the preceding run. A player who joins a club that has significantly more wins than average will add runs that are more valuable than runs added to an average team.

In Sabathia's case, he joined the Yankees, who won 89 games with a run differential of 62 runs in 2008. Sabathia wasn't the only change to the 2009 club roster, either. The Yankees also added top free agents Mark Teixeira and A.J. Burnett, and important contributors Jason Giambi and Mike Mussina departed. Though it is difficult to know for certain, I believe the additions outweighed the subtractions even without the addition of Sabathia, but for parsimony I use the 2008 run differential baseline for evaluating Sabathia's marginal contribution to the Yankees.

Figure 7-1 magnifies the portion of the revenue function depicted in Figure 6-1 that is relevant for valuing the addition of C.C. Sabathia to the Yankees. The dashed vertical lines mark the points where Sabathia contributes runs above average to two different-quality teams. The first line identifies the marginal

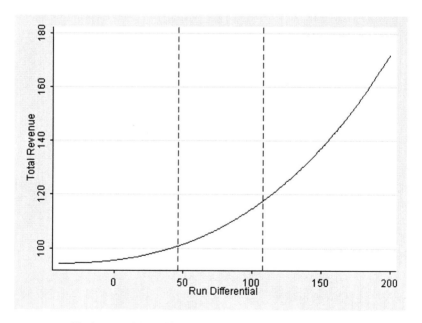

FIGURE 7-1   The Impact of Run Differential on Revenue

contribution of the 45th run that he prevents (the mean of the previous three seasons) for a .500 team. The second line identifies the same contribution to a team that has a run differential of 62 runs prior to his arrival, which increases the run differential to 107 (62 + 45 = 107). The increasing slope of the curve with each run demonstrates that runs contributed to a club of the Yankees' caliber are significantly more valuable than runs contributed to an average team. This is the contribution that the Yankees should focus on when deciding whether or not it is worthwhile to increase their contract offer when bidding against other teams.

To adjust for the added value of wins to the Yankees, I use the runs-to-revenue conversion function from Chapter 4 to estimate the revenue generated to a team scoring 62 runs more than it allowed the Yankee's 2008 run differential. Then, I add the number to Sabathia's expected additional contribution—45 runs (three-year average) and 51 runs (two-year average)—to this value to measure the added revenue produced by pushing the team further along the revenue curve. The adjustment measures Sabathia's marginal revenue contribution to a team that is experiencing increasing returns to winning in the range of games that the Yankees expect to win in the near future. Table 7-7 lists the expected value of Sabathia's additional contribution to a team that scores 62 more runs than it allows.

Year	Three Years ($)	Two Years ($)
2009	22.30	25.79
2010	24.20	27.99
2011	26.26	30.37
2012	28.50	32.96
2013	30.92	35.77
2014	33.56	38.82
2015	36.43	42.14
Total	202.17	233.85
Per year	28.88	33.41

TABLE 7-7   Projected Revenue of C.C. Sabathia to the New York Yankees
Dollars in millions

After adjusting for team quality, Sabathia's numbers don't look so out-of-step with his compensation; if anything, he appears to be underpaid. The estimates show that he is expected to generate more than what the Yankees will pay out to him over the term of his contract. This estimate is probably on the high side, because it assumes that without Sabathia the Yankees will have a 62-run differential over his contract term. While the Yankees have been a very good team over the past several seasons, it is probably not a good policy to project that the Yankees will continue to be this good too far into the future.

At the end of the day, the Yankees front office decided that Sabathia was worth the contract they offered him. And they likely reached this conclusion via "methodical, analytical and careful" examination as opposed to suffering from intoxication. Yes, the Yankees paid a steep price for Sabathia, but the value is defensible. In fact, we might want to ask why Sabathia accepted a contract that was less than his projected revenue to a team of the Yankees' caliber.

Risk and Long-Run Contracts

How players and teams view risk also influences salaries guaranteed over several seasons. Teams face significant risks when signing players to long-run contracts. Injuries, player apathy, and just plain bad projection may mean that a player doesn't produce enough output to cover his salary. While past performance offers some guide to a player's injury risk, sometimes even healthy players break down without much warning. Prior to the 2005 season, the Yankees signed free-agent starter Carl Pavano to a four-year, $40 million contract. Thanks to several injuries, Pavano would throw a disappointing 146 innings for the Yankees over the next four seasons, which was far less than the 211 innings pitched he had averaged for the Florida Marlins in the two preceding seasons. In hindsight, the Yankees would certainly prefer not to have signed the deal; however, predicting whether or not a player will suffer significant injuries is difficult.

Players are also aware of the possibility and consequences of injuries. Baseball players have their net worth tied up in a single attribute: the ability to play baseball. Since their youths, most players have devoted their lives to learning skills that are only useful for playing baseball. They practice, exercise, and travel at the expense of improving their "real world" skills in school or work. Even players who attend college and excel academically don't have the time to properly nurture their intellect. Should one's baseball ability disappear, the player is left with limited skills and experience needed to succeed outside baseball.

Though baseball players have high salaries, they also spend lots of money and enjoy a high standard of living. If a player's main income source dries up because of injury, he will face the prospect of altering spending habits that he has become accustomed to. Multiple houses, rare wine collections, and charitable donations may have to be scaled back, and that is something that players wish to avoid. Fans may not feel sorry for players forgoing luxuries, but players who appreciate these things would prefer not to give them up.

When it comes to signing contracts, the difference in risk perceptions between players and teams leads to an opportunity for trade. As a result of having their value tied up in a single skill, players are risk averse, which means they are willing to sacrifice some wealth for guaranteed income. A team, however, can insure against the loss of any one player by diversifying its risk among many players. Though some players will not live up to their projected values, others will exceed expectations. In the long run, the good deals will cancel out the bad deals. The end result is that teams may be willing to pay players high salaries even though they expect that some players will not live up to their contracts because of injuries.

For example, suppose a team signs three players each to three-year contracts; and if healthy, each player would be worth $10 million per year. If they all stay healthy, then the team will receive $90 million in player performance; however, if one of these players suffers an injury and never plays a game, the team will reap only $60 million in total value. If the team signed each player to contracts of $20 million apiece, then despite losing one player to injury the team still breaks even. Two players receive salaries less than their marginal revenue products, and the injured player receives substantially more. The former contracts offset the latter. Though the players may be disappointed that they could have earned higher salaries on a series of one-year contracts, they chose to accept lower salaries in return for a certain return.

The risks faced by teams and players explain why many players have recently signed long-term guaranteed contracts that paid them far less than they could expect to get as free agents in the future. Prior to the 2009 season, the Boston Red Sox signed Dustin Pedroia and Kevin Youkilis to long-run deals that guaranteed them over $40 million apiece, even though both players were not yet free agents. Both players' deals extended into what would have been their free-agency years when they would likely earn well above what they would be paid. These represent good deals for both sides. The Red Sox hired two players for less than market value; even if one player should get hurt, the other's success should make up for the loss. The players agree to give up some of their future earnings as free agents in order to guarantee them a tidy nest egg should they suffer an injury that prevents them from reaping the returns of the free-agent market.

In Sabathia's case, he may be taking less than his projected worth to the Yankees, but he still commanded a remarkable sum, much more than that would be needed to induce other players to agree to a seven-year deal. Risk preferences are subjective, and Sabathia may not have been willing to trade much income for security. He had already earned $36.5 million over the course of his career, so he may not have been willing to sacrifice much additional wealth for peace of mind. In addition, unlike Youkilis and Pedroia, Sabathia had other teams competing for his services; all of whom could diversify his risk of injury by hiring other players. But there is another reason why the Yankees may not have been willing to raise their offer.

The Luxury "Competitive Balance" Tax

In the late 1990s, Major League Baseball owners and players instituted a "luxury tax" framework for penalizing clubs that exceeded a maximum total salary level. The tax was briefly phased out, but was reinstituted in 2003 in a form close to what it is today. Under the terms of the current collective bargaining agreement, and renamed the "Competitive Balance Tax," clubs must pay a penalty in a percentage of the amount that a club's payroll exceeds a maximum salary threshold. First-time offenders pay a tax rate of 22.5 percent, a second consecutive violation increases the tax rate to 30 percent, and for every additional consecutive violation the tax rate is 40 percent. For the 2009 season that threshold was $162 million, and the Yankees cleared that by a wide margin with a total payroll of $226.2 million—a difference of $64.2 million resulting in nearly $26 million in taxes paid to the league. The threshold is set so high that the Yankees have been the main club affected by the tax, paying over 90 percent of the total luxury tax penalties since 2003.

This relates to Sabathia's contract because his cost to the Yankees exceeds his salary obligations. Due to the fact that the Yankees have been over the luxury tax threshold for more than two consecutive years, the team must remit 40 percent of every salary dollar they pay out beyond the total threshold to the league. On average, the Yankees will pay out approximately $32 million annually for the right to employ Sabathia—that is, $23 million plus $9.2 million in luxury taxes $(0.4 \times \$23$ million)—which is about what his projected value approximates. And should the Yankees fall below the luxury tax threshold during the term of the contract, the Yankees would have to pay less. Thus, even while paying the tax, the Sabathia deal is consistent with the revenue he generates.

Summing Up

The high-dollar long-run contracts that baseball players frequently sign may seem exorbitant, but the astronomical salaries are grounded in the revenue that teams expect players to generate for their teams. This is not to say that teams do not make mistakes; but just salary being high doesn't mean it is inconsistent with a rational calculation of player worth. Salaries are high because major-league teams earn substantial revenue. The more teams win, the more revenue they make, which explains why star players earn significantly higher salaries than marginal players. When teams and players agree to long-run contracts they must account for aging, the growth of league revenue, the quality of the signing team, risk, and luxury tax implications.

The example of C.C. Sabathia shows the many factors that go into valuing free-agent veterans. But as complicated as this calculation is, free agents are not the most difficult group of players to project. After six years of major-league service, we have a pretty good idea of how players should be expected to perform. Young prospects who haven't played a day in the big leagues pose a more complicated challenge. In the next chapter, the analysis is extended to this group, where uncertainty is much greater than it is for experienced major-leaguers.

Hot Stove Myth: Player Salaries Raise Prices at the Gate

According to Team Marketing Associates' Fan Cost Index, from 2000 to 2009, the cost of attending a baseball game rose approximately 150 percent. Over that same period, player salaries rose between eight and nine percent per year. So, it's not surprising that many fans complain that players' high salaries are raising the price of going to the ballpark.

One of the chief assumptions that I rely on in this book is that player salaries are tied to team revenues, so that as revenues begin to rise, players become more valuable and thus command higher salaries. Fans' willingness to pay to see sports (especially winning teams) has continued to grow over time with the wealth of the economy, as sports are normal goods. Therefore, the high and growing wages that players receive are simply a product of a wealthy and voracious fan base willing to spend increasingly more money on sports.

How can I be so sure that I don't have the causality backwards? Maybe it isn't player salaries that are driving up the prices fans pay to watch baseball at the stadium or on television. Sports commentators frequently blame the wages of players—especially those who don't appear to be living up to their contracts—for the rising prices of tickets, concessions, and cable subscriptions. The argument is that if players didn't make so much money, then tickets would be cheaper; thus, capping salaries would keep prices low for fans.

I don't believe the causality flows in this direction, and, therefore, capping salaries wouldn't lower ticket prices. But, how might I convince readers skeptical about the direction of the causality between wages and ticket prices?

There is an easy test that we can run to see whether higher prices are driven by fans' desire for better baseball or if fans are having more-expensive baseball thrust upon them to fund greedy players. If fans are disgusted by rising prices caused by exorbitant player wages, then as the price of attending a game rises we should see attendance fall. However, if teams are responding to the demand for a superior baseball experience that is more expensive, then fans will not be deterred by higher prices; instead, attendance should increase.

The graph below shows that attendance at Major League Baseball games has increased over the past decade. Though attendance hasn't increased every year, there is a clear upward trend. Certainly, other factors affect the desire of fans to attend games, but if salaries were driving ticket prices, then we'd see fans turning away from the game. Rather than being deterred by higher prices, even more fans are going to games. In addition to the excitement on the field, the game experience has transformed from a beer-and-peanuts crowd to one where martinis and sushi are common fare. The high prices also reflect the additional stadium amenities which fans are consuming. Furthermore, the relationship between ticket prices and attendance actually understates the amount of revenue that fans are willing to spend on baseball. Cable subscriptions, internet applications, and throwback merchandise are some other baseball products that fans have been consuming in recent years.

So, the next time you think your ticket is too expensive, don't blame the high-priced stars. If you don't value the experience as much as it costs you to attend, then don't go. As people stop going, salaries will stabilize and fall ... but I don't see that happening anytime soon.

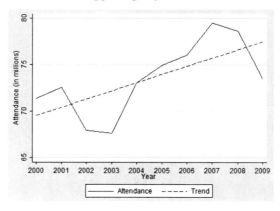

Chapter 8
You Don't Need A Name To Be Traded: Valuing Minor-League Prospects

When a trade is reported on the sports ticker, the acronym PTBNL often accompanies the running scroll. The abbreviation stands for "Player To Be Named Later;" which means one club has agreed to give up one or more players now in return for another player who will switch teams at a later date. A player-to-be-named-later is an IOU issued by a club that allows its trading partner to select an individual from a pre-determined list of players to complete a trade. This gives a club an opportunity to scout players with whom it is unfamiliar, and thus lessens the risk of doing a deal. A player-to-be-named-later can be included in a trade as long as the deal is consummated within six months and the player has never played in the league he's moving to. It's this last requirement that makes most players-to-be-named-later minor leaguers.

Being a player-to-be-named-later isn't as degrading as being swapped for batting practice balls or several pounds of catfish, but it certainly isn't the mark of a high-quality player. You can almost hear the general manager quoting a punch line to a Mitch Hedberg joke about people handing out street flyers, "Here, you throw this away." Though some players-to-be-named-later have become good major-league players (like Moises Alou), they don't frequently have productive careers. Minor-league players are extremely talented baseball players, but even among this elite group very few individuals will rise to become major-league caliber players.

Table 8-1 lists the percentage of minor-league hitters who played in the minors between 1992 and 1999 and made it to the majors prior to 2008 by league classification level. The numbers reveal that only 28 percent of minor-league players even made it to the big leagues; and only five percent of the players produced

J.C. Bradbury, *Hot Stove Economics*, DOI 10.1007/978-1-4419-6269-0_8,
© Springer Science+Business Media, LLC 2011

League Classification	Played MLB (%)	Significant MLB Career (%)
Rookie/Short-Season	10.45	1.29
Single-A	15.73	2.36
High-A	20.92	4.41
Double-A	33.50	6.56
Triple-A	72.53	13.28
Total	28.36	5.10

TABLE 8-1   Percentage of Players Played in MLB by Minor-League Classification

significant careers with at least 1,000 plate appearances and played through their 32nd birthdays.

Though the success rate of minor-league prospects is low, because the compensation rules allow teams to pay players far less than their financial worth for their first few years in the big leagues, major-league organizations don't mind taking a risk on minor-league players. Minor-league prospects are high-risk assets—junk bonds of baseball talent—that teams are willing to hold and train only because the occasional successes yield tremendous payoffs.

The preceding chapters focus on valuing major-league baseball players as assets according to their on-field performances. Minor-league players can be valued similarly, but their worth is more difficult to peg. Major-league players have already proved they are among the elite baseball players in the world. Some major-league players do deviate from past performances in unexpected ways, but typically it is easy to identify good and bad major-leaguers soon after they enter the league. Projecting major-league performance from minor-league play requires extra care to account for the additional uncertainty created by evaluating players against inferior competition and projecting their performances farther into the future.

With the long odds of making it to the big leagues, fans are often upset when their favorite club accepts minor-league prospects in return for a major-league veteran. Sure, minor leaguers may be worth it *if* they pan out, but that uncertainty is hard to live with. We need to quantify that "if," in order to know whether the prospect offers sufficient return for a major-leaguer who has already proved he can play.

Marte for Renteria

One such trade occurred in December 2005, when the Boston Red Sox traded Edgar Renteria to the Atlanta Braves for Andy Marte. After hitting a game-winning single to win the 1997 World Series for the Florida Marlins, Renteria carved out a fine career as a shortstop—garnering four All-Star selections, two silver slugger awards, and two gold gloves. His performance led the Red Sox to sign Renteria to a four-year, $40-million contract during the previous off-season. Marte, on the other hand, played the majority in the 2005 season with the Braves' Triple-A farm team in Richmond, logging 24 games in Atlanta where he posted a paltry .438 OPS. Based solely on the quality of the players, this trade seems even more lopsided than the Millwood-for-Estrada swap discussed in Chapter 1. The justification for making the swap is similar—a young and cheap player can be more valuable than a veteran with a big contract—but estimating the exact value of the two assets requires detailed analysis.

Renteria's worth over the remaining term of his contract can be estimated easily from the method detailed in Chapter 4. Table 8-2 lists Renteria's marginal revenue product estimates and salary commitments from 2006 through 2008. Renteria's performance during the contract term was consistent with his career performance up to that time; thus, the marginal revenue product estimates are consistent with what teams should have expected from him over the contract period.

Overall, Renteria was projected to generate just under $21 million for the duration of his contract—$5 million *less* than the $26 million still owed to Renteria at the time of the trade. In order for any team to be willing to take

Team	Year	MRP ($)	Salary		Difference (MRP–Salary)	
			Overall ($)	Braves ($)	Overall ($)	Braves ($)
Detroit	2008	5.421	9.000	6.333	−3.579	−0.912
Atlanta	2007	7.541	9.000	6.333	−1.459	1.208
Atlanta	2006	7.664	8.000	5.333	−0.336	2.331
Total		20.626	26.000	18.000	−5.374	2.627
Present Value					−4.794	2.538

TABLE 8-2   MRP Estimates and Salary Commitments to Edgar Renteria (2006–2008)
Dollars in millions

on Renteria, it would need a subsidy to cover the financial losses Renteria projected to generate. This explains why the Red Sox agreed to send $8 million to the Braves along with Marte, which I apply equally to each year of the contract in the table.[89] With the Red Sox subsidy, Renteria generated a $2.63 million revenue surplus for the Braves and Tigers—to whom the Braves would trade Renteria after the 2007 season. Because the asset will generate revenue at a later date, it is necessary to discount the estimate to take into account that $2.63 million accrued over several years isn't the same as receiving $2.63 million today. The expected net present value in 2006 was $2.54 million (see Appendix A for an explanation of the present value calculation).

But what did the Braves give up? Several years have passed since the trade, revealing the type of player Marte has become. Before the 2006 season even started, the Red Sox traded Marte with a package of players to the Cleveland Indians. Marte would start the season with the Indians' Triple-A club in Buffalo before getting a mid-season call-up where he performed unspectacularly—a frustrating sequence that Marte would repeat for the next four seasons. Before the 2009 season, Marte was "designated for assignment" by the Indians, which gave every major-league organization the opportunity to claim Marte. There were no takers, and Marte would return to the all-to-familiar Buffalo. It's easy to look back in hindsight to declare Marte a bust, but at the time many people thought the Braves got the short-end of the trade. To understand why any team would be willing to take on Andy Marte, it is necessary to investigate what baseball pundits thought of Marte at the time the trade was made.

In 2005, *Baseball Prospectus* declared Marte to be baseball's top prospect. *Baseball America* ranked Marte to be the ninth best prospect in baseball—one spot above the eventual 2006 Rookie of the Year, Florida Marlins shortstop Hanley Ramirez. It is easy to see why scouts were so high on Marte. At 21, he had already reached the end of the Braves minor-league system, which put Marte three years ahead of the typical major-league rookie. At High-A Myrtle Beach, Double-A Greenville, and Triple-A Richmond, he produced OPS of .840, .889, and .878, respectively. Marte also impressed scouts who looked beyond the numbers to project major-league players. Razor Shines, who had watched Marte develop as an opposing manager for the Birmingham Barons, stated, "There's nothing not to like about Andy Marte. He's an outstanding defender with a chance to be an impact player offensively."[90]

Subjective opinions will only go so far in expecting what a player will become. Many scouts excel at identifying major-league talent among prospects without even looking at player numbers; however, the historical record of minor-league performances offers a wealth of information available for objectively identifying factors that produce major-league success. It is possible to use this data to learn which factors foretell success and to what degree, and then use these factors to answer the question of what Andy Marte was projected to become.

The first step to projecting major-league production from prospects is to look at the past to see how minor-league performance translated into success in the majors. Using a sample of minor-league performance data from 1992 through 1999, I observed how minor-league performance, personal characteristics, and playing environment predicted peak major-league performance. An advantage of using peak performance as a career reference point is that players typically become free agents just as they hit their peaks; thus, the aging function can be used to value performance that typically accrues to teams during the preceding reserved years when players earn below-market salaries. After projecting peak performance, I used the aging function developed in Chapter 3 to adjust for performance expectations over players' careers.

Projecting Major-League Performance from Minor-League Performance

Players possess a basket of skills that age differently. Linear weights credits individual events according to their expected run contribution; however, the specificity of the information contained in linear weights makes projecting precise outcomes far into the future difficult. Therefore, I estimated the impact of minor-league performance on three more-general metrics of major-league peak performance: batting average, isolated power, and on-base percentage. Summed, these statistics generate OPS, which is highly correlated with run production (see Chapter 2). Because performance fluctuates from year to year, a five-year average from ages 28 to 32 served as a proxy of every player's peak-performance level.

Minor-league baseball is composed of several levels ranging from short-season leagues to Triple-A. My preliminary analysis found that performance below the

High-A level had no predictive impact on major-league performance; thus, I only feel comfortable using the data to value prospects playing in High-A, Double-A, and Triple-A. This does not mean that performance at low levels is irrelevant for predicting success; instead, it reveals that the performance metrics commonly used to evaluate players at higher levels do not tell us much about future performance at the early stages of development. That performance in the low minors does not predict major-league success with much certainty should not be surprising given the wide talent disparities and age differences in these leagues. When evaluating low-level prospects, I listen to scouting experts and give little credence to performance statistics. I suspect that most major-league teams collect useful subjective scouting information from their scouts, which they quantify and use to project performance of low-level players, but they do not make this data available to the public.

Years of scouting wisdom offers a variety of opinions as to what factors foretell major-league success; therefore, it is necessary to have some statistical evidence to justify which minor-league performance factors should be used for projecting performance. I estimated several hypothetical projections using many combinations of potential leading indicators of success to find the factors that best-predicted major-league-level performance.[91] After testing many possible predicting factors, I used the minor-league strikeout rate, walk rate, and batting average to project major-league batting average. For projecting major-league isolated power, I used minor-league-level walk rate and isolated power. I employed the minor-league-level walk rate and batting average to project major-league on-base percentage. The skills associated with future performance for each skill are not surprising, as the best hitters tend to have high batting averages, batting power, many walks, and few strikeouts.

Other potential predictors of major-league success include personal characteristics. Player endowments that may project future performance include age, height, and weight. The impact of age, which was measured in years and was estimated as a quadratic function, is relevant because identical performances at the same minor-league level by younger players ought to project superior major-league performance. Figure 8-1 confirms this relationship between age and expected value by minor-league level as younger players project to be worth more than older players within minor-league levels. In addition, scouts often use phys-

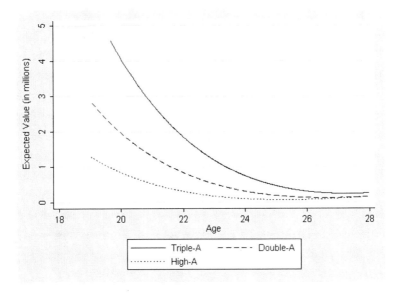

FIGURE 8-1   Impact of Age on Expected Value by Minor-League Level

ical attributes to aid in estimating a player's ability to grow and adjust as he progresses in his career; therefore, I included height (measured in inches) and weight (measured in pounds) in the projection.

Another factor influencing potential performance is the competitive environment in which players compete. I used a group of indicator variables for each team and year in which players play to pick up the impacts of external factors that affect player performance for reasons other than talent. This should minimize the impact of extreme differences in home parks and years that inflate or deflate minor-league performance statistics.

I used multiple-regression analysis to estimate the impact of all the above factors on future major-league performance. The full results are available in Appendix C.

Converting Projections into Dollars

The next step was to convert the major-league performance projections into dollars using a procedure similar to the one discussed in Chapter 4. Because the hitting projections are not denominated in runs like linear weights, it was necessary to estimate how the performance projections translate into runs.

In *The Baseball Economist*, I used on-base percentage and slugging average to estimate run production, which I then employed to estimate player worth. I did so again using a direct projection of on-base percentage and summing isolated power and batting average to produce slugging average. I used team on-base percentage and slugging percentage to estimate their impacts on runs scored with data from 2003 to 2007, and then used the weights to generate the expected runs produced above average from the projected numbers for minor-league players.[92] Then, the expected runs were converted to dollars using the weights in Equation 4.1. Though it would be nice to project precise defensive contributions, minor-league data and the frequency of position changes from the minors to majors do not allow for a simple conversion. Therefore, I projected every player to provide average defense at the average of all positions, listed in Table 4-2.[93]

The conversion of performance projections may be more easily understood through the example of Andy Marte. Based on his 2005 performance in Triple-A, Andy Marte was expected to produce a .370 on-base percentage and a .488 slugging average—a healthy .858 OPS—for 7.29 percent of his team's plate appearances at his peak. This converts to approximately 15 runs above average, producing $7.9 million with his bat at his peak (in 2013 dollars). His defensive contribution of $1.75 million increased his overall contribution to $9.65 million; however, this doesn't mean that Marte's expected worth was nearly $10 million at his peak.

Expected Value: Quantifying "If"

Estimating the predicted performance of major-league players from minor-league performance has one serious bias: all minor-league players in the sample played major-league baseball while many minor-league players with similar performances and characteristics did not. Therefore, it would be incorrect to expect all minor-league players to reach their projected major-league performance levels. Going back in time to see how already-successful players once performed ignores the uncertainty of making it to the next level. To assess the expected value of a minor-league player, the projection must account for the fact that many players wash out of baseball, so that the peak-performance projections can be weighted to account for the probability of achieving the predicted performance.

A correction is needed to weight the projected values according to the likelihood that players make it to the big leagues. Using variables similar to the ones I employed to estimate peak performance, I used a probit regression method to estimate weights for explanatory factors according to how they impact the probability that a player reached his peak-performance level in the majors. The full results are reported in Appendix C.

The preceding projections yield two pieces of information from minor-league performance that can be employed to project big-league worth: (1) projected performance converted into dollar terms, and (2) the likelihood that the player will reach the majors where he can generate that performance. Multiplying the projected value of a player by the likelihood that he will reach his peak generates an expected value of performance, which weights the projected value according to the probability of reaching his peak-performance level. Because no player has a 100-percent chance of reaching this milestone, the second step dampens the expected worth of a player. It takes into account both quality of future performance and the likelihood that it will be reaped.

Marte's 2005 Triple-A performance predicted that he had a 36 percent of reaching his peak performance—if this seems low, recall that only five percent of minor-league players play through their projected peak seasons. Multiplying $9.65 million by 36 percent yields an expected performance value of $3.5 million at his peak. With the expected value of Marte's revenue projection it is possible to take the next step and estimate how his production and salary responsibilities change over the course of his indenture to his team.

Valuing Prospects as Assets

At the time of the trade, Marte was succeeding in the top level of the minor-leagues, and he would be reserved to his parent club for six more years of major-league service. Therefore, most teams likely expected Marte to step into the big leagues at 22 for good, which meant his reserve rights would expire after his age-27 season. The average aging effects in Table 3-5 deflate Marte's projected performance downward according to how his performance ought to progress toward its peak during his first six years in the league. In addition, league revenue was growing at an annual rate of nine percent, therefore, his expected worth should rise over the term of his service.

Marte's expected salary responsibility is close to the league minimum for his first three years. In 2006, the league minimum salary was $327,000; and it would rise to $380,000 and $390,000 in the following two years. Projecting his arbitration awards is more difficult. I assume that Marte will earn 75 percent less than his projected marginal revenue product, which is approximately the average wage percentage of marginal revenue product for arbitration-eligible players.[94]

The difference between his expected marginal revenue product and salary is the net revenue that a team owning Marte's rights expects to reap from employing Marte over this period. Table 8-3 lists Marte's expected value and its components in 2005. In his first three years of service, his expected worth to his team is at its highest, even though the value of his production is at its lowest. The extreme salary restrictions during this time in players' careers net significant revenue to teams. In the last three years, the returns are still positive, but not of the same magnitude as the earlier years. The last column lists the net present value of Marte's performance in each year, and reports his total expected net present value at the time of the deal to be $6.36 million.

When compared to Renteria's net present value of $2.63 million, Marte was actually the more valuable asset. But, before we praise or scold either party in this transaction, it is important to remember these approximations are rough and do not take into account other relevant factors. The estimates ignore

Age	Year	Expected MRP ($)	Salary ($)	Difference ($)	PV (Difference) ($)
27	2011	2.901	2.017	0.884	0.679
26	2010	2.642	1.837	0.805	0.646
25	2009	2.399	1.668	0.731	0.613
24	2008	2.172	0.390	1.782	1.561
23	2007	1.960	0.380	1.580	1.447
22	2006	1.798	0.327	1.471	1.408
Sum		13.873	6.619	7.254	6.355

TABLE 8-3   Expected Value of Andy Marte in 2005

Dollars in millions

team-specific impacts and are based on assumptions regarding playing time, progression through the majors, and defensive ability that may have been too simple. Rather than say that the Red Sox got the better end of the deal based on the information available at the time the deal was made—in hindsight, the Braves clearly got the better end of the deal—it's probably best to say that this trade was defensible from the Red Sox's perspective. Trading a proven veteran for an unproven prospect was a sound business decision in this case, and other veteran-for-prospect swaps likely produce positive payoffs, as well.

As the above analysis indicates, evaluating the value of any particular prospect requires knowing detailed information. One reason that I chose to use the Marte-for-Renteria swap as an example is that the trade involved a simple exchange of two players and cash. Most trades involve many prospects, which complicates the analysis. But, it would be helpful to have general rules of thumb for evaluating the trade of prospects at different levels of performance.

Table 8-4 lists the expected value of average position-player "prospects"— whom I define to be players on the path to begin their major-league career at 24—by level.[95] The expected marginal revenue products reported reflect the

Age	Year	Expected MRP ($)	Expected salary ($)	Difference ($)	PV (Difference) ($)
Triple-A					
29	2016	2.324	2.697	−0.373	−0.251
28	2015	2.128	2.474	−0.346	−0.243
27	2014	1.944	2.270	−0.326	−0.240
26	2013	1.770	0.438	1.332	1.023
25	2012	1.607	0.425	1.182	0.949
24	2011	1.455	0.412	1.043	0.875
Sum	*6-Year*	*11.228*	*8.717*	*2.511*	*2.112*
	3-Year	*4.832*	*1.275*	*3.557*	*2.846*
Double-A					
29	2017	1.811	2.940	−1.129	−1.032
28	2016	1.659	2.697	−1.039	−0.958
27	2015	1.515	2.474	−0.960	−0.893
26	2014	1.379	0.451	0.928	0.872
25	2013	1.252	0.438	0.814	0.772
24	2012	1.134	0.425	0.709	0.678
Sum	*6-Year*	*8.750*	*9.425*	*−0.676*	*−0.562*
	3-Year	*3.766*	*1.314*	*2.452*	*2.321*
High-A					
29	2018	1.174	3.204	−2.030	−1.840
28	2017	1.075	2.940	−1.865	−1.705
27	2016	0.982	2.697	−1.715	−1.582
26	2015	0.894	0.465	0.429	0.400
25	2014	0.812	0.451	0.361	0.339
24	2013	0.735	0.438	0.297	0.282
Sum	*6-Year*	*5.673*	*10.195*	*−4.523*	*−4.107*
	3-Year	*2.441*	*1.354*	*1.087*	*1.020*

TABLE 8-4   Expected Value of Average Baseball Prospects by Minor-League Level in 2010

Dollars in millions

mean peak value adjusted for aging and league revenue growth from 2011 to 2018.[96] The projections assume the hypothetical player spends one year at each minor-league level and then accrues consecutive years of major-league service. The difference is the net return that a club can expect the average prospect to generate while under the control of his parent club. Some players repeat levels before moving up, others bounce between the majors and minors for several years before sticking in the big leagues, and many other factors will likely affect players' value; however, the table provides a simple benchmark for evaluating the expected value of minor-league players.

Marte was an above-average prospect who was young for his minor-league level; therefore, he was worth more than the typical Triple-A prospect. Higher-level players are more valuable than equally-performing players at lower levels, because there is less uncertainty about succeeding in the future. An interesting finding is that the expected return on the average prospect is negative once the player becomes arbitration eligible; however, players generate positive expected returns when they earn salaries close to league minimum. The higher three-year sum is the relevant expected value calculation because a team always has the option of cutting a player who is not worth his salary. Thus, minor-league players hold significant value as trade chips, ranging from $1.02 million for average High-A prospects to $2.85 million for average Triple-A prospects.

This leads to a question, why does the Major League Baseball Players Association—the most powerful players union in sports—agree to a collective bargaining pact that allows teams to pay players salaries significantly below their estimated worth during their first six years of service? Economists Anthony Krautmann, Lawrence Hadley, and Elizabeth Gustafson proposed that the below-market wages may offer a form compensation for training costs, which are paid almost entirely by teams at the minor-league level. These costs include not only the training and medical costs of players who make it to the major-league level, but also cover the training of many players who will never play in the major leagues. Because it is difficult to identify who will succeed and fail, even among the best minor-league talent, team owners are willing to train players who will never generate a positive return by receiving excess compensation from players who succeed. Economist Simon Rottenberg compared minor-league players to oil wells, which require many dry holes to produce a valuable strike.

> When it is discovered, the returns on it are high, but these returns
> must compensate for the losses incurred on the attempts which failed
> ... To their cost must be added the cost of scouts and try-out camps
> and other costs of finding players and assessing their capacities. The
> monopsony gains in the minor leagues are merely compensation for
> investments losses in scouting and in the operation of farm teams ...[97]

It's easy to gawk at the "exploitation" of Cy Young winners like Tim Lincecum earning $400,000 a year while generating many millions of dollars for the San Francisco Giants. But for every Tim Lincecum there are several Chris Enochs. Enochs was pitcher who was selected in the first round of the draft by the Giants' cross-town rival Oakland A's ten years before Lincecum. He toiled nine seasons in minor-league ball but never threw a pitch in the big leagues. In addition to a $1.2 million signing bonus, the Athletics paid for seven years of equipment, coaching, travel, and medical care in order to prepare Enochs to pitch at the big-league level, but he just didn't make it.

The risk of investing in potential future talent is that it may not pan out. The analysis above shows that though the expected return on the average prospect is positive, the returns are much less than is often assumed given some of the good deals that exist. It is natural to ignore the players who don't succeed, but they still represent a financial burden to ballclubs, which organizations hope to recoup from the returns from successful players.

In addition, teams would be unwilling to train players to improve their worth if after training them the players were able to accept a higher contract offer with another club at a later date—an offer that would not exist without minor-league training. Yankees pitching legend turned scout Spud Chandler opined that training costs represented a significant cost to teams and that they would not be willing to incur if they received no compensation after developing a prospect: "It's hard to blame the players for taking all that money, but they talk like there's no such thing as development costs. A boy in the minors is financial dead weight, and it's not fair to find him, train him, and then just lose him to some team richer than you."[98] This fact was not lost on union leader Marvin Miller, who, after forcing the end of the reserve clause, urged players to accept limited control by teams to pay for development costs.[99]

The unique arrangement of deferred compensation in the form of sharing a portion of a player's future output likely arose from the unique relationship between the participants. The individuals who are most capable of training baseball players typically work for Major League Baseball organizations. These instructors spend time on the farm molding raw talent and teaching valuable skills, without which players might never achieve success. The required training isn't acquired overnight and may take years to perfect. Furthermore, most players are not in a favorable financial situation to purchase their own training.

In a world where players have no period of reduced-wage employment, we might imagine prospects participating in student-loan type programs, borrowing against their future earnings to purchase private training outside of Major League Baseball's purview. The problem with such an arrangement is that the people who are most capable of projecting the future worth of prospects work for baseball organizations. Just as teams are more capable of insuring players against long-term injuries than private insurers, teams have a better idea of how to gauge the financial risk of prospects than student-loan officers; therefore, it makes sense for players and teams to enter into a bartering arrangement where players purchase training for a share of their future income.

Summing Up

At first glace, veteran-for-prospect swaps may not appear to make much sense when comparing the talent of the players involved. But after projecting minor-league play into major-league performance and accounting for the probability of becoming a successful major-league player, it appears that minor-league players can be valuable commodities. In the players-as-assets framework, minor-league prospects represent highly volatile assets who yield positive expected returns despite their considerable low rate of success.

The rules that permit teams paying players below-market salaries may seem exploitive; however, the excess returns that some players generate may reflect necessary compensation for teams to recover training costs. Therefore, the current agreement between players and owners that restricts player salaries for their first few years in the league likely reflects a mutually beneficial arrangement.

Hot Stove Myth: College Players are Better Draft Bets than High School Players

Each June, the majority of new talent enters Major League Baseball through the amateur draft. Begun in 1965, it was designed to give teams equal access to talent and prevent the big-money clubs from buying up all the best prospective talent and applies only to players in the United States (including its territories) and Canada. While the rules of the draft have been modified over time, the general eligibility rules include players who have just graduated high school, players attending community or junior college, and college players who have completed at least three years of school.

Some analysts feel that teams ought to focus more on college players than high school players. The reason for this is that college draftees tend to succeed at a higher rate than high school draftees. The implication is that teams are drafting too many high school players when college players are actually the better bargain. In *Moneyball*, Michael Lewis emphasized the Oakland A's strategy of focusing on college players to exploit a market inefficiency.

> [Bill James] looked into the history of the draft and discovered that "college players are a better investment by a huge, huge, laughably huge margin." The conventional wisdom of baseball insiders—that high school players were more likely to become superstars—was also demonstrably false.[100]

The data do seem to back-up this assertion somewhat. Jim Callis of *Baseball America* compiled success rates in the big leagues according to several categories for the first ten rounds of the draft from 1990 to 1997.[101] Given that the definition of major-league success is somewhat subjective, I will focus only on players whom Callis defines as "Regulars or Better."

For the first ten rounds, college players tend to be about as successful as high school draftees. However, when we limit the analysis to the first few rounds (see the table below), where the best talent is selected, the college-to-high school distinction becomes more pronounced. At the top of the draft, where the best players enter the league, college players are a bit more likely to be successful than high school players, which seems to support the suggestion that teams could improve their draft success by drafting more college players.

Draft Success Rate (1990–1997)

	Total Drafted	Succeeded	Success Rate (%)
First Five Rounds			
College	518	69	13.34
High School	566	63	11.13
First Two Rounds			
College	239	53	22.21
High School	268	47	17.55

However, the fact that selected collegians have been more successful than high school players does not mean that adopting a strategy of drafting more college players will improve your team in the long run. College and high school students are not merely separate talent pools from which teams can continuously draw consistent talent; they are also classes of players with differing levels of uncertainty among finite populations of worthy prospects.

Most players who are drafted out of high school decide between college or the minors; although, a small number of players opt for community or junior college. As 18- and 19-year-olds, the draftees are assets with considerable risk. Prospects who choose scholarships over contracts not only put off a payday, but they give major-league clubs three or four years to evaluate their play and project what they may become. In my analysis of minor-league players in Chapter 8 I found that performance didn't seem to predict major-league success until players reached High-A ball. This is about the same age at which college players return to the baseball labor market to be re-evaluated by scouts.

In college, some prospects may improve their statuses, but many more will wash out—just as many of their colleagues from their high school draft cohort three years earlier have washed out of the minors. The additional time that scouts have to watch players mature and grow reduces uncertainty about what college players are likely to become. Not only can teams identify top talent that is more mature and closer to the big leagues than high school talent, but also they can eliminate some players as legitimate prospects and remove them from their draft wish lists. Rating college prospects is like choosing a car from a group you've test-driven. After driving the cars, you're likely to find one you like, but you also know the cars that you don't want.

When viewing college as an information-gathering tool rather than just another talent pool, you can't necessarily improve your drafting success simply by picking up more college players. The higher success rate among college draftees is due partially to the better information scouts have about the talent pool. If the college talent pool has been depleted, reaching back into the pool won't bring the same success rate as previously selected college players—after the good ones are gone, they're gone! It's likely that teams have higher success rates with college players because they learn whom they don't want. Instead, drafting high school players, whose odds are longer than good collegiate players, may be preferred to drafting marginal college players.

Teams definitely should not shy away from college players either, because the ones who are selected have been quite successful. Furthermore, economists John Burger and Stephen Walters have found that college players reach the majors faster and frequently sign for less money than high school draftees—possibly because they don't have the threat of going to college as a bargaining chip.[102] But I think it is bad general advice to suggest that teams adopt a more college-centric drafting strategy to improve their returns to the draft. In the end, by drafting more collegians teams may end up with more identifiable duds, when additional picks would have been better spent on a raw high school prospects whose returns are less certain, but at least give the opportunity of a high upside.

Chapter 9
Epilogue

> *Every signing means that player is worth that amount*
> *to somebody. Otherwise you're trying to convince us that*
> *the owners are not rational people, that they're all*
> *fucking idiots.*
> —Donald Fehr (Executive Director, Major League
> Baseball Players Association (1986–2009)[103])

Winning in professional sports requires knowing how to excel off the field as well as on it. The scarcity of major-league caliber talent and Major League Baseball's complex organizational structure requires understanding the financial worth of players as assets in order to succeed as a ballclub. Sure, some teams have inherent advantages over others—bigger markets, more loyal fans, wealthier and more charitable owners, etc.—but baseball has shown that no team can win without understanding how to value the chief asset of the game, players. Whether you are going to buy, sell, or develop talent, improper valuations of players as assets will hider success, while gaining a better understanding of the market will give you an edge.

Baseball fans seem to hold a passion for roster management that is nearly as strong as it is for the game itself. I believe this stems from the fact that though we may not be able to suit up as athletes, we can put our minds to the task of building a better team. Few fans delude themselves into thinking they can hit a fastball out of the park or slip a biting slider past a major-league slugger, but we can convince ourselves that we know more about constructing a team than the guys who get paid to do it.

J.C. Bradbury, *Hot Stove Economics*, DOI 10.1007/978-1-4419-6269-0_9,
© Springer Science+Business Media, LLC 2011

The dollar values reported in this book aren't meant to be the final word on player value, and I hope that no one thinks that I have implied this. When Gerald Scully first attempted to value players in the 1970s, he described his estimates as crude. There are a myriad of factors that affect players' worth, but ballpark estimates set useful benchmarks so that we can conduct informed analysis. Scully's main contribution to our understanding of baseball players' worth was grounding the value in terms of the revenue that players generate for their owners using the tools of labor economics. It wasn't just some divide-the-pie game, throwing dollars at players according to the total sum spent on salaries. The marginal revenue product framework provides a coherent system that we can use for estimating player worth: players are worth the additional revenue they provide to their owners. If we know how much players can contribute to winning and how much wins are worth, then we should have a good idea as to what individual players are worth in general. Where we can see other factors contributing to player worth—playing on a winning team, returning to a beloved hometown, or serving as living monument to adoring fans—we can make adjustments to the general estimates.

If there is an underlying theme to this book, it is that human beings are rational—especially individuals making important financial decisions, like baseball executives. This should come as no surprise to economists who typically rely on the assumption of rationality when predicting and analyzing human behavior. But this is not to say that these individuals don't make mistakes. To the contrary, humans err all the time, it is just that the mistakes are unlikely to be predictable and thus exploitable. Myopia and ignorance may cause some general managers to make bad decisions, but with so much at stake in the business of baseball—"where no quarter is asked and no quarter is given" as Branch Rickey famously said—focusing on mistakes to understand how baseball teams operate is the wrong place to begin.

In general, I believe big-league ballclubs do a good job of managing their franchises. Mistakes occur, but they don't last for long as the market quickly corrects inefficiencies. Most claims of irrational spending, often in the wake of string of high-priced contracts, are based on a misunderstanding of how valuable professional baseball players are to their teams. But the fact that most teams are run by knowledgeable personnel doesn't mean that hot stove league participants should be resigned to believing all front-office decisions are good ones. Assuming competence is just a good starting point.

It is my hope that after reading this book, you will view hot stove transactions through an informed lens. Baseball players are valuable commodities whose values differ according to factors such as age, ability, and contract status. Maybe the concepts presented will help you with your fantasy baseball team or give you some more points to argue among your friends. But most of all, I hope this book furthers your enjoyment of the game by giving you more to think about during that desolate and dismal period between the World Series and Opening Day.

Appendices

Appendix A
Technical Concepts

Present Value Discounting

A dollar today is worth less than a dollar promised in the future and, therefore, they should not be valued equivalently—a concept commonly referred to as "the time value of money." Present value discounting is a method used to account for the diminished value of money that will be received in the future. Discounting reflects the funds required to purchase an asset today that will yield the future sum, using the going interest rate to discount the future value of the expected payout. For example, to value receiving $100 in one year, we look at how much it would cost to purchase a low-risk bond that would pay out $100 one year from now. If the interest rate was ten percent, the bond would sell for approximately $91; thus, the present value of $100 is $91. In this book, I use an interest rate of 4.5 percent, which was the approximate interest rate on a one-year Treasury Bill in 2007—the base year for all financial calculations in the book. The formula for present value is as follows:

$$PV = \frac{\text{Future value}}{(1+i)^{(f-t)}},$$

where f = payout year, t = present year, and i = interest rate.

In many instances in the book, I examine players who generate payouts over several seasons. Summing the present value estimates from each year generates the expected present value of the asset.

J.C. Bradbury, *Hot Stove Economics*, DOI 10.1007/978-1-4419-6269-0_10,

Z-Score

A z-score reports the value of a variable as the difference from the sample average in terms of the standard deviation of the sample. The standard deviation (σ) is the average difference from the sample mean, where $\sigma = \sqrt{\dfrac{\left[\sum (X_i - \overline{X})^2\right]}{N-1}}$. Thus, a z-score $= \dfrac{(X_i - \overline{X})}{\sigma_t}$, where i is the individual player and t is the year of analysis.

I use a z-score in the analysis of aging in Chapter 3 to compare players in different playing environments over time so that changes in performance metrics better reflect changes in ability rather than changes in the playing environment.

Multiple Regression Analysis

Throughout the book, I use and refer to studies that use multiple regression analysis to analyze relationships between variables. It is the main technique that I use for estimating the financial worth of players, and Gerald Scully and Anthony Krautmann also used multiple regression analysis to generate their marginal revenue product estimates.

The attribute of this technique that makes it so useful for studying baseball is that it allows us to isolate quantitative impacts of specific factors separate from many other contributing factors. For example, if we wanted to know how important hitting power is to run scoring, we might compare teams' runs scored and slugging percentages to see how strong the relationship is. But the problem with such a simple comparison is that though slugging average does reflect hitting power, it also reflects the general ability of players to get hits. Some players with high slugging averages hit with power to make up for their low batting averages, while other players have high slugging averages because of high batting averages. With multiple regression analysis, we can compare the effects of both factors, batting average and slugging average, while "holding constant" the impact of the other factor. That is, when batting averages are equal, we can know how much slugging average adds to run scoring. Multiple regression analysis uses a statistical procedure—ordinary least square (OLS) is the most commonly employed multiple-regression estimator—to observe how run scoring changes while taking into account the other factor.

The simple model described above—Runs scored $= \alpha + (\beta_1 \times \text{AVG}) + (\beta_2 \times \text{SLG})$, where α is the vertical intercept and the βs are coefficients—is by no means the best way to predict run scoring. We should probably at least break out slugging average into its components—batting average and isolated power—to limit the impact of the correlation between batting average and slugging average and include other omitted factors, such as on-base percentage, to ensure that the coefficient estimates aren't biased. The point of this simple example is to demonstrate how the statistical method can be employed to gauge the individual impacts of factors that occur simultaneously.

In an appendix of *The Baseball Economist*, I include a simple guide to understanding multiple regression analysis that goes beyond the brief explanation provided here. I must stress that though the intuition behind the method is simple, applying the technique is complicated. If you are looking to learn more about the multiple regression analysis, then I suggest picking up an introductory econometrics textbook, and it is probably best to take a college econometrics course before attempting to use multiple regression analysis.

Interpreting Multiple Regression Analysis Tables

In the book chapters, I report summaries of my regression estimates; however, the following appendices report more-detailed results. I use a standard format to present the estimates, and I want to explain how to interpret the numbers reported in the tables.

The far-left column lists the variables that may affect the outcome that the estimates are attempting to predict. The columns to the right display two sets of numbers for each explanatory variable, with each column representing estimates of separate models. The top number is the weight for each factor, which is a coefficient. Multiplying the coefficient times the actual value of the variable changes the predicted value according to the estimated impact of the explanatory factor. The coefficient estimates for each variable in a vertical column multiplied by actual values for each factor can be summed to generate a predicted outcome for the entire model.

The numbers below the weights in brackets are t- or z-test statistics that measure the expected error of the estimate. The higher the number, the smaller the error, and thus the more confidence we have in the estimate. As a general rule of thumb, once a test statistic approaches two, the estimate is considered to be "statistically significant," which means that there is a high degree of confidence that the impact is not zero—indicating no influence of the explanatory variable on the outcome. Often times symbols like asterisks will be printed outside the brackets to denote levels of statistical significance. An estimate that is significant at the one-percent level indicates that there is less than a 1-in-100 chance that the estimated relationship is equal to zero, assuming that the model is specified correctly. Statistical significance at the five- and ten-percent levels indicates 1-in-20 and 1-in-10 chances, respectively, that the estimate is not zero. Therefore, lower level of significance indicates a more certain relationship than a higher level.

The next-to-last row of the tables reports the number of observations used to estimate the weights. For example, if we were estimating the impact of average income on mortality using US states as our observational units, then there would be 50 observations. If we observed 50 states over five years then this would result in 250 observations. In general, more observations are preferred to less. Many observations will result in a greater likelihood that the estimated weights will be statistically significant. It is important to note that in small samples statistical significance is difficult to achieve, but in larger estimates statistical significance is likely. If the sample is large enough, it is possible to estimate impacts that are statistically significant, but the effects can be so small that they are meaningless for practical purposes.

The last row normally reports the metric known as R^2, which measures the "fit" of the estimated model to the actual data. It ranges from zero to one, and can be interpreted as a percent. For example, an R^2 of 0.74 indicates that 74 percent of the difference in the outcomes across observational units being predicted is explained by changes in the explanatory variables. In some cases, I report modified R^2 that slightly deviate from raw R^2, but are necessary to correct for issues with the estimating technique. Though they differ, they can be interpreted in a similar manner.

Appendix B
Converting Performance To Dollars From Chapter 4

Table B-1 reports estimates of the impact of several factors on team revenue using different specifications and multiple regression analysis techniques. Model 1 reports the weights that I use for converting performance to dollars in the book. I list alternate specifications for curious readers.

	1 Cubic	2 Linear	3 Quadratic	4 Interaction	5 Random Effects
Run Difference	0.0641 [2.21]*	0.1188 [4.68]**	0.1441 [5.48]**	0.0329 [0.86]	0.0427 [3.87]**
Run Difference^2	9.79E-004 [5.05]**		5.76E-004 [3.28]**	9.01E-004 [4.37]**	1.17E-004 [1.82]
Run Difference^3	3.12E-006 [4.05]**			2.90E-006 [3.65]**	
MSA Population	6.10E-006 [7.20]**	6.00E-006 [6.08]**	5.90E-006 [6.61]**	5.70E-006 [8.85]**	7.10E-006 [8.32]**
Honeymoon	19.5457691 [3.72]**	18.8587261 [3.51]**	18.0367189 [3.37]**	19.0931002 [3.63]**	18.4669104 [4.75]**
(Run Difference* Population)				7.21E-009 [1.41]	
Constant	95.5015047 [14.77]**	105.888217 [15.28]**	100.1521188 [14.89]**	97.4766728 [16.66]**	98.6257928 [15.25]**
Observations	150	150	150	150	150
R^2	0.63	0.57	0.60	0.63	0.55

TABLE B-1   The Impact of Performance on Team Revenue (2003–2007)

* Significant at five percent; ** significant at one percent. Absolute value of z-statistics in brackets. R^2 is "adjusted R^2" for models 1,2, 3, and 5 and "overall R^2" for model 4. Revenue estimates from *Forbes* "The Business of Baseball" reports, various years. Revenue converted to 2007 dollars.

J.C. Bradbury, *Hot Stove Economics*, DOI 10.1007/978-1-4419-6269-0_11,
© Springer Science+Business Media, LLC 2011

Models 2 and 3 are estimates with the linear and quadratic functions of the run differential. Models 1–3 use Newey-West corrections of the standard errors for first-order serial correlation. While all the coefficient estimates are positive and statistically significant, as expected, the cubic estimate offers the superior fit, indicated by a higher R^2. I also estimated the impact of runs using higher polynomial powers, but the estimates were not significant, which indicates that the cubic functional form appears to be the best choice.

It is possible that wins in bigger markets may generate more revenue than wins in smaller markets, not just that bigger markets take in more revenue by virtue of being bigger.[104] Typically, economists handle such interactions by including a term that multiplies the interacting variables (i.e., population × wins) to capture the impact of the joint effect.[105] Model 4 reports the results of a specification with an interaction term of the run difference times the population. The interaction term is not statistically significant, and the R^2 of the model is no better than Model 1. When I calculated hypothetical player values including the sample mean of the interaction term, the estimates were similar to estimates generated by Model 1. This is not to say that there is no interaction between population and wins, but it appears difficult to estimate this exact effect. I believe it is better to acknowledge that the effect may exist and to make rough adjustments to add/diminish the impact of a player in certain markets after estimating the average effect.

There is also the possibility that market-specific factors that are difficult to quantify in a few variables impact revenue. To address this possibility, I estimated several models with fixed- and random-effects estimators, which hold constant unobserved team-specific factors. Model 5 reports the estimates the impact of run differential on revenue using a random-effects estimate of a quadratic function using the Baltagi and Wu (1999) method that corrects for first-order serial correlation. I report the quadratic form, as opposed to the cubic form, because the higher-order terms do not appear to be relevant. In fact, even the squared term is not statistically significant in the reported model; however, I feel that it would be wrong to use a linear estimate given the expected shape of the relationship. In most estimates of panel data—data of a cross-section of units over multiple observations—random- and fixed-effects estimation procedures are preferred. But, this creates a problem: the known characteristics of teams includes their propensity to win.

The fact that franchise success is stable in the short-run causes the performance and team-specific effects to be correlated, thereby making it difficult to identify the explanatory power of the run differential. Thus, random- and fixed-effects methods attribute a large part of a team's unique characteristics to revenue generation, which leads to a near-equal apportionment of revenue all players. That is, excellent players are valued similar to marginal players in a way that is inconsistent with the variance of observed players' salaries.

The results reported here represent a small sample of models that I used to estimate the impact of performance on revenue. I report these particular models because they represent the best of the rejected alternative models. After reviewing numerous specifications, I believe the pooled common effects estimate reported in Model 1 best captures the relationship between winning and revenue among the alternatives that I considered.

Appendix C
Projecting The Value Of Prospects From Chapter 8

Tables C-1, C-2, and C-3 report weights, estimated using ordinary least squares regression, on the impacts of minor-league performance variables on major-league peak performance. To be included in the sample used for projecting major-league performance, a player must have a minimum of 100 plate appearances in the minor-league level during the season of observation, a minimum of 1,000

	Triple-A	Double-A	High-A
Strikeout Rate	−0.101	−0.120	−0.119
	[4.91]*	[2.65]*	[2.45]**
Walk Rate	0.026	0.063	0.106
	[1.00]	[1.03]	[1.68]†
Batting Average	0.120	0.163	0.240
	[4.83]*	[2.71]*	[3.97]*
Age	−0.012	−0.020	−0.005
	[5.17]*	[4.17]*	[0.49]
Age^2	1.80E-004	3.60E-004	4.00E-005
	[4.57]*	[4.40]*	[0.20]
Height	−1.11E-003	2.90E-004	−2.50E-004
	[2.34]**	[0.28]	[0.17]
Weight	1.60E-004	1.60E-004	1.30E-004
	[3.05]*	[1.54]	[0.86]
Constant	0.474	0.437	0.322
	[9.36]*	[3.69]*	[1.56]
Observations	518	191	128
Adjusted R^2	0.29	0.27	0.18

TABLE C-1   Impact of Minor-League Performance on Major-League Batting Average

Robust *t* statistics in brackets; † significant at ten percent; * significant at five percent; ** significant at one percent; team and year dummies not reported.

J.C. Bradbury, *Hot Stove Economics*, DOI 10.1007/978-1-4419-6269-0_12,
© Springer Science+Business Media, LLC 2011

	Triple-A	Double-A	High-A
Walk Rate	0.103	0.178	0.193
	[2.12]*	[1.86]†	[1.41]
Isolated Power	0.314	0.336	0.421
	[10.85]**	[6.02]**	[4.32]**
Age	−0.026	−0.035	0.013
	[5.94]**	[3.92]**	[0.61]
Age^2	3.80E-004	6.10E-004	−3.90E-004
	[5.35]**	[4.13]**	[0.96]
Height	5.70E-004	1.08E-003	8.20E-004
	[0.57]	[0.55]	[0.29]
Weight	7.40E-004	7.60E-004	6.30E-004
	[6.97]**	[3.76]**	[2.32]*
Constant	0.308	0.293	−0.198
	[3.12]**	[1.58]	[0.53]
Observations	518	191	128
Adjusted R^2	0.55	0.56	0.44

TABLE C-2   Impact of Minor-League Performance on Major-League Isolated Power

Robust t statistics in brackets; † significant at ten percent; * significant at five percent; ** significant at one percent; team and year dummies not reported.

	Triple-A	Double-A	High-A
Walk Rate	0.375	0.426	0.450
	[10.88]*	[5.99]*	[5.25]*
Batting Average	0.131	0.220	0.262
	[4.13]*	[3.76]*	[2.77]*
Age	−0.011	−0.025	−0.019
	[3.27]*	[3.10]*	[1.18]
Age^2	1.50E-004	4.50E-004	3.10E-004
	[2.75]*	[3.01]*	[0.93]
Height	−1.53E-003	6.20E-004	−4.10E-004
	[2.29]**	[0.51]	[0.24]
Weight	1.80E-004	6.00E-005	1.10E-004
	[2.65]*	[0.41]	[0.57]
Constant	0.518	0.421	0.536
	[7.26]*	[2.92]*	[2.14]**
Observations	518	191	128
Adjusted R^2	0.33	0.37	0.29

TABLE C-3   Impact of Minor-League Performance on Major-League On-Base Percentage

Robust t statistics in brackets; † significant at ten percent; * significant at five percent; ** significant at one percent; team and year dummies not reported.

career major-league plate appearances, and play major-league baseball to age 32 or beyond (to generate a peak-age estimate). In order to ensure that players have sufficient time to reach the major-league peak, samples from Triple-A, Double-A, and High-A include players prior to 1999, 1998, and 1997, respectively.

The weights in the tables reflect how marginal differences in each predicting factor impact future performance. For example, a ten-point increase in the minor-league batting average raises a hitter's projected batting average by about a 1.2 points ($0.010 \times 0.120 = 0.0012$), and a three percentage-point increase in the strikeout rate decreases the batting average by three points ($0.03 \times -0.101 = 0.00303$).

Table C-4 reports the weights of each factor on the likelihood that a player reaches his major-league peak, estimated using probit regression.[106] Just as better minor-league performance begets better major-league performance, it also indicates a stronger likelihood that a player will make it in the big leagues. For example, having a strikeout rate that is one percentage-point above average lowers the likelihood of reaching his peak by 0.8 percent ($0.01 \times -0.835 = 0.00835$).

	Triple-A	Double-A	High-A
Strikeout Rate	−0.835 [7.28]*	−0.419 [5.65]*	−0.210 [5.14]*
Walk Rate	0.274 [1.50]	0.356 [0.78]	0.302 [3.84]*
Batting Average	0.260 [1.77]†	0.088 [3.68]*	0.163 [5.36]*
Isolated Power	0.207 [2.73]*	0.066 [1.26]	
Age	−0.231 [11.50]*	−0.073 [3.31]*	−0.044 [2.65]*
Age^2	3.92E-003 [10.86]*	1.16E-003 [2.56]**	7.42E-004 [2.01]**
Height	−1.02E-002 [3.53]*	−4.63E-003 [2.50]**	−1.84E-003 [1.66]†
Weight	1.98E-003 [5.92]*	1.15E-003 [5.74]*	5.87E-004 [5.33]*
Observations	3,063	2,397	2,227
Pseudo R^2	0.19	0.25	0.28

TABLE C-4   Impact of Minor-League Performance on Reaching Major-League Peak

Weights represent marginal impact of change in predicting variable on likelihood of reaching peak. Robust z-statistics in brackets; † significant at ten percent; * significant at five percent; ** significant at one percent; constant and team and year dummies not reported.

Appendix D
Marginal Revenue Product Estimates

PA%	– Percentage of team's plate appearances taken by the hitter.
BFP%	– Percentage of team's batters faced by the pitcher.
Runs Above Average	– Expected runs contributed above what an average player contributes with the same playing time.
Average Value	– The revenue that an average player contributes with the same playing time. Separated into hitting and fielding for position players.
Value Above Average	– The revenue generated beyond what an average player contributes with the same playing time.
MRP	– Marginal revenue product estimate of performance to the average team.
MRP (raw)	– Marginal revenue product estimate of pitching performance to the average team, not adjusted for value of pitching role.
MRP (adjusted)	– Marginal revenue product estimate of pitching performance to the average team, adjusted for value of pitching role.

All dollar values in millions of current dollars.

J.C. Bradbury, *Hot Stove Economics*, DOI 10.1007/978-1-4419-6269-0_13,
© Springer Science+Business Media, LLC 2011

POSITION PLAYERS (2009)

Player	PA%	Runs Above Average	Average Value Hitting ($)	Average Value Fielding ($)	Value Above Average ($)	MRP ($)
Arizona Diamondbacks						
Justin Upton	9.38	29.81	5.35	1.53	3.40	10.28
Mark Reynolds	10.56	11.26	6.02	1.80	1.01	8.83
Stephen Drew	9.49	−1.41	5.41	2.02	−0.10	7.32
Miguel Montero	7.50	0.22	4.28	2.22	0.02	6.52
Chris Young	7.99	−6.69	4.56	1.67	−0.46	5.77
Ryan Roberts	5.60	15.73	3.19	0.97	1.50	5.67
Gerardo Parra	7.83	−14.84	4.47	1.32	−0.89	4.90
Felipe Lopez	6.11	−0.22	3.48	1.13	−0.02	4.60
Augie Ojeda	4.93	−0.10	2.81	1.02	−0.01	3.83
Eric Byrnes	4.12	−3.94	2.35	0.59	−0.28	2.65
Chad Tracy	4.59	−10.31	2.62	0.51	−0.66	2.46
Chris Snyder	3.22	−8.05	1.84	1.05	−0.54	2.35
Alex Romero	2.50	−6.44	1.43	0.36	−0.44	1.35
Rusty Ryal	1.08	3.91	0.62	0.16	0.32	1.10
Josh Whitesell	2.12	−6.34	1.21	0.22	−0.44	0.99
Trent Oeltjen	1.16	0.73	0.66	0.19	0.06	0.91
Brandon Allen	1.85	−9.42	1.06	0.22	−0.62	0.66
Tony Clark	1.24	−2.68	0.71	0.12	−0.20	0.63
Conor Jackson	1.75	−11.35	1.00	0.26	−0.72	0.54
John Hester	0.48	−1.32	0.27	0.13	−0.10	0.30
Luke Carlin	0.34	−3.48	0.19	0.08	−0.25	0.02
Atlanta Braves						
Yunel Escobar	9.53	27.09	5.44	2.11	2.99	10.54
Brian McCann	8.70	8.09	4.96	2.57	0.69	8.22
Chipper Jones	9.41	10.40	5.37	1.61	0.92	7.89
Martin Prado	7.94	15.71	4.53	1.34	1.50	7.37
Matt Diaz	6.71	10.76	3.83	1.07	0.96	5.85
Nate McLouth	6.25	5.82	3.56	1.20	0.48	5.24
Garret Anderson	8.43	−13.75	4.81	1.24	−0.84	5.21
Casey Kotchman	5.30	8.75	3.02	0.61	0.76	4.39
Adam LaRoche	3.82	15.26	2.18	0.45	1.45	4.07
Kelly Johnson	5.46	−7.82	3.11	1.03	−0.53	3.62
Dave Ross	2.38	9.65	1.36	0.84	0.85	3.05
Jeff Francoeur	5.11	−14.51	2.92	0.90	−0.87	2.95
Omar Infante	3.61	1.70	2.06	0.67	0.13	2.86
Ryan Church	2.27	4.42	1.30	0.43	0.36	2.08
Jordan Schafer	3.08	−11.03	1.76	0.70	−0.70	1.75
Greg Norton	1.53	−5.75	0.87	0.02	−0.40	0.49
Diory Hernandez	1.47	−11.63	0.84	0.35	−0.73	0.45
Brooks Conrad	0.92	−3.25	0.52	0.13	−0.24	0.42
Brandon Jones	0.27	0.63	0.15	0.04	0.05	0.24
Gregor Blanco	0.76	−5.08	0.43	0.14	−0.36	0.21
Clint Sammons	0.19	−0.17	0.11	0.07	−0.01	0.17
Reid Gorecki	0.43	−3.39	0.24	0.13	−0.24	0.13
Barbaro Canizares	0.33	−3.35	0.19	0.04	−0.24	−0.02
Brian Barton	0.00	−0.38	0.00	0.00	−0.03	−0.03
Baltimore Orioles						
Brian Roberts	11.50	10.89	6.56	2.15	0.97	9.68
Nick Markakis	11.41	1.81	6.51	1.84	0.14	8.49
Adam Jones	8.33	−6.26	4.75	1.66	−0.43	5.98
Luke Scott	8.12	7.71	4.63	0.30	0.66	5.59
Melvin Mora	7.96	−11.64	4.54	1.52	−0.73	5.32
Nolan Reimold	6.59	3.17	3.76	0.92	0.25	4.93
Cesar Izturis	6.61	−8.92	3.77	1.67	−0.59	4.85
Matt Wieters	6.18	−7.27	3.52	1.80	−0.49	4.83
Aubrey Huff	7.70	−14.83	4.39	0.73	−0.89	4.24
Ty Wigginton	7.00	−16.81	3.99	0.85	−0.97	3.87
Felix Pie	4.51	−8.62	2.57	0.85	−0.57	2.85
Gregg Zaun	3.16	−3.05	1.80	1.06	−0.22	2.64
Robert Andino	3.45	−14.99	1.97	0.93	−0.89	2.01
Michael Aubrey	1.52	2.42	0.87	0.17	0.19	1.23
Chad Moeller	1.60	−4.98	0.91	0.58	−0.35	1.15

| Player | PA% | Runs Above Average | Average Value | | Value Above Average ($) | MRP ($) |
			Hitting ($)	Fielding ($)		
Jeff Fiorentino	1.20	−4.22	0.69	0.23	−0.30	0.62
Luis Montanez	1.46	−6.50	0.83	0.20	−0.45	0.58
Oscar Salazar	0.53	2.66	0.30	0.05	0.21	0.56
Justin Turner	0.35	−0.10	0.20	0.06	−0.01	0.25
Ryan Freel	0.32	−1.87	0.18	0.05	−0.14	0.10
Guillermo Rodriguez	0.11	−0.79	0.06	0.04	−0.06	0.04
Boston Red Sox						
Kevin Youkilis	9.27	47.19	5.29	1.30	6.57	13.16
Dustin Pedroia	11.26	23.35	6.42	2.15	2.46	11.03
Jason Bay	10.06	26.84	5.74	1.58	2.95	10.27
J.D. Drew	8.50	29.42	4.85	1.42	3.34	9.60
Jacoby Ellsbury	10.90	1.43	6.21	2.14	0.11	8.47
David Ortiz	9.89	1.96	5.64	0.03	0.15	5.83
Mike Lowell	7.63	−13.22	4.35	1.29	−0.81	4.83
Jason Varitek	6.70	−27.51	3.82	2.24	−1.29	4.77
Victor Martinez	3.74	8.16	2.13	0.79	0.70	3.62
Alex Gonzalez	2.51	−2.65	1.43	0.64	−0.19	1.88
Rocco Baldelli	2.59	−2.68	1.47	0.40	−0.20	1.68
George Kottaras	1.69	−6.08	0.96	0.60	−0.42	1.14
Jeff Bailey	1.43	−0.44	0.82	0.19	−0.03	0.97
Julio Lugo	1.94	−9.08	1.11	0.43	−0.60	0.94
Casey Kotchman	1.50	−4.97	0.85	0.17	−0.35	0.67
Mark Kotsay	1.25	−6.21	0.71	0.18	−0.43	0.46
Jed Lowrie	1.20	−8.81	0.68	0.31	−0.58	0.41
Brian N. Anderson	0.33	0.60	0.19	0.09	0.05	0.32
Joey Gathright	0.27	1.08	0.15	0.06	0.08	0.30
Josh Reddick	0.98	−6.14	0.56	0.16	−0.42	0.29
Adam LaRoche	0.30	−0.25	0.17	0.03	−0.02	0.18
Aaron Bates	0.19	0.13	0.11	0.03	0.01	0.14
Chris Woodward	0.25	−1.01	0.14	0.08	−0.08	0.14
Gil Velazquez	0.05	−1.03	0.03	0.03	−0.08	−0.02
Chris Carter	0.09	−1.49	0.05	0.01	−0.11	−0.05
Chicago Cubs						
Derrek Lee	9.85	40.50	5.62	1.08	5.24	11.94
Ryan Theriot	10.84	−8.25	6.18	2.32	−0.55	7.95
Kosuke Fukudome	9.66	3.30	5.51	1.82	0.26	7.59
Milton Bradley	7.58	−5.62	4.32	1.19	−0.39	5.12
Alfonso Soriano	8.36	−18.38	4.77	1.23	−1.03	4.97
Aramis Ramirez	5.48	8.29	3.12	0.98	0.71	4.81
Geovany Soto	6.23	−13.36	3.55	1.95	−0.82	4.69
Mike Fontenot	6.71	−14.99	3.83	1.35	−0.89	4.29
Koyie Hill	4.55	−12.61	2.59	1.51	−0.78	3.32
Jeff Baker	3.59	5.96	2.05	0.71	0.50	3.25
Jake Fox	3.86	−1.23	2.20	0.53	−0.09	2.64
Micah Hoffpauir	4.12	−4.82	2.35	0.47	−0.34	2.48
Reed Johnson	2.98	−1.56	1.70	0.58	−0.12	2.16
Sam Fuld	1.84	2.62	1.05	0.36	0.21	1.62
Bobby Scales	2.21	−1.23	1.26	0.35	−0.09	1.52
Andres Blanco	2.21	−5.67	1.26	0.52	−0.40	1.38
Aaron Miles	2.72	−22.34	1.55	0.50	−1.16	0.89
Tyler Colvin	0.32	−0.49	0.18	0.07	−0.04	0.22
Joey Gathright	0.24	−1.36	0.14	0.04	−0.10	0.07
So Taguchi	0.19	−1.44	0.11	0.02	−0.11	0.02
Ryan Freel	0.51	−5.47	0.29	0.09	−0.38	0.00
Chicago White Sox						
Paul Konerko	10.13	15.58	5.78	1.01	1.48	8.26
Alexei Ramirez	9.88	−6.28	5.64	2.30	−0.43	7.50
Scott Podsednik	9.57	4.67	5.46	1.43	0.38	7.27
A.J. Pierzynski	8.72	−15.24	4.98	2.67	−0.90	6.74
Jermaine Dye	9.36	−14.19	5.34	1.46	−0.86	5.94
Gordon Beckham	7.01	4.07	4.00	1.27	0.33	5.60
Jim Thome	6.80	13.19	3.88	0.00	1.21	5.09
Chris Getz	6.77	−14.80	3.86	1.43	−0.88	4.40
Jayson Nix	4.73	2.82	2.70	1.02	0.22	3.94
Carlos Quentin	6.51	−11.12	3.71	0.93	−0.71	3.93
Josh Fields	4.37	−20.88	2.49	0.69	−1.12	2.06

Player	PA%	Runs Above Average	Average Value Hitting ($)	Fielding ($)	Value Above Average ($)	MRP ($)
Dewayne Wise	2.50	−1.80	1.42	0.56	−0.13	1.85
Brian N. Anderson	3.42	−16.87	1.95	0.76	−0.97	1.74
Mark Kotsay	2.07	−1.75	1.18	0.25	−0.13	1.30
Alexis Rios	2.51	−14.84	1.43	0.56	−0.89	1.10
Ramon Castro	1.37	−5.56	0.78	0.53	−0.39	0.93
Brent Lillibridge	1.83	−10.79	1.04	0.41	−0.69	0.76
Corky Miller	0.68	−4.30	0.39	0.21	−0.31	0.30
Tyler Flowers	0.33	−1.20	0.19	0.07	−0.09	0.16
Wilson Betemit	0.82	−6.62	0.47	0.10	−0.45	0.11
Jerry Owens	0.24	−3.26	0.14	0.04	−0.24	−0.05
Cincinnati Reds						
Joey Votto	8.79	40.51	5.01	0.96	5.24	11.21
Brandon Phillips	10.41	2.78	5.94	2.09	0.22	8.25
Jay Bruce	6.26	1.46	3.57	1.04	0.11	4.72
Laynce Nix	5.45	6.00	3.11	0.81	0.50	4.42
Ryan Hanigan	4.74	−2.68	2.70	1.60	−0.20	4.11
Willy Taveras	7.06	−27.95	4.03	1.36	−1.30	4.09
Jerry Hairston	5.50	−2.56	3.13	1.03	−0.19	3.98
Ramon Hernandez	5.35	−6.89	3.05	1.30	−0.47	3.88
Chris Dickerson	4.83	4.64	2.76	0.74	0.38	3.87
Jonny Gomes	5.08	1.00	2.89	0.65	0.08	3.63
Drew Stubbs	3.17	4.04	1.81	0.60	0.33	2.73
Scott Rolen	2.62	5.98	1.49	0.48	0.50	2.47
Adam Rosales	4.30	−13.54	2.45	0.74	−0.83	2.37
Alex Gonzalez	4.36	−22.28	2.49	1.03	−1.16	2.36
Edwin Encarnacion	2.67	−5.98	1.52	0.51	−0.41	1.62
Wladimir Balentien	2.02	1.02	1.15	0.33	0.08	1.56
Darnell McDonald	1.79	−1.85	1.02	0.28	−0.14	1.17
Corky Miller	1.12	−5.01	0.64	0.39	−0.35	0.67
Craig Tatum	1.24	−7.52	0.71	0.41	−0.51	0.61
Juan Francisco	0.40	4.11	0.23	0.04	0.33	0.61
Drew Sutton	1.23	−3.71	0.70	0.17	−0.27	0.60
Kevin Barker	0.58	−0.35	0.33	0.02	−0.03	0.33
Danny Richar	0.15	−1.24	0.08	0.03	−0.09	0.02
Cleveland Indians						
Shin−Soo Choo	10.84	43.77	6.18	1.64	5.87	13.69
Asdrubal Cabrera	9.19	7.73	5.24	1.94	0.66	7.84
Grady Sizemore	7.96	13.23	4.54	1.33	1.22	7.09
Jhonny Peralta	10.21	−12.78	5.82	1.90	−0.79	6.93
Victor Martinez	6.88	8.58	3.93	1.39	0.74	6.05
Jamey Carroll	5.66	5.50	3.23	1.06	0.45	4.75
Luis Valbuena	6.30	−6.85	3.59	1.41	−0.47	4.53
Travis Hafner	6.06	11.54	3.46	0.00	1.04	4.50
Kelly Shoppach	5.17	−3.70	2.95	1.63	−0.27	4.32
Ben Francisco	5.62	0.58	3.20	1.01	0.04	4.26
Mark DeRosa	4.97	2.32	2.83	0.80	0.18	3.81
Ryan Garko	4.32	9.41	2.46	0.46	0.82	3.74
Matt LaPorta	3.13	−1.51	1.79	0.49	−0.11	2.17
Trevor Crowe	3.20	−8.64	1.82	0.66	−0.57	1.91
Andy Marte	2.77	−3.58	1.58	0.35	−0.26	1.67
Michael Brantley	1.91	−4.76	1.09	0.35	−0.34	1.11
Chris Gimenez	2.06	−9.45	1.17	0.39	−0.62	0.94
Lou Marson	0.82	1.66	0.47	0.30	0.13	0.90
Wyatt Toregas	0.95	−6.23	0.54	0.37	−0.43	0.48
David Dellucci	0.71	−0.58	0.41	0.01	−0.04	0.37
Josh Barfield	0.32	1.18	0.18	0.06	0.09	0.33
Tony Graffanino	0.38	−2.73	0.22	0.08	−0.20	0.10
Niuman Romero	0.24	−1.34	0.14	0.05	−0.10	0.09
Colorado Rockies						
Troy Tulowitzki	10.06	36.35	5.74	2.30	4.48	12.52
Todd Helton	10.33	29.13	5.89	1.13	3.30	10.32
Brad Hawpe	9.42	15.89	5.37	1.56	1.52	8.45
Clint Barmes	9.68	−4.10	5.52	2.01	−0.29	7.24
Seth Smith	6.20	20.75	3.54	0.77	2.11	6.42
Ian Stewart	7.87	−4.53	4.49	1.48	−0.32	5.65
Dexter Fowler	8.30	−12.64	4.73	1.61	−0.78	5.56

Player	PA%	Runs Above Average	Average Value Hitting ($)	Fielding ($)	Value Above Average ($)	MRP ($)
Carlos Gonzalez	5.08	14.16	2.90	0.91	1.32	5.13
Chris Iannetta	5.61	−2.26	3.20	1.85	−0.17	4.88
Ryan Spilborghs	6.30	−7.93	3.59	0.95	−0.53	4.01
Garrett Atkins	6.39	−19.77	3.65	0.94	−1.08	3.51
Yorvit Torrealba	3.88	−11.17	2.21	1.32	−0.71	2.82
Paul Phillips	0.87	−2.10	0.49	0.27	−0.15	0.61
Omar Quintanilla	1.11	−5.00	0.63	0.22	−0.35	0.49
Matt Murton	0.90	−1.74	0.51	0.11	−0.13	0.49
Jason Giambi	0.50	2.08	0.28	0.03	0.16	0.48
Eric Young	0.98	−5.86	0.56	0.13	−0.41	0.28
Edwin Bellorin	0.14	−0.56	0.08	0.04	−0.04	0.08
Jeff Baker	0.38	−3.26	0.22	0.05	−0.24	0.04
Mike McCoy	0.10	−0.38	0.05	0.00	−0.03	0.03
Detroit Tigers						
Miguel Cabrera	10.99	41.47	6.27	1.16	5.42	12.84
Curtis Granderson	11.39	10.87	6.50	2.26	0.97	9.73
Placido Polanco	10.83	−7.46	6.18	2.04	−0.50	7.71
Brandon Inge	10.22	−3.65	5.83	1.98	−0.26	7.55
Magglio Ordonez	8.31	3.78	4.74	1.03	0.30	6.08
Gerald Laird	7.65	−16.67	4.36	2.62	−0.96	6.03
Adam Everett	6.26	−12.61	3.57	1.66	−0.78	4.45
Ryan Raburn	4.67	2.42	2.66	0.72	0.19	3.58
Clete Thomas	4.97	−5.15	2.84	0.87	−0.36	3.34
Carlos Guillen	5.17	−1.95	2.95	0.41	−0.14	3.21
Ramon Santiago	4.75	−11.37	2.71	1.14	−0.72	3.13
Marcus Thames	4.72	−1.08	2.69	0.16	−0.08	2.76
Josh Anderson	2.81	−8.96	1.60	0.50	−0.59	1.51
Alex Avila	1.16	3.54	0.66	0.37	0.28	1.31
Jeff Larish	1.44	1.09	0.82	0.07	0.08	0.98
Don Kelly	0.99	−1.67	0.57	0.16	−0.12	0.61
Aubrey Huff	1.88	−8.19	1.07	0.00	−0.55	0.52
Wilkin Ramirez	0.21	1.61	0.12	0.02	0.13	0.27
Dusty Ryan	0.48	−3.41	0.27	0.19	−0.25	0.22
Brent Dlugach	0.05	−0.12	0.03	0.01	−0.01	0.03
Dane Sardinha	0.55	−7.89	0.31	0.22	−0.53	0.00
Matt Treanor	0.22	−4.37	0.13	0.08	−0.31	−0.11
Florida Marlins						
Hanley Ramirez	10.33	49.73	5.89	2.22	7.12	15.23
Dan Uggla	10.58	1.43	6.04	2.22	0.11	8.37
Jorge Cantu	10.19	−5.24	5.81	1.25	−0.37	6.70
Chris Coghlan	8.95	1.43	5.10	1.28	0.11	6.50
Jeremy Hermida	7.78	−3.16	4.44	1.22	−0.23	5.43
John Baker	6.70	−9.17	3.82	2.08	−0.60	5.30
Emilio Bonifacio	8.06	−28.25	4.60	1.45	−1.31	4.74
Ronny Paulino	4.21	−2.94	2.40	1.40	−0.21	3.59
Cameron Maybin	3.15	−0.32	1.80	0.68	−0.02	2.45
Brett Carroll	2.50	3.78	1.43	0.46	0.30	2.19
Nick Johnson	2.38	7.02	1.36	0.23	0.59	2.18
Wes Helms	3.71	−7.22	2.11	0.55	−0.49	2.17
Alfredo Amezaga	1.19	−4.29	0.68	0.22	−0.31	0.60
Alejandro De Aza	0.43	0.52	0.24	0.06	0.04	0.35
Gaby Sanchez	0.36	0.17	0.21	0.01	0.01	0.23
Brett Hayes	0.19	0.70	0.11	0.00	0.05	0.16
Andy Gonzalez	0.19	−2.20	0.11	0.03	−0.16	−0.02
Houston Astros						
Hunter Pence	10.72	20.09	6.11	1.81	2.03	9.95
Lance Berkman	9.31	31.00	5.31	1.01	3.59	9.91
Michael Bourn	11.23	11.59	6.40	2.19	1.04	9.64
Carlos Lee	10.96	7.68	6.25	1.58	0.65	8.48
Miguel Tejada	11.15	−6.74	6.36	2.45	−0.46	8.34
Kazuo Matsui	8.83	−19.93	5.03	1.77	−1.08	5.72
Geoff Blum	7.07	−15.07	4.03	1.25	−0.90	4.39
Ivan Rodriguez	5.70	−15.38	3.25	1.82	−0.91	4.16
Jeff Keppinger	5.70	−15.61	3.25	1.03	−0.92	3.36
Humberto Quintero	2.78	−4.78	1.59	1.04	−0.34	2.29
Jason Michaels	2.52	−3.55	1.44	0.31	−0.26	1.49
Darin Erstad	2.48	−8.40	1.42	0.21	−0.56	1.07

Player	PA%	Runs Above Average	Average Value Hitting ($)	Fielding ($)	Value Above Average ($)	MRP ($)
Edwin Maysonet	1.31	−1.37	0.75	0.25	−0.10	0.89
Chris Coste	1.85	−10.95	1.06	0.45	−0.70	0.81
J.R. Towles	0.88	−4.89	0.50	0.28	−0.35	0.43
Matt Kata	0.86	−3.66	0.49	0.08	−0.26	0.31
Tommy Manzella	0.08	−0.68	0.05	0.01	−0.05	0.01
Aaron Boone	0.23	−2.68	0.13	0.02	−0.20	−0.04
Chris Johnson	0.38	−6.02	0.22	0.07	−0.42	−0.13
Jason Smith	0.45	−7.22	0.26	0.05	−0.49	−0.18
Kansas City Royals						
Billy Butler	11.01	18.83	6.28	1.11	1.87	9.26
Alberto Callaspo	10.39	0.88	5.93	2.14	0.07	8.14
David DeJesus	10.28	1.45	5.86	1.55	0.11	7.52
Mark Teahen	9.36	−14.65	5.34	1.68	−0.88	6.14
Miguel Olivo	6.82	−4.19	3.89	2.06	−0.30	5.65
Willie Bloomquist	7.67	−17.04	4.37	1.42	−0.98	4.82
Mitch Maier	6.51	−12.45	3.71	1.35	−0.77	4.29
Mike Jacobs	7.83	−8.00	4.47	0.10	−0.54	4.03
Coco Crisp	3.52	7.36	2.01	0.68	0.62	3.32
Jose Guillen	5.11	−24.28	2.92	0.70	−1.22	2.41
John Buck	3.31	−5.79	1.89	0.90	−0.40	2.38
Yuniesky Betancourt	4.31	−23.51	2.46	1.09	−1.19	2.36
Brayan Pena	3.00	−0.17	1.71	0.52	−0.01	2.22
Alex Gordon	3.10	−5.45	1.77	0.59	−0.38	1.97
Josh Anderson	2.02	−7.17	1.15	0.45	−0.49	1.11
Mike Aviles	2.08	−14.36	1.19	0.50	−0.86	0.82
Luis Hernandez	1.33	−9.60	0.76	0.33	−0.63	0.47
Ryan Freel	0.80	−4.22	0.46	0.15	−0.30	0.31
Tony Pena	0.87	−11.34	0.50	0.30	−0.72	0.07
Tug Hulett	0.31	−6.24	0.18	0.04	−0.43	−0.21
Los Angeles Angels of Anaheim						
Chone Figgins	11.56	46.58	6.59	1.94	6.44	14.97
Kendry Morales	9.87	36.05	5.63	1.13	4.43	11.18
Torii Hunter	8.03	25.50	4.58	1.60	2.76	8.93
Bobby Abreu	10.58	12.43	6.03	1.51	1.13	8.67
Juan Rivera	9.07	18.83	5.17	1.32	1.87	8.36
Erick Aybar	8.82	−0.25	5.03	2.10	−0.02	7.11
Maicer Izturis	6.93	7.76	3.95	1.33	0.66	5.95
Mike Napoli	6.85	1.97	3.91	1.83	0.15	5.89
Howie Kendrick	6.34	5.44	3.62	1.28	0.45	5.35
Vladimir Guerrero	6.46	1.38	3.68	0.02	0.11	3.81
Gary Matthews	5.71	−13.00	3.26	1.10	−0.80	3.55
Jeff Mathis	4.31	−20.09	2.46	1.58	−1.09	2.95
Robb Quinlan	1.90	−4.95	1.09	0.27	−0.35	1.01
Reggie Willits	1.46	−8.39	0.83	0.26	−0.56	0.53
Brandon Wood	0.73	−2.49	0.42	0.14	−0.18	0.38
Sean Rodriguez	0.46	0.04	0.26	0.09	0.00	0.35
Chris Pettit	0.11	0.64	0.06	0.03	0.05	0.14
Bobby Wilson	0.10	−0.54	0.05	0.06	−0.04	0.08
Freddy Sandoval	0.17	−1.30	0.10	0.05	−0.10	0.05
Terry Evans	0.11	−1.66	0.06	0.03	−0.12	−0.03
Ryan Budde	0.05	−1.09	0.03	0.01	−0.08	−0.04
Los Angeles Dodgers						
Andre Ethier	10.73	27.87	6.12	1.74	3.10	10.96
Matt Kemp	10.45	17.67	5.96	2.24	1.73	9.93
Orlando Hudson	9.88	17.09	5.64	1.98	1.66	9.28
Casey Blake	8.85	23.92	5.05	1.63	2.54	9.22
Rafael Furcal	10.65	1.48	6.07	2.22	0.11	8.41
Manny Ramirez	6.75	28.14	3.85	0.98	3.14	7.97
James Loney	10.20	9.43	5.82	1.16	0.82	7.80
Russell Martin	9.21	−10.33	5.25	2.84	−0.67	7.42
Juan Pierre	6.66	8.92	3.80	0.95	0.77	5.52
Ron Belliard	1.30	8.72	0.74	0.25	0.75	1.74
Juan Castro	1.90	−0.67	1.08	0.48	−0.05	1.51
Brad Ausmus	1.68	−1.39	0.96	0.58	−0.10	1.43
Blake DeWitt	0.83	−2.27	0.47	0.12	−0.17	0.42

Player	PA%	Runs Above Average	Average Value Hitting ($)	Fielding ($)	Value Above Average ($)	MRP ($)
Tony Abreu	0.17	1.40	0.10	0.03	0.11	0.24
Mitch Jones	0.23	0.99	0.13	0.01	0.08	0.22
Jamie Hoffmann	0.38	−0.91	0.21	0.04	−0.07	0.19
Doug Mientkiewicz	0.31	−0.22	0.18	0.01	−0.02	0.17
Xavier Paul	0.25	−0.09	0.14	0.03	−0.01	0.16
Chin-Lung Hu	0.09	0.49	0.05	0.02	0.04	0.11
Jason Repko	0.11	−0.85	0.06	0.03	−0.06	0.02
A.J. Ellis	0.16	−2.29	0.09	0.07	−0.17	−0.01
Milwaukee Brewers						
Prince Fielder	11.42	60.72	6.51	1.27	9.74	17.52
Ryan Braun	11.25	28.58	6.41	1.68	3.21	11.31
Mike Cameron	9.97	13.40	5.69	2.09	1.24	9.01
Jason Kendall	8.35	−22.48	4.76	2.82	−1.17	6.42
Craig Counsell	7.29	7.26	4.16	1.33	0.61	6.10
Corey Hart	7.50	−2.10	4.28	1.22	−0.16	5.34
Casey McGehee	6.26	7.62	3.57	1.06	0.65	5.27
J.J. Hardy	7.39	−11.16	4.21	1.69	−0.71	5.19
Felipe Lopez	4.72	12.00	2.69	0.87	1.09	4.64
Rickie Weeks	2.57	11.99	1.47	0.49	1.09	3.04
Bill Hall	3.72	−6.65	2.12	0.71	−0.46	2.37
Jody Gerut	2.81	−3.12	1.60	0.42	−0.23	1.80
Mat Gamel	2.35	0.98	1.34	0.28	0.08	1.69
Alcides Escobar	2.13	−2.14	1.21	0.53	−0.16	1.59
Frank Catalanotto	2.57	−3.65	1.47	0.36	−0.26	1.56
Mike Rivera	2.10	−4.50	1.20	0.66	−0.32	1.53
Jason Bourgeois	0.64	−1.52	0.36	0.06	−0.11	0.31
Chris Duffy	0.59	−3.83	0.34	0.09	−0.27	0.15
Hernan Iribarren	0.22	−0.35	0.13	0.01	−0.03	0.11
Carlos Corporan	0.02	0.47	0.01	0.00	0.04	0.05
Corey Patterson	0.24	−2.69	0.14	0.03	−0.20	−0.03
Brad Nelson	0.37	−5.34	0.21	0.02	−0.37	−0.15
Minnesota Twins						
Joe Mauer	9.55	53.82	5.45	2.25	8.04	15.74
Denard Span	10.65	29.11	6.07	1.80	3.29	11.17
Justin Morneau	9.30	25.50	5.30	0.94	2.76	9.00
Jason Kubel	9.11	26.74	5.19	0.54	2.94	8.67
Michael Cuddyer	10.24	12.70	5.84	1.57	1.16	8.57
Joe Crede	5.78	4.62	3.30	1.04	0.38	4.71
Nick Punto	6.93	−18.06	3.95	1.71	−1.02	4.64
Brendan Harris	7.14	−29.84	4.07	1.38	−1.33	4.12
Carlos Gomez	5.50	−6.43	3.14	1.38	−0.44	4.07
Delmon Young	6.56	−13.47	3.74	0.98	−0.82	3.90
Orlando Cabrera	4.10	−12.04	2.34	0.88	−0.75	2.46
Matt Tolbert	3.64	−9.61	2.08	0.74	−0.63	2.18
Alexi Casilla	4.03	−27.26	2.30	0.91	−1.29	1.92
Jose Morales	2.11	−0.24	1.20	0.44	−0.02	1.63
Brian Buscher	2.58	−3.21	1.47	0.34	−0.23	1.58
Mike Redmond	2.32	−14.04	1.32	0.79	−0.85	1.26
Justin Huber	0.03	−0.55	0.02	0.00	−0.04	−0.02
New York Mets						
David Wright	10.04	13.35	5.72	1.79	1.23	8.74
Carlos Beltran	5.80	25.35	3.31	1.12	2.74	7.16
Luis Castillo	9.42	−3.76	5.37	1.84	−0.27	6.95
Daniel Murphy	9.03	7.58	5.15	1.02	0.65	6.82
Angel Pagan	6.11	21.16	3.48	1.08	2.17	6.73
Fernando Tatis	6.15	9.95	3.51	0.86	0.88	5.25
Jeff Francoeur	5.00	6.24	2.85	0.84	0.52	4.21
Omir Santos	4.97	−9.25	2.83	1.66	−0.61	3.89
Gary Sheffield	5.07	−0.48	2.89	0.63	−0.04	3.49
Ryan Church	4.14	4.12	2.36	0.70	0.33	3.39
Alex Cora	5.00	−9.85	2.85	1.05	−0.64	3.26
Brian Schneider	3.15	−7.83	1.80	1.07	−0.53	2.34
Jose Reyes	2.70	2.93	1.54	0.55	0.23	2.32
Cory Sullivan	2.55	−0.40	1.45	0.38	−0.03	1.80
Anderson Hernandez	2.42	−3.41	1.38	0.61	−0.25	1.74
Carlos Delgado	1.82	4.32	1.04	0.19	0.35	1.58

Player	PA%	Runs Above Average	Average Value Hitting ($)	Fielding ($)	Value Above Average ($)	MRP ($)
Jeremy Reed	2.87	−6.86	1.64	0.40	−0.47	1.57
Ramon Castro	1.41	0.74	0.81	0.44	0.06	1.30
Wilson Valdez	1.54	−2.39	0.88	0.39	−0.18	1.09
Josh Thole	0.96	0.43	0.55	0.31	0.03	0.89
Fernando Martinez	1.62	−5.43	0.93	0.28	−0.38	0.83
Nick Evans	1.12	−1.96	0.64	0.13	−0.14	0.62
Ramon Martinez	0.71	−7.72	0.41	0.17	−0.52	0.06
Emil Brown	0.10	−0.34	0.06	0.01	−0.03	0.04
Angel Berroa	0.50	−5.16	0.29	0.10	−0.36	0.03
Andy Green	0.08	−0.82	0.05	0.01	−0.06	−0.01
Argenis Reyes	0.29	−3.57	0.17	0.05	−0.26	−0.04
New York Yankees						
Derek Jeter	11.11	41.46	6.33	2.22	5.42	13.97
Mark Teixeira	10.97	46.76	6.25	1.14	6.48	13.88
Robinson Cano	10.45	30.89	5.96	2.21	3.57	11.75
Alex Rodriguez	8.30	30.00	4.73	1.39	3.43	9.55
Johnny Damon	9.71	22.83	5.54	1.36	2.39	9.29
Jorge Posada	6.79	14.31	3.87	1.89	1.34	7.10
Hideki Matsui	8.16	21.40	4.65	0.00	2.20	6.85
Melky Cabrera	8.38	−1.21	4.78	1.79	−0.09	6.48
Brett Gardner	4.41	8.01	2.51	1.03	0.69	4.22
Jose Molina	2.40	−10.85	1.37	0.86	−0.69	1.54
Francisco Cervelli	1.57	−2.68	0.89	0.58	−0.20	1.28
Jerry Hairston	1.44	1.26	0.82	0.30	0.10	1.22
Eric Hinske	1.52	1.35	0.87	0.24	0.10	1.21
Ramiro Pena	1.88	−6.46	1.07	0.50	−0.44	1.13
Cody Ransom	1.33	−7.50	0.76	0.28	−0.51	0.54
Kevin Cash	0.43	−3.00	0.25	0.16	−0.22	0.19
Xavier Nady	0.45	−1.82	0.26	0.06	−0.13	0.18
Juan Miranda	0.14	0.63	0.08	0.02	0.05	0.15
Freddy Guzman	0.11	−0.45	0.06	0.02	−0.03	0.05
Shelley Duncan	0.23	−2.01	0.13	0.03	−0.15	0.02
Angel Berroa	0.37	−5.28	0.21	0.09	−0.37	−0.07
Oakland Athletics						
Ryan Sweeney	8.55	16.37	4.88	1.57	1.57	8.02
Kurt Suzuki	9.83	−11.31	5.61	2.82	−0.72	7.71
Rajai Davis	6.92	18.98	3.94	1.44	1.89	7.28
Matt Holliday	6.40	20.48	3.65	0.99	2.08	6.72
Adam Kennedy	9.38	−6.95	5.35	1.66	−0.47	6.54
Jack Cust	9.80	−2.43	5.59	0.52	−0.18	5.93
Mark Ellis	6.56	−5.70	3.74	1.44	−0.40	4.78
Orlando Cabrera	7.17	−28.11	4.09	1.57	−1.30	4.35
Jason Giambi	5.25	−10.47	2.99	0.40	−0.67	2.72
Daric Barton	3.07	5.33	1.75	0.37	0.44	2.56
Cliff Pennington	3.67	−10.51	2.09	0.94	−0.68	2.36
Scott Hairston	3.97	−9.06	2.26	0.62	−0.60	2.28
Bobby Crosby	4.35	−18.64	2.48	0.77	−1.04	2.21
Landon Powell	2.48	−0.25	1.42	0.69	−0.02	2.09
Jack Hannahan	2.15	−1.30	1.22	0.48	−0.10	1.61
Nomar Garciaparra	2.71	−4.34	1.54	0.13	−0.31	1.37
Eric Patterson	1.76	−0.45	1.00	0.33	−0.03	1.30
Travis Buck	1.84	−5.03	1.05	0.32	−0.35	1.01
Tommy Everidge	1.55	−5.45	0.89	0.15	−0.38	0.65
Matt Carson	0.35	0.03	0.20	0.07	0.00	0.28
Aaron Cunningham	0.91	−7.87	0.52	0.18	−0.53	0.17
Gregorio Petit	0.50	−3.97	0.28	0.11	−0.28	0.11
Chris Denorfia	0.03	−0.57	0.02	0.01	−0.04	−0.02
Eric Chavez	0.50	−6.39	0.28	0.10	−0.44	−0.06
Philadelphia Phillies						
Chase Utley	10.84	50.95	6.18	2.14	7.39	15.71
Ryan Howard	11.09	35.13	6.33	1.21	4.27	11.81
Jayson Werth	10.67	28.89	6.08	1.80	3.26	11.14
Shane Victorino	10.95	−1.85	6.24	2.16	−0.14	8.27
Raul Ibanez	8.91	18.06	5.08	1.37	1.78	8.23
Jimmy Rollins	11.44	−13.66	6.52	2.39	−0.83	8.09
Pedro Feliz	9.86	−13.06	5.62	1.91	−0.80	6.73

Player	PA%	Runs Above Average	Average Value Hitting ($)	Fielding ($)	Value Above Average ($)	MRP ($)
Carlos Ruiz	5.98	−1.13	3.41	2.11	−0.08	5.44
Greg Dobbs	2.67	−3.74	1.52	0.28	−0.27	1.53
Paul Bako	2.05	−6.29	1.17	0.72	−0.43	1.45
Chris Coste	1.86	−2.43	1.06	0.51	−0.18	1.40
Matt Stairs	2.04	−0.23	1.16	0.12	−0.02	1.26
Ben Francisco	1.64	−0.24	0.94	0.25	−0.02	1.17
John Mayberry	0.95	−0.58	0.54	0.16	−0.04	0.65
Eric Bruntlett	1.86	−14.23	1.06	0.31	−0.86	0.51
Miguel Cairo	0.74	−0.71	0.42	0.09	−0.05	0.46
Lou Marson	0.32	−0.25	0.18	0.12	−0.02	0.29
Andy Tracy	0.19	1.57	0.11	0.01	0.12	0.24
Paul Hoover	0.06	0.67	0.04	0.03	0.05	0.11
Andy LaRoche	9.74	1.81	5.55	1.82	0.14	7.51
Andrew McCutchen	8.14	8.45	4.64	1.59	0.73	6.96
Garrett Jones	5.91	25.15	3.37	0.84	2.71	6.92
Freddy Sanchez	6.31	6.53	3.60	1.20	0.55	5.34
Jack Wilson	4.72	11.28	2.69	1.17	1.01	4.88
Brandon Moss	7.00	−7.36	3.99	1.09	−0.50	4.59
Nyjer Morgan	5.30	6.57	3.02	0.78	0.55	4.35
Adam LaRoche	6.07	0.56	3.46	0.68	0.04	4.19
Delwyn Young	6.40	−8.52	3.65	1.05	−0.57	4.13
Ryan Doumit	5.02	−5.73	2.86	1.52	−0.40	3.99
Nate McLouth	3.22	6.65	1.84	0.63	0.56	3.03
Jason Jaramillo	3.70	−8.02	2.11	1.28	−0.54	2.85
Lastings Milledge	3.95	−2.11	2.25	0.62	−0.16	2.72
Ramon Vazquez	3.95	−13.15	2.25	0.72	−0.81	2.17
Steven Pearce	3.07	−0.58	1.75	0.34	−0.04	2.04
Ronny Cedeno	2.81	−5.40	1.60	0.66	−0.38	1.88
Robinzon Diaz	2.28	−6.85	1.30	0.69	−0.47	1.53
Eric Hinske	2.08	0.27	1.19	0.21	0.02	1.42
Luis Cruz	1.29	−3.63	0.73	0.30	−0.26	0.78
Craig Monroe	1.44	−4.61	0.82	0.16	−0.33	0.65
Brian Bixler	0.76	−3.72	0.43	0.19	−0.27	0.35
Neil Walker	0.66	−6.09	0.38	0.10	−0.42	0.06
Jeff Salazar	0.43	−4.04	0.24	0.03	−0.29	−0.02
San Diego Padres						
Adrian Gonzalez	11.02	66.14	6.29	1.19	11.19	18.67
Chase Headley	9.91	11.74	5.65	1.52	1.06	8.23
Kevin Kouzmanoff	9.27	7.69	5.29	1.69	0.66	7.64
Tony Gwynn	7.30	15.70	4.16	1.43	1.50	7.09
David Eckstein	9.19	−11.79	5.24	1.73	−0.74	6.23
Everth Cabrera	7.09	−5.00	4.04	1.58	−0.35	5.27
Will Venable	5.24	10.71	2.99	0.87	0.95	4.81
Scott Hairston	3.50	14.99	1.99	0.63	1.41	4.04
Nick Hundley	4.68	−5.01	2.67	1.55	−0.35	3.86
Henry Blanco	3.76	1.23	2.14	1.22	0.10	3.46
Kyle Blanks	2.78	8.86	1.59	0.40	0.77	2.75
Luis Rodriguez	4.06	−15.55	2.32	0.82	−0.92	2.22
Brian Giles	4.10	−23.57	2.34	0.65	−1.20	1.79
Edgar Gonzalez	2.74	−6.29	1.56	0.35	−0.43	1.48
Oscar Salazar	1.96	0.78	1.12	0.22	0.06	1.40
Jody Gerut	1.96	−2.23	1.12	0.35	−0.16	1.30
Eliezer Alfonzo	1.89	−11.59	1.08	0.61	−0.73	0.96
Drew Macias	1.46	−2.09	0.83	0.21	−0.15	0.88
Chris Burke	1.44	−6.61	0.82	0.34	−0.45	0.71
Luis Durango	0.23	1.79	0.13	0.02	0.14	0.29
Jose Lobaton	0.28	−2.40	0.16	0.11	−0.18	0.09
Cliff Floyd	0.28	−2.48	0.16	0.00	−0.18	−0.02
San Francisco Giants						
Pablo Sandoval	10.45	27.18	5.96	1.72	3.00	10.68
Aaron Rowand	9.01	−2.56	5.14	1.84	−0.19	6.80
Randy Winn	9.86	−7.93	5.62	1.56	−0.53	6.65
Juan Uribe	7.13	11.06	4.07	1.50	0.99	6.56
Bengie Molina	8.59	−20.67	4.90	2.51	−1.11	6.30
Edgar Renteria	8.42	−29.63	4.80	1.89	−1.33	5.36
Travis Ishikawa	5.99	1.26	3.42	0.72	0.10	4.23

Player	PA%	Runs Above Average	Average Value Hitting ($)	Fielding ($)	Value Above Average ($)	MRP ($)
Fred Lewis	5.55	−2.27	3.16	0.72	−0.17	3.72
Nate Schierholtz	5.09	−4.60	2.90	0.78	−0.33	3.35
Eugenio Velez	5.07	−7.55	2.89	0.82	−0.51	3.20
Andres Torres	2.81	7.89	1.60	0.49	0.67	2.77
Emmanuel Burriss	3.63	−18.49	2.07	0.78	−1.03	1.82
Eli Whiteside	2.21	−7.89	1.26	0.76	−0.53	1.49
Ryan Garko	2.10	−5.45	1.20	0.20	−0.38	1.02
Freddy Sanchez	1.77	−5.41	1.01	0.33	−0.38	0.96
Rich Aurilia	2.20	−10.25	1.25	0.23	−0.66	0.82
John Bowker	1.21	−2.54	0.69	0.16	−0.19	0.66
Matt Downs	0.99	−4.93	0.56	0.23	−0.35	0.44
Steve Holm	0.15	0.87	0.08	0.06	0.07	0.21
Kevin Frandsen	0.89	−7.36	0.51	0.19	−0.50	0.20
Ryan Rohlinger	0.33	−1.10	0.19	0.08	−0.08	0.19
Jesus Guzman	0.33	−2.10	0.19	0.01	−0.15	0.05
Buster Posey	0.28	−3.33	0.16	0.10	−0.24	0.02
Seattle Mariners						
Ichiro Suzuki	11.09	39.75	6.33	1.67	5.10	13.09
Franklin Gutierrez	10.29	29.27	5.87	2.20	3.32	11.39
Jose Lopez	10.68	1.15	6.09	2.05	0.09	8.24
Russell Branyan	8.26	19.60	4.71	0.91	1.97	7.58
Adrian Beltre	7.80	11.59	4.45	1.41	1.04	6.90
Ken Griffey	7.43	−3.63	4.24	0.10	−0.26	4.08
Kenji Johjima	4.22	−1.12	2.41	1.39	−0.08	3.71
Rob Johnson	4.74	−14.45	2.71	1.64	−0.87	3.48
Mike Sweeney	4.35	0.75	2.48	0.03	0.06	2.57
Jack Hannahan	2.73	2.54	1.56	0.49	0.20	2.25
Endy Chavez	2.98	0.26	1.70	0.50	0.02	2.21
Yuniesky Betancourt	4.01	−21.05	2.29	0.96	−1.12	2.13
Ronny Cedeno	3.37	−21.48	1.92	0.81	−1.14	1.60
Wladimir Balentien	2.78	−6.64	1.59	0.45	−0.46	1.58
Josh Wilson	2.26	−4.11	1.29	0.56	−0.29	1.56
Jack Wilson	1.90	−0.09	1.08	0.47	−0.01	1.54
Ryan Langerhans	2.00	−1.19	1.14	0.36	−0.09	1.41
Michael Saunders	2.11	−4.09	1.20	0.38	−0.29	1.29
Bill Hall	2.14	−5.96	1.22	0.36	−0.41	1.17
Mike Carp	1.06	4.98	0.61	0.11	0.41	1.13
Chris Woodward	1.21	−2.86	0.69	0.25	−0.21	0.73
Matt Tuiasosopo	0.41	0.28	0.23	0.09	0.02	0.34
Adam Moore	0.39	−1.11	0.22	0.14	−0.08	0.28
Jamie Burke	0.70	−5.86	0.40	0.24	−0.41	0.23
Guillermo Quiroz	0.25	−1.16	0.14	0.08	−0.09	0.14
Chris Shelton	0.46	−2.15	0.26	0.03	−0.16	0.13
St. Louis Cardinals						
Albert Pujols	11.35	92.01	6.48	1.21	19.74	27.43
Yadier Molina	8.82	3.87	5.03	2.85	0.31	8.20
Brendan Ryan	6.96	19.54	3.97	1.63	1.96	7.55
Ryan Ludwick	8.74	1.18	4.99	1.41	0.09	6.49
Skip Schumaker	9.51	−11.90	5.42	1.75	−0.75	6.42
Matt Holliday	4.38	27.61	2.50	0.66	3.07	6.23
Colby Rasmus	8.43	−9.44	4.81	1.67	−0.62	5.86
Rick Ankiel	6.55	−10.57	3.74	1.18	−0.68	4.24
Joe Thurston	4.98	−9.86	2.84	0.90	−0.64	3.10
Chris Duncan	4.93	−8.42	2.81	0.65	−0.56	2.90
Mark DeRosa	4.25	−10.36	2.42	0.78	−0.67	2.53
Julio Lugo	2.76	−7.26	1.57	0.55	−0.49	1.63
Khalil Greene	3.13	−15.06	1.79	0.56	−0.90	1.45
Jason LaRue	1.82	−5.79	1.04	0.62	−0.40	1.25
Brian Barden	1.85	−3.23	1.05	0.37	−0.23	1.19
Tyler Greene	1.88	−6.21	1.07	0.45	−0.43	1.09
Nick Stavinoha	1.48	−5.09	0.84	0.18	−0.36	0.67
David Freese	0.55	0.04	0.31	0.07	0.00	0.38
Jarrett Hoffpauir	0.26	1.66	0.15	0.04	0.13	0.32
Troy Glaus	0.52	−2.82	0.30	0.07	−0.21	0.16
Shane Robinson	0.42	−3.21	0.24	0.06	−0.23	0.07
Matt Pagnozzi	0.08	−0.37	0.05	0.02	−0.03	0.04

Player	PA%	Runs Above Average	Average Value Hitting ($)	Fielding ($)	Value Above Average ($)	MRP ($)
Tampa Bay Rays						
Ben Zobrist	9.63	65.44	5.49	1.84	11.00	18.33
Evan Longoria	10.78	46.21	6.15	1.89	6.37	14.40
Carl Crawford	10.80	37.54	6.16	1.59	4.69	12.44
Jason Bartlett	9.11	34.81	5.20	2.06	4.21	11.47
Carlos Pena	9.16	18.45	5.22	1.03	1.82	8.08
B.J. Upton	10.06	−13.00	5.74	2.04	−0.80	6.97
Dioner Navarro	6.59	−31.21	3.76	2.25	−1.36	4.65
Pat Burrell	7.65	−11.34	4.36	0.01	−0.72	3.65
Gabe Gross	5.24	−3.23	2.99	0.84	−0.23	3.59
Akinori Iwamura	4.18	3.09	2.38	0.89	0.25	3.52
Gabe Kapler	3.82	5.70	2.18	0.75	0.47	3.40
Willy Aybar	5.40	−11.14	3.08	0.57	−0.71	2.94
Gregg Zaun	1.59	−2.29	0.91	0.51	−0.17	1.25
Michel Hernandez	1.72	−6.57	0.98	0.64	−0.45	1.17
Reid Brignac	1.49	−2.99	0.85	0.39	−0.22	1.03
Joe Dillon	0.56	0.68	0.32	0.02	0.05	0.39
Fernando Perez	0.56	−1.98	0.32	0.13	−0.15	0.30
Matthew Joyce	0.59	−3.48	0.34	0.10	−0.25	0.19
Shawn Riggans	0.22	−2.07	0.13	0.08	−0.15	0.06
Chris Richard	0.37	−3.43	0.21	0.05	−0.25	0.01
Texas Rangers						
Ian Kinsler	10.45	29.30	5.96	2.01	3.32	11.29
Marlon Byrd	9.78	10.39	5.58	1.91	0.92	8.41
Nelson Cruz	8.41	21.24	4.79	1.38	2.18	8.35
Michael Young	9.68	7.51	5.52	1.68	0.64	7.84
Elvis Andrus	8.83	3.51	5.04	2.20	0.28	7.52
David Murphy	8.05	4.10	4.59	1.16	0.33	6.08
Josh Hamilton	5.96	1.94	3.40	1.05	0.15	4.60
Hank Blalock	8.08	−10.82	4.61	0.52	−0.69	4.43
Chris Davis	6.84	−16.94	3.90	0.85	−0.97	3.78
Jarrod Saltalamacchia	5.06	−19.82	2.89	1.73	−1.08	3.54
Andruw Jones	5.40	2.62	3.08	0.22	0.21	3.51
Omar Vizquel	3.18	0.92	1.82	0.70	0.07	2.58
Taylor Teagarden	3.56	−9.85	2.03	1.19	−0.64	2.58
Julio Borbon	2.92	5.16	1.67	0.20	0.42	2.29
Ivan Rodriguez	1.70	−3.16	0.97	0.52	−0.23	1.26
Esteban German	0.82	−1.39	0.47	0.16	−0.10	0.52
Kevin Richardson	0.10	0.07	0.06	0.04	0.01	0.10
Craig Gentry	0.31	−2.46	0.18	0.07	−0.18	0.07
Greg Golson	0.02	−0.29	0.01	0.00	−0.02	−0.01
Brandon Boggs	0.29	−3.55	0.17	0.05	−0.26	−0.04
Joaquin Arias	0.15	−3.88	0.08	0.03	−0.28	−0.16
Toronto Blue Jays						
Aaron Hill	11.54	32.04	6.58	2.17	3.75	12.50
Marco Scutaro	10.69	29.39	6.10	2.21	3.34	11.64
Adam Lind	10.28	32.81	5.86	0.58	3.88	10.32
Lyle Overbay	7.86	24.81	4.48	0.92	2.66	8.07
Scott Rolen	5.86	25.61	3.34	1.11	2.77	7.23
Vernon Wells	10.75	−24.19	6.13	2.21	−1.21	7.13
Alexis Rios	7.53	−1.74	4.29	1.28	−0.13	5.45
Rod Barajas	7.23	−18.29	4.12	2.34	−1.03	5.44
Jose Bautista	6.35	3.51	3.62	1.11	0.28	5.02
Travis Snider	4.34	−2.94	2.47	0.76	−0.21	3.02
Kevin Millar	4.45	−8.95	2.54	0.37	−0.59	2.31
Randy Ruiz	2.04	10.93	1.17	0.01	0.98	2.15
Raul Chavez	2.64	−7.13	1.51	0.96	−0.48	1.98
John McDonald	2.45	−2.46	1.40	0.57	−0.18	1.79
Edwin Encarnacion	2.72	−3.92	1.55	0.52	−0.28	1.79
Joe Inglett	1.56	1.23	0.89	0.27	0.10	1.26
Kyle Phillips	0.28	−0.93	0.16	0.09	−0.07	0.18
Michael Barrett	0.30	−2.05	0.17	0.09	0.15	0.11
Russ Adams	0.33	−2.35	0.19	0.04	−0.17	0.05
David Dellucci	0.46	−5.64	0.26	0.06	−0.39	−0.07

Player	PA%	Runs Above Average	Average Value Hitting ($)	Fielding ($)	Value Above Average ($)	MRP ($)
Washington Nationals						
Ryan Zimmerman	11.05	51.79	6.30	1.94	7.58	15.82
Adam Dunn	10.65	12.88	6.07	1.35	1.18	8.60
Josh Willingham	8.00	17.20	4.56	1.21	1.67	7.44
Cristian Guzman	8.85	−16.16	5.05	1.78	−0.94	5.89
Nick Johnson	6.76	4.69	3.86	0.72	0.38	4.96
Willie Harris	6.27	1.55	3.57	1.17	0.12	4.87
Elijah Dukes	6.63	−8.48	3.78	1.19	−0.56	4.41
Nyjer Morgan	3.38	14.77	1.93	0.65	1.39	3.97
Josh Bard	4.80	−14.29	2.74	1.54	−0.86	3.42
Alberto Gonzalez	5.04	−17.45	2.87	1.09	−0.99	2.97
Wil Nieves	3.97	−13.08	2.26	1.35	−0.80	2.81
Anderson Hernandez	4.07	−10.13	2.32	0.80	−0.66	2.47
Ron Belliard	3.25	−5.06	1.85	0.56	−0.36	2.06
Jesus Flores	1.69	4.65	0.96	0.50	0.38	1.85
Austin Kearns	3.36	−10.77	1.92	0.51	−0.69	1.74
Justin Maxwell	1.63	4.86	0.93	0.35	0.40	1.68
Ian Desmond	1.42	−1.36	0.81	0.32	−0.10	1.03
Pete Orr	1.29	−0.12	0.74	0.24	−0.01	0.97
Mike Morse	0.88	2.47	0.50	0.09	0.19	0.78
Roger Bernadina	0.08	0.54	0.05	0.02	0.04	0.11
Corey Patterson	0.24	−1.04	0.14	0.05	−0.08	0.10
Lastings Milledge	0.41	−3.05	0.24	0.07	−0.22	0.09
Jamie Burke	0.21	−1.63	0.12	0.08	−0.12	0.08
Jorge Padilla	0.41	−4.61	0.24	0.05	−0.33	−0.04
Alex Cintron	0.45	−6.09	0.25	0.03	−0.42	−0.13

Pitchers (2009)

Player	BFP %	Runs Above Average	Average Value ($)	Value Above Average ($)	MRP (raw) ($)	MRP (adjusted) ($)
Arizona Diamondbacks						
Danny Haren	14.50	44.22	6.03	5.96	11.99	13.63
Juan Gutierrez	4.90	14.94	2.04	1.41	3.45	8.61
Max Scherzer	11.82	21.05	4.92	2.15	7.07	7.07
Chad Qualls	3.46	11.87	1.44	1.07	2.51	6.28
Doug Davis	14.19	−5.06	5.90	−0.36	5.54	5.54
Jon Garland	11.62	5.85	4.83	0.49	5.32	5.47
Jon Rauch	3.75	5.46	1.56	0.45	2.01	4.02
Clay Zavada	3.53	5.14	1.47	0.42	1.89	3.78
Esmerling Vasquez	3.80	3.45	1.58	0.28	1.86	3.71
Blaine Boyer	2.55	7.34	1.06	0.62	1.68	3.37
Leo Rosales	2.97	4.24	1.23	0.34	1.58	3.16
Tony Pena	2.44	4.74	1.02	0.39	1.40	2.81
Billy Buckner	5.46	1.64	2.27	0.13	2.40	2.40
Yusmeiro Petit	6.49	−5.53	2.70	−0.39	2.31	2.31
Daniel Schlereth	1.37	1.00	0.57	0.08	0.65	0.65
Bryan Augenstein	1.29	−0.05	0.54	0.00	0.53	0.53
Kevin Mulvey	1.66	−3.53	0.69	−0.25	0.44	0.44
Daniel Cabrera	0.81	1.03	0.34	0.08	0.42	0.42
Scott Schoeneweis	1.87	−5.77	0.78	−0.40	0.38	0.38
Bobby Korecky	0.51	0.51	0.21	0.04	0.25	0.25
Doug Slaten	0.48	0.63	0.20	0.05	0.25	0.25
Tom Gordon	0.16	−0.95	0.07	−0.07	0.00	0.00
Josh Wilson	0.05	−0.34	0.02	−0.03	−0.01	−0.01
Brandon Webb	0.32	−2.46	0.13	−0.18	−0.05	−0.05
Atlanta Braves						
Javier Vazquez	14.08	47.84	5.85	6.71	12.56	14.13
Rafael Soriano	4.95	16.89	2.06	1.64	3.69	9.23
Jair Jurrjens	14.24	16.42	5.92	1.58	7.50	7.88
Peter Moylan	4.98	11.86	2.07	1.07	3.14	7.85
Derek Lowe	13.77	9.16	5.73	0.80	6.53	6.53

Player	BFP %	Runs Above Average	Average Value ($)	Value Above Average ($)	MRP (raw) ($)	MRP (adjusted) ($)
Mike Gonzalez	5.07	8.97	2.11	0.78	2.89	5.78
Tommy Hanson	8.41	13.74	3.50	1.27	4.77	4.83
Kenshin Kawakami	10.78	3.34	4.48	0.27	4.75	4.75
Eric O'Flaherty	3.80	8.56	1.58	0.74	2.32	4.64
Kris Medlen	4.74	8.27	1.97	0.71	2.68	2.68
Tim Hudson	2.90	2.76	1.21	0.22	1.42	1.44
Manny Acosta	2.80	−0.43	1.17	−0.03	1.13	1.13
Jeff Bennett	2.63	−1.07	1.09	−0.08	1.01	1.01
Jo−Jo Reyes	1.92	−2.71	0.80	−0.20	0.60	0.60
James Parr	1.06	1.95	0.44	0.15	0.59	0.59
Boone Logan	1.32	−0.06	0.55	0.00	0.54	0.54
Buddy Carlyle	1.72	−6.86	0.72	−0.47	0.25	0.25
Jorge Campillo	0.34	0.15	0.14	0.01	0.15	0.15
Luis Valdez	0.21	−0.48	0.09	−0.04	0.05	0.05
Blaine Boyer	0.18	−0.62	0.07	−0.05	0.03	0.03
Vladimir Nunez	0.11	−3.96	0.05	−0.28	−0.24	−0.24
Baltimore Orioles						
Jeremy Guthrie	13.74	−16.88	5.72	−0.97	4.74	4.79
Matt Albers	4.86	3.89	2.02	0.31	2.33	4.67
Brad Bergesen	8.16	7.80	3.39	0.67	4.06	4.37
George Sherrill	2.69	6.70	1.12	0.56	1.68	3.36
Jason Berken	8.81	−9.35	3.66	−0.61	3.05	3.05
Mark Hendrickson	7.19	−5.07	2.99	−0.36	2.63	2.63
Koji Uehara	4.39	8.52	1.82	0.74	2.56	2.56
Jim Johnson	4.72	2.29	1.96	0.18	2.14	2.14
Brian Bass	6.29	−7.54	2.62	−0.51	2.11	2.11
Danys Baez	4.64	0.30	1.93	0.02	1.95	1.95
David Hernandez	7.27	−27.99	3.02	−1.30	1.72	1.72
Brian Matusz	3.08	2.30	1.28	0.18	1.46	1.46
Rich Hill	4.32	−7.29	1.80	−0.49	1.30	1.30
Chris Ray	3.37	−4.64	1.40	−0.33	1.07	1.07
Chris Tillman	4.48	−12.95	1.86	−0.80	1.06	1.06
Adam Eaton	3.05	−7.91	1.27	−0.53	0.74	0.74
Cla Meredith	1.86	−1.03	0.77	−0.08	0.69	0.69
Kameron Mickolio	0.93	2.78	0.39	0.22	0.61	0.61
Alberto Castillo	0.77	2.37	0.32	0.19	0.51	0.51
Dennis Sarfate	1.59	−2.22	0.66	−0.16	0.50	0.50
Sean Henn	0.30	0.33	0.12	0.03	0.15	0.15
Jamie Walker	0.86	−3.06	0.36	−0.22	0.14	0.14
Chris Lambert	0.41	−0.70	0.17	−0.05	0.12	0.12
Chris Waters	0.77	−3.81	0.32	−0.27	0.05	0.05
Radhames Liz	0.25	−1.64	0.10	−0.12	−0.02	−0.02
Bob McCrory	0.77	−6.76	0.32	−0.46	−0.14	−0.14
Alfredo Simon	0.44	−7.04	0.18	−0.48	−0.30	−0.30
Boston Red Sox						
Jon Lester	13.42	35.89	5.58	4.40	9.98	10.54
Josh Beckett	14.05	28.48	5.84	3.20	9.04	9.91
Jonathan Papelbon	4.54	13.67	1.89	1.27	3.15	7.88
Brad Penny	9.39	5.02	3.90	0.41	4.32	4.32
Tim Wakefield	9.10	3.60	3.79	0.29	4.07	4.19
Daniel Bard	3.37	7.55	1.40	0.64	2.05	4.09
Justin Masterson	4.97	9.24	2.06	0.81	2.87	2.87
Clay Buchholz	6.35	−1.06	2.64	−0.08	2.56	2.56
Ramon Ramirez	4.79	1.28	1.99	0.10	2.09	2.09
Hideki Okajima	4.11	3.37	1.71	0.27	1.98	1.98
Manny Delcarmen	4.42	0.19	1.84	0.01	1.85	1.85
Takashi Saito	3.82	3.21	1.59	0.26	1.85	1.85
Daisuke Matsuzaka	4.50	−2.92	1.87	−0.21	1.66	1.66
John Smoltz	2.96	0.83	1.23	0.06	1.30	1.30
Paul Byrd	2.47	−0.96	1.03	−0.07	0.95	0.95
Junichi Tazawa	2.07	−0.79	0.86	−0.06	0.80	0.80
Billy Wagner	0.89	3.19	0.37	0.26	0.63	0.63
Michael Bowden	1.19	−0.87	0.50	−0.07	0.43	0.43
Javier Lopez	1.02	−1.59	0.42	−0.12	0.31	0.31
Fernando Cabrera	0.45	1.39	0.19	0.11	0.29	0.29
Hunter Jones	1.00	−2.79	0.42	−0.20	0.21	0.21
Dustin Richardson	0.22	0.24	0.09	0.02	0.11	0.11

Player	BFP %	Runs Above Average	Average Value ($)	Value Above Average ($)	MRP (raw) ($)	MRP (adjusted) ($)
Dusty Brown	0.08	0.52	0.03	0.04	0.07	0.07
Enrique Gonzalez	0.29	−1.41	0.12	−0.10	0.01	0.01
Jonathan Van Every	0.06	−0.31	0.03	−0.02	0.00	0.00
Nick Green	0.14	−1.08	0.06	−0.08	−0.02	−0.02
Billy Traber	0.32	−2.36	0.13	−0.17	−0.04	−0.04
Chicago Cubs						
Ryan Dempster	13.63	21.06	5.67	2.15	7.82	8.37
Ted Lilly	11.43	23.38	4.75	2.46	7.22	7.83
Carlos Zambrano	11.87	22.16	4.93	2.30	7.23	7.29
Randy Wells	11.24	18.62	4.67	1.84	6.52	6.65
Carlos Marmol	5.42	4.58	2.26	0.37	2.63	5.26
Rich Harden	9.86	4.94	4.10	0.40	4.50	4.50
Sean Marshall	6.04	5.24	2.51	0.43	2.94	2.94
Aaron Heilman	5.07	1.63	2.11	0.13	2.23	2.23
Esmailin Caridad	1.20	6.80	0.50	0.57	1.07	2.14
Kevin Gregg	4.82	−1.99	2.01	−0.15	1.86	1.86
Angel Guzman	3.97	0.71	1.65	0.05	1.70	1.70
Tom Gorzelanny	2.72	3.03	1.13	0.24	1.37	1.37
Justin Berg	0.74	3.80	0.31	0.31	0.62	1.23
John Grabow	1.70	2.01	0.71	0.16	0.86	0.86
Jeff Samardzija	2.61	−4.66	1.08	−0.33	0.75	0.75
David Patton	2.17	−3.05	0.90	−0.22	0.68	0.68
Jose Ascanio	1.18	2.26	0.49	0.18	0.67	0.67
Kevin Hart	1.94	−4.18	0.81	−0.30	0.51	0.51
Jeff Stevens	0.96	−1.80	0.40	−0.13	0.26	0.26
Luis Vizcaino	0.21	1.47	0.09	0.11	0.20	0.20
Jason Waddell	0.13	0.94	0.05	0.07	0.13	0.13
Mitch Atkins	0.11	0.40	0.05	0.03	0.08	0.08
Neal Cotts	0.89	−4.14	0.37	−0.30	0.07	0.07
Chad Fox	0.10	−1.23	0.04	−0.09	−0.05	−0.05
Chicago White Sox						
Matt Thornton	4.73	19.02	1.97	1.89	3.86	9.65
Gavin Floyd	12.95	18.83	5.38	1.87	7.25	7.74
Mark Buehrle	14.20	6.16	5.90	0.51	6.42	6.88
John Danks	13.63	−1.42	5.67	−0.11	5.56	5.79
Jose Contreras	8.33	8.41	3.47	0.72	4.19	4.19
D.J. Carrasco	6.58	14.11	2.74	1.32	4.05	4.05
Tony Pena	2.58	4.68	1.07	0.38	1.46	2.91
Clayton Richard	6.29	1.62	2.61	0.13	2.74	2.74
Freddy Garcia	3.72	8.93	1.55	0.78	2.32	2.41
Octavio Dotel	4.35	2.79	1.81	0.22	2.03	2.03
Scott Linebrink	4.21	1.00	1.75	0.08	1.83	1.83
Bobby Jenks	3.70	1.57	1.54	0.12	1.66	1.66
Bartolo Colon	4.48	−7.82	1.86	−0.53	1.34	1.34
Jake Peavy	1.22	3.80	0.51	0.31	0.81	0.86
Lance Broadway	1.23	1.59	0.51	0.12	0.64	0.64
Randy Williams	1.30	0.20	0.54	0.02	0.56	0.56
Carlos Torres	2.11	−4.66	0.88	−0.33	0.55	0.55
Aaron Poreda	0.80	1.40	0.33	0.11	0.44	0.44
Daniel Hudson	1.33	−1.72	0.55	−0.13	0.43	0.43
Jimmy Gobble	0.96	−2.92	0.40	−0.21	0.19	0.19
Jhonny Nunez	0.47	−0.36	0.20	−0.03	0.17	0.17
Mike MacDougal	0.41	−1.65	0.17	−0.12	0.05	0.05
Jack Egbert	0.29	−1.73	0.12	−0.13	−0.01	−0.01
Wes Whisler	0.11	−0.73	0.05	−0.06	−0.01	−0.01
Cincinnati Reds						
Nick Masset	4.67	10.31	1.94	0.91	2.85	7.14
Francisco Cordero	4.41	9.73	1.84	0.85	2.69	6.72
Bronson Arroyo	14.76	−5.18	6.14	−0.36	5.77	6.36
Aaron Harang	11.24	10.44	4.68	0.93	5.60	5.82
Johnny Cueto	11.83	0.08	4.92	0.01	4.93	4.93
Jared Burton	4.24	4.73	1.76	0.39	2.15	4.30
Arthur Rhodes	3.44	7.76	1.43	0.66	2.09	4.18
Danny Herrera	4.19	3.77	1.74	0.30	2.05	4.09
Homer Bailey	7.93	0.10	3.30	0.01	3.31	3.31
Micah Owings	8.67	−18.40	3.60	−1.03	2.57	2.57
Carlos Fisher	3.61	0.72	1.50	0.06	1.56	1.56

Player	BFP %	Runs Above Average	Average Value ($)	Value Above Average ($)	MRP (raw) ($)	MRP (adjusted) ($)
Josh Roenicke	0.86	4.23	0.36	0.34	0.70	1.41
Edinson Volquez	3.49	−3.78	1.45	−0.27	1.18	1.18
Kip Wells	3.15	−3.40	1.31	−0.25	1.06	1.06
Justin Lehr	4.57	−14.70	1.90	−0.88	1.02	1.02
Matt Maloney	2.72	−3.03	1.13	−0.22	0.91	0.91
Dave Weathers	2.56	−5.42	1.06	−0.38	0.69	0.69
Ramon Ramirez	0.77	−0.89	0.32	−0.07	0.25	0.25
Robert Manuel	0.29	0.92	0.12	0.07	0.19	0.19
Pedro Viola	0.48	−2.06	0.20	−0.15	0.05	0.05
Mike Lincoln	1.84	−13.45	0.76	−0.82	−0.06	−0.06
Paul Janish	0.27	−2.71	0.11	−0.20	−0.08	−0.08
Cleveland Indians						
Cliff Lee	10.09	21.88	4.20	2.26	6.46	7.23
Carl Pavano	8.40	1.82	3.49	0.14	3.64	3.66
David Huff	9.03	−7.75	3.76	−0.52	3.24	3.24
Aaron Laffey	8.48	−7.99	3.53	−0.54	2.99	2.99
Jeremy Sowers	8.58	−10.49	3.57	−0.67	2.89	2.89
Fausto Carmona	9.38	−19.75	3.90	−1.08	2.82	2.82
Kerry Wood	3.79	−0.32	1.58	−0.02	1.55	1.55
Justin Masterson	4.03	−3.17	1.68	−0.23	1.45	1.45
Jensen Lewis	4.49	−9.66	1.87	−0.63	1.23	1.23
Rafael Perez	3.62	−3.99	1.51	−0.29	1.22	1.22
Joe Smith	2.23	0.13	0.93	0.01	0.94	0.94
Chris Perez	2.09	0.71	0.87	0.05	0.92	0.92
Tony Sipp	2.64	−2.51	1.10	−0.18	0.92	0.92
Tomokazu Ohka	4.82	−20.06	2.00	−1.09	0.91	0.91
Rafael Betancourt	2.03	0.66	0.84	0.05	0.90	0.90
Matt Herges	1.68	1.07	0.70	0.08	0.78	0.78
Jess Todd	1.56	0.12	0.65	0.01	0.66	0.66
Anthony Reyes	2.77	−8.03	1.15	−0.54	0.61	0.61
Jose Veras	1.68	−2.48	0.70	−0.18	0.52	0.52
Mike Gosling	1.79	−6.36	0.75	−0.44	0.31	0.31
Zach Jackson	0.74	−0.95	0.31	−0.07	0.24	0.24
Greg Aquino	1.16	−4.06	0.48	−0.29	0.19	0.19
Carlos Carrasco	1.76	−8.75	0.73	−0.58	0.15	0.15
Masahide Kobayashi	0.71	−2.67	0.29	−0.19	0.10	0.10
Vinnie Chulk	0.87	−3.93	0.36	−0.28	0.08	0.08
Rich Rundles	0.09	−0.03	0.04	0.00	0.04	0.04
Luis Vizcaino	0.88	−5.44	0.37	−0.38	−0.01	−0.01
Scott Lewis	0.31	−2.35	0.13	−0.17	−0.04	−0.04
Winston Abreu	0.27	−3.07	0.11	−0.22	−0.11	−0.11
Colorado Rockies						
Ubaldo Jimenez	14.81	36.77	6.16	4.56	10.72	11.70
Jason Marquis	14.92	16.67	6.21	1.61	7.82	8.47
Jason Hammel	12.49	28.73	5.20	3.24	8.43	8.43
Jorge de la Rosa	12.95	19.02	5.38	1.89	7.28	7.28
Huston Street	3.89	13.21	1.62	1.22	2.83	7.08
Aaron Cook	10.94	4.23	4.55	0.34	4.89	4.89
Matt Daley	3.42	6.89	1.42	0.58	2.00	4.01
Manuel Corpas	2.37	5.99	0.98	0.50	1.48	2.96
Rafael Betancourt	1.59	8.54	0.66	0.74	1.40	2.80
Franklin Morales	2.90	2.20	1.21	0.17	1.38	1.38
Josh Fogg	3.03	−3.83	1.26	−0.27	0.99	0.99
Matt Belisle	2.16	1.11	0.90	0.09	0.98	0.98
Joel Peralta	1.83	1.01	0.76	0.08	0.84	0.84
Glendon Rusch	1.49	2.26	0.62	0.18	0.80	0.80
Jason Grilli	1.60	1.24	0.67	0.10	0.76	0.76
Juan Rincon	1.88	−0.65	0.78	−0.05	0.73	0.73
Alan Embree	1.80	−1.51	0.75	−0.11	0.64	0.64
Jose Contreras	1.23	1.28	0.51	0.10	0.61	0.61
Joe Beimel	1.10	1.43	0.46	0.11	0.57	0.57
Randy Flores	0.84	2.25	0.35	0.18	0.53	0.53
Matt Herges	0.65	0.11	0.27	0.01	0.28	0.28
Jhoulys Chacin	0.78	−1.30	0.32	−0.10	0.23	0.23
Ryan Speier	0.41	0.39	0.17	0.03	0.20	0.20
Adam Eaton	0.66	−1.61	0.28	−0.12	0.16	0.16
Esmil Rogers	0.26	0.62	0.11	0.05	0.16	0.16

Player	BFP %	Runs Above Average	Average Value ($)	Value Above Average ($)	MRP (raw) ($)	MRP (adjusted) ($)
Detroit Tigers						
Justin Verlander	15.74	53.89	6.54	8.06	14.60	16.43
Edwin Jackson	14.26	6.58	5.93	0.55	6.48	6.97
Rick Porcello	11.54	−4.46	4.80	−0.32	4.48	4.48
Bobby Seay	3.33	6.43	1.39	0.54	1.92	3.85
Armando Galarraga	10.29	−16.84	4.28	−0.97	3.31	3.31
Zach Miner	6.55	−4.62	2.73	−0.33	2.40	2.40
Brandon Lyon	5.03	3.09	2.09	0.25	2.34	2.34
Fernando Rodney	5.29	−2.06	2.20	−0.15	2.05	2.05
Ryan Perry	4.37	−2.13	1.82	−0.16	1.66	1.66
Nate Robertson	3.75	−0.24	1.56	−0.02	1.54	1.54
Lucas French	2.13	2.73	0.89	0.22	1.10	1.10
Fu−Te Ni	1.94	0.96	0.81	0.07	0.88	0.88
Joel Zumaya	2.39	−4.45	0.99	−0.32	0.68	0.68
Eddie Bonine	2.32	−5.31	0.97	−0.37	0.59	0.59
Jarrod Washburn	3.09	−12.53	1.29	−0.78	0.51	0.53
Dontrelle Willis	2.56	−8.74	1.07	−0.58	0.49	0.49
Alfredo Figaro	1.33	−1.79	0.55	−0.13	0.42	0.42
Freddy Dolsi	0.75	1.12	0.31	0.09	0.40	0.40
Casey Fien	0.85	−1.38	0.35	−0.10	0.25	0.25
Juan Rincon	0.79	−1.34	0.33	−0.10	0.23	0.23
Clay Rapada	0.26	−1.34	0.11	−0.10	0.01	0.01
Jeremy Bonderman	0.85	−6.72	0.35	−0.46	−0.11	−0.11
Chris Lambert	0.58	−5.18	0.24	−0.36	−0.12	−0.12
Florida Marlins						
Josh Johnson	13.57	38.24	5.64	4.82	10.46	11.01
Ricky Nolasco	12.46	28.44	5.18	3.19	8.37	8.37
Kiko Calero	3.79	11.95	1.58	1.08	2.66	6.65
Brian Sanches	3.94	3.43	1.64	0.27	1.91	3.82
Dan Meyer	3.84	3.82	1.60	0.31	1.91	3.81
Chris Volstad	10.83	−17.32	4.50	−0.99	3.51	3.51
Sean West	7.41	−0.07	3.08	−0.01	3.08	3.08
Burke Badenhop	4.81	8.89	2.00	0.77	2.77	2.77
Andrew Miller	5.81	−0.97	2.42	−0.07	2.34	2.34
Anibal Sanchez	6.08	−3.61	2.53	−0.26	2.27	2.27
Brendan Donnelly	1.65	5.20	0.69	0.43	1.11	2.23
Renyel Pinto	4.37	−2.09	1.82	−0.15	1.66	1.66
Leo Nunez	4.65	−5.66	1.93	−0.39	1.54	1.54
Matt Lindstrom	3.48	−0.04	1.45	0.00	1.44	1.44
Rick VandenHurk	4.06	−3.82	1.69	−0.27	1.42	1.42
Cristhian Martinez	1.78	2.73	0.74	0.22	0.96	0.96
Tim Wood	1.54	0.36	0.64	0.03	0.67	0.67
Hayden Penn	1.91	−2.74	0.79	−0.20	0.59	0.59
Graham Taylor	1.00	−2.00	0.42	−0.15	0.27	0.27
Christopher Leroux	0.56	0.14	0.23	0.01	0.24	0.24
Logan Kensing	0.64	−0.52	0.26	−0.04	0.23	0.23
Luis Ayala	0.67	−0.96	0.28	−0.07	0.21	0.21
Cody Ross	0.06	0.21	0.03	0.02	0.04	0.04
Dave Davidson	0.17	−0.84	0.07	−0.06	0.01	0.01
Carlos Martinez	0.21	−1.55	0.09	−0.12	−0.03	−0.03
Ross Gload	0.06	−0.88	0.03	−0.07	−0.04	−0.04
John Koronka	0.65	−7.25	0.27	−0.49	−0.22	−0.22
Houston Astros						
Wandy Rodriguez	13.61	23.63	5.66	2.50	8.16	8.46
Roy Oswalt	12.14	19.63	5.05	1.97	7.02	7.07
Jeff Fulchino	5.39	9.01	2.24	0.78	3.02	6.05
Chris Sampson	3.98	6.33	1.65	0.53	2.18	4.37
Brian Moehler	11.13	−4.17	4.63	−0.30	4.33	4.33
Alberto Arias	3.35	8.67	1.39	0.75	2.14	4.29
LaTroy Hawkins	4.15	4.40	1.73	0.36	2.08	4.17
Jose Valverde	3.51	5.77	1.46	0.48	1.94	3.88
Mike Hampton	7.92	−2.69	3.29	−0.20	3.10	3.10
Felipe Paulino	7.18	−6.88	2.99	−0.47	2.52	2.52
Russ Ortiz	6.20	−3.26	2.58	−0.24	2.34	2.34
Samuel Gervacio	1.33	4.65	0.55	0.38	0.93	1.87
Bud Norris	3.99	−2.14	1.66	−0.16	1.50	1.50
Tim Byrdak	4.18	−8.27	1.74	−0.55	1.19	1.19

Player	BFP %	Runs Above Average	Average Value ($)	Value Above Average ($)	MRP (raw) ($)	MRP (adjusted) ($)
Wesley Wright	3.27	−6.27	1.36	−0.43	0.93	0.93
Yorman Bazardo	2.47	−3.22	1.03	−0.23	0.79	0.79
Wilton Lopez	1.56	−3.82	0.65	−0.27	0.37	0.37
Geoff Geary	1.56	−4.15	0.65	−0.30	0.35	0.35
Billy Sadler	0.11	0.32	0.05	0.02	0.07	0.07
Doug Brocail	1.35	−7.27	0.56	−0.49	0.07	0.07
Brandon Backe	1.04	−5.78	0.43	−0.40	0.03	0.03
Chad Paronto	0.58	−4.64	0.24	−0.33	−0.09	−0.09
Kansas City Royals						
Zack Greinke	14.60	62.41	6.07	10.18	16.26	18.48
Joakim Soria	3.54	11.87	1.47	1.07	2.55	6.37
Brian Bannister	10.66	6.14	4.43	0.51	4.95	4.95
Luke Hochevar	10.07	−4.92	4.19	−0.35	3.84	3.84
Gil Meche	9.27	−6.89	3.86	−0.47	3.39	3.39
Kyle Farnsworth	2.68	6.58	1.12	0.55	1.67	3.33
Kyle Davies	8.59	−17.57	3.57	−1.00	2.57	2.57
Robinson Tejeda	5.00	3.87	2.08	0.31	2.39	2.39
Jamey Wright	5.59	−4.70	2.32	−0.33	1.99	1.99
Sidney Ponson	4.36	−1.92	1.81	−0.14	1.67	1.67
Bruce Chen	4.45	−8.35	1.85	−0.56	1.30	1.30
Roman Colon	3.51	−5.40	1.46	−0.38	1.08	1.08
Juan Cruz	3.50	−5.32	1.45	−0.37	1.08	1.08
Ron Mahay	3.19	−6.81	1.33	−0.47	0.86	0.86
John Bale	2.17	−1.97	0.90	−0.15	0.76	0.76
Lenny DiNardo	1.87	−3.74	0.78	−0.27	0.51	0.51
Horacio Ramirez	1.66	−2.55	0.69	−0.19	0.50	0.50
Dusty Hughes	1.01	−0.74	0.42	−0.06	0.36	0.36
Yasuhiko Yabuta	1.23	−2.73	0.51	−0.20	0.31	0.31
Carlos Rosa	0.69	−0.14	0.29	−0.01	0.27	0.27
Victor Marte	0.93	−5.31	0.39	−0.37	0.01	0.01
Anthony Lerew	0.99	−6.25	0.41	−0.43	−0.02	−0.02
Doug Waechter	0.45	−2.85	0.19	−0.21	−0.02	−0.02
Los Angeles Angels of Anaheim						
John Lackey	11.96	20.67	4.98	2.10	7.08	7.65
Jered Weaver	14.11	11.29	5.87	1.01	6.88	7.30
Kevin Jepsen	3.79	10.93	1.58	0.98	2.55	6.38
Joe Saunders	12.88	−15.31	5.35	−0.91	4.45	4.45
Ervin Santana	9.82	−6.12	4.08	−0.42	3.66	3.66
Darren Oliver	4.69	11.59	1.95	1.04	2.99	2.99
Matt Palmer	8.08	−6.04	3.36	−0.42	2.94	2.94
Jason Bulger	4.19	3.03	1.74	0.24	1.98	1.98
Shane Loux	4.33	1.95	1.80	0.15	1.96	1.96
Brian Fuentes	3.87	1.30	1.61	0.10	1.71	1.71
Scott Kazmir	2.29	6.98	0.95	0.59	1.54	1.54
Jose Arredondo	3.23	0.02	1.34	0.00	1.35	1.35
Justin Speier	2.91	−0.35	1.21	−0.03	1.18	1.18
Sean O'Sullivan	3.63	−9.40	1.51	−0.62	0.89	0.89
Rafael Rodriguez	2.32	−1.44	0.96	−0.11	0.86	0.86
Trevor Bell	1.76	−1.68	0.73	−0.12	0.61	0.61
Scot Shields	1.33	−2.48	0.55	−0.18	0.37	0.37
Rich Thompson	1.47	−3.61	0.61	−0.26	0.35	0.35
Dustin Moseley	1.04	−1.18	0.43	−0.09	0.34	0.34
Nick Adenhart	0.43	1.04	0.18	0.08	0.26	0.26
Kelvim Escobar	0.37	0.29	0.15	0.02	0.17	0.17
Robert Mosebach	0.24	−0.35	0.10	−0.03	0.07	0.07
Anthony Ortega	0.99	−4.90	0.41	−0.35	0.07	0.07
Daniel Davidson	0.18	−1.07	0.07	−0.08	−0.01	−0.01
Fernando Rodriguez	0.10	−2.19	0.04	−0.16	−0.12	−0.12
Los Angeles Dodgers						
Jonathan Broxton	4.85	21.48	2.02	2.21	4.23	10.56
Randy Wolf	13.94	7.60	5.80	0.65	6.45	6.76
Clayton Kershaw	11.34	17.90	4.72	1.76	6.47	6.47
Chad Billingsley	13.31	6.97	5.54	0.59	6.12	6.12
Ramon Troncoso	5.77	6.57	2.40	0.55	2.95	5.90
Ronald Belisario	4.84	7.50	2.01	0.64	2.65	5.30

Player	BFP %	Runs Above Average	Average Value ($)	Value Above Average ($)	MRP (raw) ($)	MRP (adjusted) ($)
Hiroki Kuroda	7.85	11.29	3.26	1.01	4.28	4.28
Jeff Weaver	5.74	2.37	2.39	0.19	2.57	2.57
Hong—Chih Kuo	2.01	3.44	0.83	0.28	1.11	2.22
Guillermo Mota	4.42	−1.32	1.84	−0.10	1.74	1.74
James McDonald	4.53	−2.77	1.88	−0.20	1.68	1.68
Eric Stults	3.61	−1.14	1.50	−0.09	1.41	1.41
Vicente Padilla	2.57	3.76	1.07	0.30	1.37	1.37
Jon Garland	2.49	1.97	1.04	0.15	1.19	1.23
Eric Milton	1.75	3.51	0.73	0.28	1.01	1.01
George Sherrill	1.80	3.03	0.75	0.24	0.99	0.99
Cory Wade	1.96	−0.62	0.81	−0.05	0.77	0.77
Scott Elbert	1.34	−1.60	0.56	−0.12	0.44	0.44
Brent Leach	1.42	−3.10	0.59	−0.22	0.37	0.37
Jason Schmidt	1.34	−2.79	0.56	−0.20	0.35	0.35
Claudio Vargas	0.70	0.64	0.29	0.05	0.34	0.34
Charlie Haeger	1.28	−3.46	0.53	−0.25	0.28	0.28
Mark Loretta	0.03	0.09	0.01	0.01	0.02	0.02
Will Ohman	0.87	−7.47	0.36	−0.51	−0.14	−0.14
Travis Schlichting	0.24	−3.51	0.10	−0.25	−0.15	−0.15
Milwaukee Brewers						
Trevor Hoffman	3.31	11.37	1.37	1.02	2.40	5.99
Todd Coffey	5.29	7.61	2.20	0.65	2.85	5.70
Yovani Gallardo	12.48	2.52	5.19	0.20	5.39	5.56
Braden Looper	13.63	−35.47	5.67	−1.40	4.27	4.27
Jeff Suppan	11.78	−28.05	4.90	−1.30	3.60	3.60
Mark DiFelice	3.45	4.36	1.43	0.35	1.79	3.58
Manny Parra	10.56	−13.57	4.39	−0.83	3.56	3.56
David Bush	8.00	−5.79	3.33	−0.40	2.92	2.92
Carlos Villanueva	6.64	−0.05	2.76	0.00	2.76	2.76
Chris Narveson	3.23	0.88	1.34	0.07	1.41	1.41
Mitch Stetter	3.20	−0.84	1.33	−0.06	1.27	1.27
Mike Burns	3.57	−5.65	1.49	−0.39	1.09	1.09
Claudio Vargas	1.83	1.16	0.76	0.09	0.85	0.85
Seth McClung	4.38	−17.16	1.82	−0.98	0.84	0.84
Chris Smith	3.15	−10.85	1.31	−0.69	0.62	0.62
Dave Weathers	1.68	−3.64	0.70	−0.26	0.44	0.44
Jorge Julio	1.39	−4.31	0.58	−0.31	0.27	0.27
John Axford	0.54	0.60	0.22	0.05	0.27	0.27
Jesus Colome	0.44	0.41	0.18	0.03	0.22	0.22
Josh Butler	0.43	−1.32	0.18	−0.10	0.08	0.08
David Riske	0.09	0.29	0.04	0.02	0.06	0.06
R.J. Swindle	0.58	−3.54	0.24	−0.25	−0.01	−0.01
Tim Dillard	0.36	−3.19	0.15	−0.23	−0.08	−0.08
Minnesota Twins						
Joe Nathan	4.32	12.61	1.80	1.15	2.95	7.37
Nick Blackburn	14.06	4.05	5.85	0.33	6.17	6.40
Scott Baker	13.20	9.16	5.49	0.80	6.29	6.35
Francisco Liriano	9.71	−9.93	4.04	−0.64	3.39	3.39
Carl Pavano	5.10	10.53	2.12	0.94	3.06	3.08
Kevin Slowey	6.28	5.37	2.61	0.44	3.05	3.05
Glen Perkins	6.74	−2.18	2.80	−0.16	2.64	2.64
Brian Duensing	5.72	2.45	2.38	0.19	2.57	2.57
Matt Guerrier	4.85	1.47	2.01	0.11	2.13	2.13
Jose Mijares	4.03	2.20	1.68	0.17	1.85	1.85
Bobby Keppel	3.86	1.84	1.60	0.14	1.75	1.75
Jesse Crain	3.67	2.46	1.52	0.19	1.72	1.72
R.A. Dickey	4.67	−4.87	1.94	−0.34	1.60	1.60
Anthony Swarzak	4.27	−9.40	1.78	−0.62	1.16	1.16
Luis Ayala	2.20	1.08	0.91	0.08	1.00	1.00
Jeff Manship	2.33	−2.46	0.97	−0.18	0.79	0.79
Jon Rauch	1.02	1.79	0.42	0.14	0.56	0.56
Ron Mahay	0.62	0.66	0.26	0.05	0.31	0.31
Philip Humber	0.80	−1.91	0.33	−0.14	0.19	0.19
Sean Henn	0.80	−3.05	0.33	−0.22	0.11	0.11
Kevin Mulvey	0.16	0.50	0.07	0.04	0.10	0.10
Craig Breslow	1.02	−5.22	0.42	−0.37	0.06	0.06

Player	BFP %	Runs Above Average	Average Value ($)	Value Above Average ($)	MRP (raw) ($)	MRP (adjusted) ($)
Armando Gabino	0.40	−2.75	0.17	−0.20	−0.03	−0.03
Juan Morillo	0.19	−2.53	0.08	−0.19	−0.11	−0.11
New York Mets						
Johan Santana	11.16	13.35	4.64	1.23	5.87	6.46
Mike Pelfrey	13.11	1.37	5.45	0.11	5.56	5.56
Pedro Feliciano	3.85	5.52	1.60	0.46	2.06	4.11
Livan Hernandez	9.44	−6.69	3.92	−0.46	3.47	3.47
Bobby Parnell	6.57	0.51	2.73	0.04	2.77	2.77
Tim Redding	8.35	−12.64	3.47	−0.78	2.69	2.69
Nelson Figueroa	5.09	4.32	2.12	0.35	2.47	2.47
Sean Green	5.03	1.16	2.09	0.09	2.18	2.18
John Maine	5.55	−3.16	2.31	−0.23	2.08	2.08
Francisco Rodriguez	4.69	0.58	1.95	0.04	2.00	2.00
Brian Stokes	5.03	−4.03	2.09	−0.29	1.80	1.80
Patrick Misch	3.99	−7.46	1.66	−0.50	1.16	1.16
Oliver Perez	5.16	−20.61	2.14	−1.11	1.04	1.04
Jonathon Niese	1.75	3.44	0.73	0.28	1.00	1.00
J.J. Putz	2.15	−0.68	0.89	−0.05	0.84	0.84
Fernando Nieve	2.56	−3.44	1.07	−0.25	0.82	0.82
Ken Takahashi	1.85	0.54	0.77	0.04	0.81	0.81
Lance Broadway	1.07	2.32	0.44	0.18	0.63	0.63
Elmer Dessens	2.07	−3.98	0.86	−0.28	0.58	0.58
Darren O'Day	0.27	0.81	0.11	0.06	0.17	0.17
Billy Wagner	0.11	0.84	0.05	0.06	0.11	0.11
Tobi Stoner	0.57	−1.98	0.24	−0.15	0.09	0.09
Casey Fossum	0.30	−0.52	0.13	−0.04	0.09	0.09
Jon Switzer	0.27	−1.19	0.11	−0.09	0.02	0.02
New York Yankees						
C.C. Sabathia	15.02	28.53	6.24	3.20	9.45	10.52
Mariano Rivera	4.11	12.74	1.71	1.17	2.88	7.19
A.J. Burnett	14.34	−3.59	5.96	−0.26	5.71	5.95
Andy Pettitte	13.35	1.57	5.55	0.12	5.67	5.75
Joba Chamberlain	11.35	−10.28	4.72	−0.66	4.06	4.06
David Robertson	3.06	6.00	1.27	0.50	1.77	3.54
Philip Hughes	5.62	12.79	2.34	1.17	3.51	3.51
Alfredo Aceves	5.39	8.26	2.24	0.71	2.95	2.95
Phil Coke	3.81	−4.24	1.58	−0.30	1.28	1.28
Sergio Mitre	3.86	−4.64	1.60	−0.33	1.28	1.28
Chien-Ming Wang	3.30	−5.38	1.37	−0.38	0.99	0.99
Chad Gaudin	3.01	−5.48	1.25	−0.38	0.87	0.87
Brian Bruney	2.80	−5.56	1.16	−0.39	0.78	0.78
Jonathan Albaladejo	2.53	−6.39	1.05	−0.44	0.61	0.61
Mark Melancon	1.18	0.51	0.49	0.04	0.53	0.53
Jose Veras	1.89	−6.23	0.79	−0.43	0.36	0.36
Josh Towers	0.40	1.17	0.17	0.09	0.26	0.26
Damaso Marte	0.99	−2.19	0.41	−0.16	0.25	0.25
Brett Tomko	1.36	−5.68	0.57	−0.40	0.17	0.17
Edwar Ramirez	1.76	−9.60	0.73	−0.63	0.11	0.11
Nick Swisher	0.08	−0.07	0.03	−0.01	0.03	0.03
Ian Kennedy	0.10	−0.59	0.04	−0.04	0.00	0.00
Michael Dunn	0.32	−2.31	0.13	−0.17	−0.04	−0.04
Anthony Claggett	0.37	−3.88	0.15	−0.28	−0.12	−0.12
Oakland Athletics						
Andrew Bailey	5.17	18.10	2.15	1.78	3.93	9.83
Michael Wuertz	4.87	18.91	2.02	1.88	3.91	9.76
Brad Ziegler	5.01	10.68	2.08	0.95	3.03	7.59
Brett Anderson	11.77	16.77	4.90	1.62	6.52	6.52
Dallas Braden	9.43	11.73	3.92	1.06	4.98	5.15
Trevor Cahill	12.38	−24.47	5.15	−1.22	3.93	3.93
Craig Breslow	3.48	3.75	1.45	0.30	1.75	3.50
Russ Springer	3.06	5.51	1.27	0.46	1.73	3.46
Gio Gonzalez	7.29	−4.05	3.03	−0.29	2.74	2.74
Vin Mazzaro	6.78	−5.83	2.82	−0.41	2.41	2.41
Edgar Gonzalez	4.79	2.59	1.99	0.20	2.20	2.20
Jeff Gray	1.86	3.43	0.77	0.28	1.05	2.10
Jerry Blevins	1.44	3.77	0.60	0.30	0.90	1.81
Josh Outman	4.42	−1.72	1.84	−0.13	1.71	1.71

Player	BFP %	Runs Above Average	Average Value ($)	Value Above Average ($)	MRP (raw) ($)	MRP (adjusted) ($)
Santiago Casilla	3.73	−3.50	1.55	−0.25	1.30	1.30
Dana Eveland	3.54	−4.68	1.47	−0.33	1.14	1.14
Brad Kilby	1.04	4.57	0.43	0.37	0.81	0.81
Brett Tomko	2.27	−2.45	0.95	−0.18	0.77	0.77
Kevin Cameron	1.19	2.56	0.49	0.20	0.70	0.70
Sean Gallagher	1.14	0.53	0.47	0.04	0.51	0.51
Clayton Mortensen	2.13	−5.78	0.89	−0.40	0.48	0.48
Jonathan Meloan	0.46	3.23	0.19	0.26	0.45	0.45
Jay Marshall	0.56	0.30	0.23	0.02	0.26	0.26
Dan Giese	1.51	−6.04	0.63	−0.42	0.21	0.21
Henry Rodriguez	0.32	0.93	0.13	0.07	0.20	0.20
Chad Reineke	0.35	−2.06	0.15	−0.15	−0.01	−0.01
Philadelphia Phillies						
Ryan Madson	5.11	12.99	2.12	1.19	3.32	8.29
Cole Hamels	13.00	22.10	5.40	2.29	7.69	7.76
Joe Blanton	13.36	3.32	5.56	0.27	5.82	6.10
J.A. Happ	10.94	2.35	4.55	0.19	4.73	4.73
Cliff Lee	5.24	18.95	2.18	1.89	4.06	4.55
Jamie Moyer	11.16	−7.79	4.64	−0.52	4.12	4.12
Chan Ho Park	5.78	11.18	2.40	1.00	3.41	3.41
Chad Durbin	5.01	−6.76	2.08	−0.46	1.62	1.62
Pedro Martinez	3.05	3.44	1.27	0.28	1.54	1.54
Brad Lidge	4.52	−6.48	1.88	−0.45	1.43	1.43
Tyler Walker	2.40	3.17	1.00	0.25	1.25	1.25
Clay Condrey	2.78	1.17	1.16	0.09	1.25	1.25
Brett Myers	4.85	−13.77	2.02	−0.84	1.18	1.18
Kyle Kendrick	1.79	3.09	0.74	0.25	0.99	0.99
Rodrigo Lopez	2.19	1.01	0.91	0.08	0.99	0.99
Scott Eyre	2.04	−1.43	0.85	−0.11	0.74	0.74
Jack Taschner	2.28	−3.61	0.95	−0.26	0.69	0.69
Sergio Escalona	0.96	2.94	0.40	0.23	0.63	0.63
Antonio Bastardo	1.69	−1.17	0.70	−0.09	0.62	0.62
J.C. Romero	1.17	−3.56	0.48	−0.26	0.23	0.23
Andrew Carpenter	0.51	−0.90	0.21	−0.07	0.14	0.14
Steven Register	0.18	0.28	0.07	0.02	0.09	0.09
Pittsburgh Pirates						
Paul Maholm	13.61	15.65	5.66	1.49	7.15	7.47
Zach Duke	14.50	5.62	6.03	0.47	6.50	7.14
Ross Ohlendorf	11.80	−7.79	4.91	−0.52	4.38	4.45
Charlie Morton	6.77	2.64	2.82	0.21	3.02	3.02
Joel Hanrahan	2.18	5.26	0.91	0.43	1.34	2.68
Jeff Karstens	7.67	−8.82	3.19	−0.58	2.60	2.60
Ian Snell	5.86	−5.20	2.44	−0.36	2.07	2.07
Jesse Chavez	4.65	−4.60	1.94	−0.33	1.61	1.61
Matt Capps	4.09	−2.04	1.70	−0.15	1.55	1.55
Evan Meek	3.17	1.05	1.32	0.08	1.40	1.40
Kevin Hart	4.13	−5.47	1.72	−0.38	1.34	1.34
John Grabow	3.40	−1.41	1.41	−0.11	1.31	1.31
Virgil Vasquez	3.35	−2.52	1.39	−0.18	1.21	1.21
Steven Jackson	3.03	−1.03	1.26	−0.08	1.18	1.18
Sean Burnett	2.16	−0.90	0.90	−0.07	0.83	0.83
Daniel McCutchen	2.52	−3.77	1.05	−0.27	0.78	0.79
Denny Bautista	0.99	1.37	0.41	0.11	0.52	0.52
Chris Bootcheck	1.14	0.14	0.47	0.01	0.48	0.48
Tom Gorzelanny	0.59	1.41	0.24	0.11	0.35	0.35
Tyler Yates	0.91	−2.24	0.38	−0.16	0.21	0.21
Jose Ascanio	0.21	1.20	0.09	0.09	0.18	0.18
Donald Veal	1.42	−6.26	0.59	−0.43	0.16	0.16
Craig Hansen	0.49	−1.17	0.20	−0.09	0.12	0.12
Eric Hacker	0.23	−0.17	0.09	−0.01	0.08	0.08
Anthony Claggett	0.08	−1.48	0.03	−0.11	−0.08	−0.08
Phil Dumatrait	1.04	−8.15	0.43	−0.54	−0.11	−0.11
San Diego Padres						
Luke Gregerson	5.07	15.33	2.11	1.45	3.56	8.90
Heath Bell	4.43	13.95	1.84	1.30	3.14	7.85
Kevin Correia	13.23	3.68	5.50	0.30	5.80	5.80

Player	BFP %	Runs Above Average	Average Value ($)	Value Above Average ($)	MRP (raw) ($)	MRP (adjusted) ($)
Mike Adams	2.17	11.92	0.90	1.08	1.98	4.95
Joe Thatcher	3.00	8.84	1.25	0.77	2.01	4.03
Chad Gaudin	7.59	2.13	3.16	0.17	3.32	3.32
Jake Peavy	5.34	10.03	2.22	0.88	3.11	3.28
Edward Mujica	6.26	0.12	2.61	0.01	2.61	2.61
Tim Stauffer	5.04	−7.85	2.09	−0.53	1.57	1.57
Josh Geer	6.98	−31.63	2.90	−1.36	1.54	1.54
Cla Meredith	2.63	2.66	1.09	0.21	1.30	1.30
Clayton Richard	4.40	−9.08	1.83	−0.60	1.23	1.23
Chris Young	5.36	−19.25	2.23	−1.06	1.17	1.17
Greg Burke	3.25	−3.87	1.35	−0.28	1.07	1.07
Mat Latos	3.38	−7.47	1.41	−0.51	0.90	0.90
Luis Perdomo	4.27	−14.95	1.78	−0.89	0.89	0.89
Wade LeBlanc	3.09	−6.45	1.29	−0.44	0.84	0.84
Cesar Ramos	0.99	3.00	0.41	0.24	0.65	0.65
Ryan Webb	1.87	−2.16	0.78	−0.16	0.62	0.62
Michael Ekstrom	1.32	−1.69	0.55	−0.13	0.42	0.42
Shawn Hill	0.89	0.60	0.37	0.05	0.42	0.42
Adam Russell	0.97	−0.26	0.40	−0.02	0.38	0.38
Edwin Moreno	1.72	−6.22	0.72	−0.43	0.29	0.29
Walter Silva	1.93	−8.75	0.80	−0.58	0.22	0.22
Josh Banks	1.59	−7.10	0.66	−0.48	0.18	0.18
Sean Gallagher	0.40	−0.93	0.17	−0.07	0.10	0.10
Ernesto Frieri	0.11	0.25	0.05	0.02	0.07	0.07
Eulogio De La Cruz	0.27	−2.47	0.11	−0.18	−0.07	−0.07
Aaron Poreda	0.19	−2.64	0.08	−0.19	−0.11	−0.11
Josh Wilson	0.11	−2.23	0.05	−0.16	−0.12	−0.12
Duaner Sanchez	0.91	−7.76	0.38	−0.52	−0.14	−0.14
Arturo Lopez	0.27	−4.97	0.11	−0.35	−0.24	−0.24
Cesar Carrillo	0.96	−11.45	0.40	−0.72	−0.33	−0.33
San Francisco Giants						
Tim Lincecum	14.83	63.21	6.17	10.39	16.56	19.01
Brian Wilson	4.96	18.31	2.06	1.81	3.87	9.68
Matt Cain	14.52	16.68	6.04	1.61	7.65	8.34
Barry Zito	13.40	5.86	5.57	0.49	6.06	6.06
Jonathan Sanchez	11.63	5.20	4.84	0.43	5.27	5.27
Sergio Romo	2.34	10.74	0.97	0.96	1.93	4.83
Brandon Medders	4.92	4.09	2.04	0.33	2.38	4.75
Bobby Howry	4.39	5.81	1.83	0.48	2.31	4.62
Jeremy Affeldt	4.06	5.93	1.69	0.49	2.18	4.37
Randy Johnson	6.75	−3.45	2.81	−0.25	2.56	2.56
Merkin Valdez	3.69	−1.34	1.53	−0.10	1.43	1.43
Justin Miller	3.87	−3.99	1.61	−0.29	1.32	1.32
Brad Penny	2.64	0.88	1.10	0.07	1.17	1.17
Joe Martinez	2.43	−0.08	1.01	−0.01	1.00	1.00
Ryan Sadowski	2.10	−1.13	0.87	−0.08	0.79	0.79
Waldis Joaquin	0.84	0.42	0.35	0.03	0.38	0.38
Dan Runzler	0.62	0.54	0.26	0.04	0.30	0.30
Madison Bumgarner	0.66	−0.16	0.27	−0.01	0.26	0.26
Osiris Matos	0.51	−0.85	0.21	−0.06	0.15	0.15
Patrick Misch	0.31	−0.58	0.13	−0.04	0.09	0.09
Alex Hinshaw	0.54	−4.78	0.22	−0.34	−0.11	−0.11
Seattle Mariners						
Felix Hernandez	15.86	40.16	6.60	5.17	11.77	13.48
David Aardsma	4.81	9.74	2.00	0.86	2.85	7.13
Mark Lowe	5.50	6.55	2.29	0.55	2.84	5.68
Jarrod Washburn	8.62	9.52	3.59	0.83	4.42	4.62
Sean White	4.24	3.77	1.76	0.30	2.07	4.13
Ryan Rowland-Smith	6.51	2.70	2.71	0.21	2.92	3.11
Erik Bedard	5.65	8.04	2.35	0.69	3.04	3.04
Jason Vargas	6.25	−8.09	2.60	−0.54	2.06	2.06
Chris Jakubauskas	6.33	−9.72	2.63	−0.63	2.00	2.00
Miguel Batista	5.29	−4.50	2.20	−0.32	1.88	1.88
Brandon Morrow	5.08	−10.33	2.11	−0.67	1.45	1.45
Doug Fister	4.16	−5.43	1.73	−0.38	1.35	1.35
Ian Snell	4.69	−10.41	1.95	−0.67	1.28	1.28
Shawn Kelley	3.10	−0.34	1.29	−0.03	1.26	1.26

Player	BFP %	Runs Above Average	Average Value ($)	Value Above Average ($)	MRP (raw) ($)	MRP (adjusted) ($)
Garrett Olson	5.63	−22.94	2.34	−1.18	1.16	1.16
Carlos Silva	2.31	−5.34	0.96	−0.37	0.59	0.59
Lucas French	2.91	−10.45	1.21	−0.67	0.54	0.54
Randy Messenger	0.70	−1.75	0.29	−0.13	0.16	0.16
Roy Corcoran	1.48	−7.19	0.61	−0.49	0.13	0.13
Dennis Stark	0.88	−4.71	0.36	−0.33	0.03	0.03
St. Louis Cardinals						
Adam Wainwright	15.94	39.16	6.63	4.99	11.61	13.06
Chris Carpenter	12.32	43.22	5.12	5.76	10.88	12.28
Joel Pineiro	14.21	37.91	5.91	4.76	10.67	11.76
Ryan Franklin	4.11	7.33	1.71	0.62	2.33	4.66
Trever Miller	2.84	6.20	1.18	0.52	1.70	3.40
Kyle Lohse	8.41	−1.81	3.50	−0.13	3.36	3.36
Todd Wellemeyer	9.22	−16.48	3.83	−0.96	2.88	2.88
Brad Thompson	5.67	−0.46	2.36	−0.03	2.32	2.32
Kyle McClellan	4.73	1.86	1.97	0.15	2.11	2.11
Mitchell Boggs	4.40	1.81	1.83	0.14	1.97	1.97
John Smoltz	2.60	8.47	1.08	0.73	1.81	1.81
Dennys Reyes	2.96	2.49	1.23	0.20	1.43	1.43
Jason Motte	4.01	−3.73	1.67	−0.27	1.40	1.40
Blake Hawksworth	2.63	1.42	1.09	0.11	1.20	1.20
Chris Perez	1.74	−0.39	0.72	−0.03	0.69	0.69
Blaine Boyer	1.15	1.38	0.48	0.11	0.59	0.59
Josh Kinney	1.33	−3.57	0.55	−0.26	0.30	0.30
Clayton Mortensen	0.26	−0.97	0.11	−0.07	0.04	0.04
P.J. Walters	1.31	−7.85	0.55	−0.53	0.02	0.02
Jess Todd	0.16	−1.86	0.07	−0.14	−0.07	−0.07
Tampa Bay Rays						
James Shields	15.13	14.96	6.29	1.41	7.70	8.46
Matt Garza	14.01	8.72	5.83	0.75	6.58	6.94
Jeff Niemann	12.51	11.80	5.20	1.07	6.27	6.27
Grant Balfour	4.70	4.79	1.96	0.39	2.35	4.69
J.P. Howell	4.52	5.13	1.88	0.42	2.30	4.60
David Price	9.06	−2.66	3.77	−0.19	3.57	3.57
Scott Kazmir	8.20	−2.73	3.41	−0.20	3.21	3.21
Lance Cormier	5.39	2.88	2.24	0.23	2.47	2.47
Andy Sonnanstine	7.47	−11.02	3.11	−0.70	2.40	2.40
Wade Davis	2.44	6.72	1.01	0.57	1.58	1.59
Dan Wheeler	3.56	−0.22	1.48	−0.02	1.46	1.46
Randy Choate	2.31	1.95	0.96	0.15	1.11	1.11
Brian Shouse	1.99	−1.43	0.83	−0.11	0.72	0.72
Joe Nelson	2.96	−7.83	1.23	−0.53	0.71	0.71
Chad Bradford	0.89	1.68	0.37	0.13	0.50	0.50
Dale Thayer	0.96	−0.40	0.40	−0.03	0.37	0.37
Jason Isringhausen	0.60	0.74	0.25	0.06	0.31	0.31
Russ Springer	1.06	−2.10	0.44	−0.16	0.28	0.28
Jeff Bennett	1.14	−4.75	0.47	−0.34	0.14	0.14
Winston Abreu	0.24	0.46	0.10	0.04	0.14	0.14
Troy Percival	0.85	−3.27	0.35	−0.24	0.12	0.12
Texas Rangers						
C.J. Wilson	5.23	16.76	2.18	1.62	3.80	9.49
Darren O'Day	3.50	11.41	1.46	1.03	2.48	6.20
Scott Feldman	12.82	7.50	5.33	0.64	5.97	5.97
Kevin Millwood	13.77	−3.03	5.73	−0.22	5.51	5.86
Frank Francisco	3.29	7.64	1.37	0.65	2.02	4.04
Derek Holland	9.90	−7.24	4.12	−0.49	3.63	3.63
Tommy Hunter	7.70	3.21	3.20	0.26	3.46	3.46
Vicente Padilla	7.70	−1.28	3.20	−0.10	3.11	3.11
Neftali Feliz	1.90	8.68	0.79	0.75	1.54	3.08
Brandon McCarthy	6.80	−1.18	2.83	−0.09	2.74	2.74
Dustin Nippert	4.86	3.02	2.02	0.24	2.26	2.26
Jason Jennings	4.41	−0.50	1.83	−0.04	1.80	1.80
Matt Harrison	4.59	−2.98	1.91	−0.22	1.69	1.69
Doug Mathis	2.79	3.83	1.16	0.31	1.47	1.47
Jason Grilli	1.83	2.20	0.76	0.17	0.93	0.93
Willie Eyre	1.17	2.73	0.49	0.22	0.70	0.70

Player	BFP %	Runs Above Average	Average Value ($)	Value Above Average ($)	MRP (raw) ($)	MRP (adjusted) ($)
Eddie Guardado	2.69	−6.98	1.12	−0.48	0.64	0.64
Guillermo Moscoso	1.04	1.67	0.43	0.13	0.56	0.56
Pedro Strop	0.49	1.76	0.20	0.14	0.34	0.34
Kris Benson	1.85	−7.23	0.77	−0.49	0.28	0.28
Warner Madrigal	1.09	−4.80	0.45	−0.34	0.11	0.11
Josh Rupe	0.50	−3.75	0.21	−0.27	−0.06	−0.06
Luis Mendoza	0.11	−1.79	0.05	−0.13	−0.09	−0.09
Toronto Blue Jays						
Roy Halladay	15.33	44.73	6.38	6.06	12.44	14.89
Brandon League	4.98	9.84	2.07	0.87	2.94	7.34
Jason Frasor	3.61	10.03	1.50	0.88	2.39	5.97
Ricky Romero	12.28	−0.61	5.10	−0.05	5.06	5.17
Jesse Carlson	4.63	3.84	1.93	0.31	2.24	4.47
Brian Tallet	11.42	−8.29	4.75	−0.55	4.19	4.19
Scott Downs	3.18	6.96	1.32	0.59	1.91	3.82
Scott Richmond	9.71	−18.97	4.04	−1.05	2.99	2.99
Shawn Camp	5.30	3.21	2.20	0.26	2.46	2.46
Brett Cecil	6.72	−11.81	2.79	−0.74	2.05	2.05
Marc Rzepczynski	4.16	−0.36	1.73	−0.03	1.70	1.70
Casey Janssen	3.06	−0.77	1.27	−0.06	1.21	1.21
David Purcey	3.55	−6.08	1.48	−0.42	1.06	1.06
Dirk Hayhurst	1.54	−0.35	0.64	−0.03	0.62	0.62
Robert Ray	1.61	−1.88	0.67	−0.14	0.53	0.54
Jeremy Accardo	1.70	−3.08	0.71	−0.22	0.49	0.49
Josh Roenicke	1.34	−1.10	0.56	−0.08	0.47	0.47
Brian Burres	0.59	0.03	0.25	0.00	0.25	0.25
Bryan Bullington	0.49	−0.56	0.21	−0.04	0.16	0.16
Bill Murphy	0.72	−2.47	0.30	−0.18	0.12	0.12
Brian Wolfe	1.23	−5.88	0.51	−0.41	0.10	0.10
Jesse Litsch	0.67	−3.26	0.28	−0.24	0.04	0.04
B.J. Ryan	1.51	−10.15	0.63	−0.66	−0.03	−0.03
Brad Mills	0.67	−5.84	0.28	−0.41	−0.13	−0.13
Washington Nationals						
John Lannan	13.78	−6.36	5.73	−0.44	5.29	5.51
Jordan Zimmermann	6.16	10.95	2.56	0.98	3.54	3.54
Joel Hanrahan	2.57	4.60	1.07	0.37	1.44	2.88
Craig Stammen	7.06	−1.25	2.93	−0.09	2.84	2.84
Garrett Mock	6.65	0.89	2.76	0.07	2.83	2.83
Ross Detwiler	5.37	5.29	2.23	0.44	2.67	2.67
Shairon Martis	5.94	−11.65	2.47	−0.73	1.73	1.73
Livan Hernandez	3.35	4.00	1.40	0.32	1.72	1.72
J.D. Martin	5.37	−9.47	2.23	−0.62	1.61	1.61
Scott Olsen	4.55	−6.43	1.89	−0.44	1.45	1.45
Tyler Clippard	3.87	−2.76	1.61	−0.20	1.41	1.41
Joe Beimel	2.71	1.70	1.13	0.13	1.26	1.26
Mike MacDougal	3.48	−2.76	1.45	−0.20	1.25	1.25
Julian Tavarez	2.66	0.34	1.11	0.03	1.13	1.13
Jay Bergmann	3.35	−4.19	1.40	−0.30	1.10	1.10
Ron Villone	3.59	−5.75	1.49	−0.40	1.09	1.09
Saul Rivera	2.77	−4.91	1.15	−0.35	0.81	0.81
Kip Wells	1.84	−0.95	0.77	−0.07	0.69	0.69
Daniel Cabrera	3.26	−11.12	1.36	−0.71	0.65	0.65
Jesus Colome	1.18	1.94	0.49	0.15	0.64	0.64
Sean Burnett	1.64	−1.67	0.68	−0.12	0.56	0.56
Logan Kensing	2.08	−8.34	0.86	−0.56	0.31	0.31
Jorge Sosa	1.62	−5.24	0.67	−0.37	0.31	0.31
Marco Estrada	0.52	0.14	0.22	0.01	0.23	0.23
Zack Segovia	0.74	−1.52	0.31	−0.11	0.19	0.19
Wilfredo Ledezma	0.47	−0.27	0.20	−0.02	0.18	0.18
Collin Balester	2.13	−12.19	0.88	−0.76	0.12	0.12
Steven Shell	0.35	−0.35	0.14	−0.03	0.12	0.12
Mike Hinckley	0.69	−4.66	0.29	−0.33	−0.04	−0.04
Victor Garate	0.24	−2.53	0.10	−0.18	−0.09	−0.09

POSITION PLAYERS (2008)

Player	PA%	Runs Above Average	Hitting ($)	Fielding ($)	Value Above Average ($)	MRP ($)
Arizona Diamondbacks						
Chris Young	11.35	5.27	5.94	2.10	0.40	8.44
Stephen Drew	10.77	3.89	5.63	2.11	0.29	8.04
Conor Jackson	9.94	16.15	5.20	1.21	1.42	7.83
Mark Reynolds	9.96	−12.43	5.21	1.70	−0.71	6.21
Chris Snyder	6.56	0.65	3.43	2.05	0.05	5.53
Orlando Hudson	7.39	3.47	3.87	1.33	0.26	5.45
Justin Upton	6.77	6.95	3.54	1.03	0.54	5.11
Augie Ojeda	4.42	−0.64	2.31	0.77	−0.04	3.04
Chad Tracy	4.74	−8.70	2.48	0.45	−0.53	2.40
Miguel Montero	3.36	−4.61	1.76	0.90	−0.30	2.36
Adam Dunn	3.04	3.47	1.59	0.40	0.26	2.24
Chris Burke	3.23	−7.07	1.69	0.44	−0.44	1.69
Eric Byrnes	3.64	−13.86	1.90	0.48	−0.77	1.61
Jeff Salazar	2.47	−6.32	1.29	0.30	−0.40	1.20
Alex Romero	2.31	−7.32	1.21	0.33	−0.46	1.09
Tony Clark	1.25	−2.19	0.65	0.11	−0.15	0.61
David Eckstein	1.19	−5.57	0.62	0.22	−0.36	0.49
Robby Hammock	0.78	−5.84	0.41	0.24	−0.37	0.27
Josh Whitesell	0.15	0.27	0.08	0.01	0.02	0.10
Emilio Bonifacio	0.19	−1.44	0.10	0.02	−0.10	0.03
Jamie D'Antona	0.31	−2.89	0.16	0.01	−0.19	−0.03
Atlanta Braves						
Chipper Jones	8.39	63.52	4.39	1.30	9.61	15.30
Brian McCann	9.00	19.05	4.71	2.53	1.74	8.98
Yunel Escobar	9.22	20.04	4.82	1.80	1.86	8.48
Mark Teixeira	7.08	35.82	3.71	0.73	4.03	8.46
Kelly Johnson	9.64	8.72	5.05	1.75	0.69	7.49
Jeff Francoeur	10.24	−33.03	5.36	1.59	−1.27	5.68
Gregor Blanco	8.15	−7.18	4.26	1.36	−0.45	5.18
Omar Infante	5.47	6.93	2.86	0.91	0.54	4.31
Mark Kotsay	5.42	−7.66	2.83	1.05	−0.47	3.41
Martin Prado	3.99	9.18	2.09	0.57	0.73	3.39
Josh Anderson	2.29	8.28	1.20	0.39	0.65	2.25
Greg Norton	3.17	0.44	1.66	0.21	0.03	1.90
Casey Kotchman	2.75	−2.32	1.44	0.29	−0.16	1.57
Brandon Jones	2.01	−4.99	1.05	0.29	−0.32	1.02
Ruben Gotay	1.84	−1.63	0.96	0.12	−0.11	0.97
Matt Diaz	2.20	−11.34	1.15	0.33	−0.66	0.82
Brent Lillibridge	1.34	−5.31	0.70	0.30	−0.34	0.66
Corky Miller	1.05	−10.55	0.55	0.36	−0.62	0.29
Clint Sammons	0.93	−8.51	0.48	0.29	−0.52	0.26
Jason Perry	0.27	−3.40	0.14	0.05	−0.23	−0.04
Baltimore Orioles						
Nick Markakis	11.23	42.14	5.87	1.66	5.09	12.62
Brian Roberts	11.34	22.10	5.93	1.95	2.10	9.99
Aubrey Huff	10.65	31.06	5.57	0.53	3.30	9.40
Luke Scott	8.63	13.36	4.52	0.96	1.13	6.61
Melvin Mora	9.18	−1.04	4.80	1.41	−0.07	6.15
Ramon Hernandez	8.17	−22.05	4.27	2.34	−1.06	5.56
Adam Jones	8.28	−8.08	4.33	1.68	−0.50	5.52
Kevin Millar	9.82	−10.88	5.14	0.93	−0.64	5.43
Jay Payton	5.85	−9.03	3.06	0.96	−0.55	3.48
Oscar Salazar	1.51	4.73	0.79	0.14	0.35	1.28
Guillermo Quiroz	2.38	−15.17	1.25	0.80	−0.83	1.22
Luis Montanez	1.88	−1.17	0.99	0.26	−0.08	1.16
Juan Castro	2.67	−17.70	1.40	0.65	−0.92	1.13
Alex Cintron	2.32	−15.57	1.21	0.48	−0.84	0.85
Luis Hernandez	1.47	−7.73	0.77	0.40	−0.48	0.69
Freddie Bynum	1.95	−15.22	1.02	0.47	−0.83	0.66
Brandon Fahey	1.82	−15.16	0.95	0.48	−0.83	0.61
Scott Moore	0.14	−0.31	0.08	0.02	−0.02	0.08
Eider Torres	0.14	−1.10	0.08	0.04	−0.08	0.04
Omir Santos	0.16	−2.37	0.08	0.06	−0.16	−0.01

Player	PA%	Runs Above Average	Average Value Hitting ($)	Fielding ($)	Value Above Average ($)	MRP ($)
Boston Red Sox						
Dustin Pedroia	11.34	37.52	5.93	2.00	4.30	12.24
Kevin Youkilis	9.70	44.95	5.08	1.13	5.60	11.81
Jacoby Ellsbury	9.51	7.23	4.98	1.54	0.56	7.08
J.D. Drew	7.12	21.56	3.73	1.06	2.04	6.83
Mike Lowell	7.31	7.62	3.82	1.23	0.60	5.65
Manny Ramirez	6.64	16.61	3.47	0.60	1.47	5.55
David Ortiz	7.67	15.45	4.01	0.00	1.35	5.36
Jason Varitek	7.54	−24.21	3.95	2.30	−1.11	5.13
Coco Crisp	6.39	−3.42	3.34	1.33	−0.23	4.44
Jed Lowrie	4.78	3.15	2.50	0.97	0.23	3.70
Julio Lugo	4.80	−7.29	2.51	1.09	−0.45	3.14
Jason Bay	3.30	6.06	1.72	0.48	0.46	2.66
Sean Casey	3.41	−2.18	1.78	0.28	−0.15	1.91
Alex Cora	2.80	−4.61	1.46	0.68	−0.30	1.84
Kevin Cash	2.53	−9.23	1.32	0.84	−0.56	1.61
Brandon Moss	1.34	−0.94	0.70	0.20	−0.06	0.84
Jeff Bailey	0.92	−0.70	0.48	0.08	−0.05	0.52
Mark Kotsay	1.42	−7.47	0.74	0.21	−0.46	0.49
Jonathan Van Every	0.28	−0.02	0.15	0.05	0.00	0.20
Chris Carter	0.31	−0.18	0.16	0.02	−0.01	0.17
George Kottaras	0.08	−0.36	0.04	0.02	−0.02	0.03
Joe Thurston	0.14	−1.51	0.07	0.02	−0.10	−0.01
Dave Ross	0.14	−2.08	0.07	0.06	−0.14	−0.01
Gil Velazquez	0.12	−2.39	0.07	0.03	−0.16	−0.06
Chicago Cubs						
Aramis Ramirez	10.10	16.02	5.29	1.68	1.41	8.37
Derrek Lee	10.93	13.67	5.72	1.08	1.16	7.96
Geovany Soto	8.82	9.59	4.61	2.53	0.77	7.92
Ryan Theriot	10.35	0.91	5.42	2.05	0.06	7.53
Mark DeRosa	9.29	8.90	4.86	1.65	0.71	7.22
Alfonso Soriano	7.88	13.75	4.12	1.05	1.17	6.34
Kosuke Fukudome	9.24	−2.87	4.84	1.40	−0.19	6.04
Mike Fontenot	4.45	21.46	2.33	0.72	2.02	5.08
Reed Johnson	5.86	−4.55	3.07	1.01	−0.30	3.78
Jim Edmonds	4.67	2.56	2.44	0.94	0.19	3.57
Ronny Cedeno	3.70	−9.05	1.93	0.71	−0.55	2.10
Henry Blanco	2.01	−2.30	1.05	0.57	−0.16	1.46
Micah Hoffpauir	1.25	2.63	0.66	0.12	0.19	0.97
Daryle Ward	1.86	−2.29	0.98	0.10	−0.15	0.92
Felix Pie	1.46	−3.85	0.76	0.30	−0.25	0.81
Eric Patterson	0.69	−1.85	0.36	0.09	−0.13	0.33
Matt Murton	0.66	−2.09	0.34	0.07	−0.14	0.28
Casey McGehee	0.39	−1.49	0.20	0.05	−0.10	0.16
Koyie Hill	0.34	−5.33	0.18	0.09	−0.34	−0.07
Chicago White Sox						
Carlos Quentin	9.13	29.42	4.78	1.28	3.06	9.12
Jermaine Dye	10.35	10.66	5.42	1.55	0.87	7.84
Orlando Cabrera	11.72	−12.63	6.13	2.23	−0.72	7.65
Jim Thome	9.66	17.89	5.05	0.00	1.61	6.67
A.J. Pierzynski	9.15	−23.81	4.79	2.49	−1.10	6.17
Nick Swisher	9.44	−12.87	4.94	1.46	−0.73	5.67
Alexei Ramirez	8.17	−10.93	4.27	1.65	−0.64	5.28
Paul Konerko	8.25	0.72	4.32	0.80	0.05	5.16
Joe Crede	5.99	6.89	3.13	1.09	0.53	4.75
Juan Uribe	5.67	−16.19	2.96	1.15	−0.87	3.24
Brian N. Anderson	3.10	−3.63	1.62	0.69	−0.24	2.07
Ken Griffey	2.41	−2.36	1.26	0.38	−0.16	1.48
Dewayne Wise	2.29	−3.03	1.20	0.38	−0.20	1.38
Toby Hall	2.18	−12.95	1.14	0.69	−0.73	1.10
Pablo Ozuna	1.11	−5.32	0.58	0.21	−0.34	0.44
Jerry Owens	0.27	−0.52	0.14	0.05	−0.04	0.16
Jason Bourgeois	0.05	0.25	0.03	0.00	0.02	0.05
Chris Getz	0.11	−0.71	0.06	0.03	−0.05	0.04
Josh Fields	0.56	−5.84	0.29	0.08	−0.37	0.00
Paul Phillips	0.03	−0.59	0.02	0.02	−0.04	−0.01

Player	PA%	Runs Above Average	Average Value		Value Above Average ($)	MRP ($)
			Hitting ($)	Fielding ($)		
Cincinnati Reds						
Joey Votto	9.52	34.36	4.98	0.99	3.80	9.77
Brandon Phillips	9.84	8.57	5.15	1.81	0.68	7.63
Edwin Encarnacion	9.41	−8.19	4.92	1.63	−0.50	6.05
Adam Dunn	7.50	9.40	3.92	1.03	0.75	5.71
Jeff Keppinger	8.11	−29.91	4.24	1.57	−1.23	4.59
Jay Bruce	7.30	−6.58	3.82	1.18	−0.41	4.59
Ken Griffey	6.87	−1.37	3.59	0.90	−0.09	4.40
Jerry Hairston	4.80	12.53	2.51	0.81	1.05	4.37
Paul Bako	5.46	−20.22	2.86	1.71	−1.00	3.56
Corey Patterson	6.33	−23.48	3.31	1.20	−1.10	3.42
Chris Dickerson	1.97	13.37	1.03	0.27	1.13	2.44
Dave Ross	2.80	−0.48	1.46	0.83	−0.03	2.26
Javier Valentin	2.33	−1.94	1.22	0.23	−0.13	1.31
Ryan Hanigan	1.58	−0.76	0.83	0.51	−0.05	1.28
Jolbert Cabrera	2.04	−1.62	1.07	0.29	−0.11	1.25
Ryan Freel	2.31	−6.46	1.21	0.35	−0.41	1.15
Andy Phillips	1.29	−2.20	0.68	0.12	−0.15	0.64
Paul Janish	1.44	−8.12	0.75	0.33	−0.50	0.59
Wilkin Castillo	0.55	−0.57	0.29	0.07	−0.04	0.31
Scott Hatteberg	0.99	−5.32	0.52	0.07	−0.34	0.24
Norris Hopper	0.94	−5.97	0.49	0.13	−0.38	0.24
Danny Richar	0.60	−4.99	0.31	0.09	−0.32	0.08
Adam Rosales	0.48	−3.75	0.25	0.06	−0.25	0.07
Juan Castro	0.18	−2.88	0.09	0.03	−0.19	−0.06
Cleveland Indians						
Grady Sizemore	11.83	41.83	6.19	2.02	5.04	13.25
Jhonny Peralta	10.54	1.78	5.52	2.09	0.13	7.73
Shin-Soo Choo	5.87	27.00	3.07	0.73	2.73	6.53
Kelly Shoppach	6.40	9.82	3.35	1.94	0.79	6.08
Ryan Garko	8.94	−0.37	4.68	0.86	−0.03	5.51
Franklin Gutierrez	6.99	8.16	3.66	1.15	0.64	5.45
Ben Francisco	7.92	3.10	4.15	1.01	0.23	5.38
Asdrubal Cabrera	6.64	0.98	3.47	1.39	0.07	4.93
Casey Blake	5.84	9.24	3.06	0.97	0.74	4.77
Jamey Carroll	6.38	−4.00	3.34	1.12	−0.26	4.19
Victor Martinez	4.67	−3.49	2.44	1.06	−0.23	3.27
David Dellucci	5.95	−4.57	3.12	0.43	−0.30	3.25
Andy Marte	4.08	−11.49	2.14	0.77	−0.67	2.24
Travis Hafner	3.70	−8.34	1.94	0.00	−0.51	1.43
Sal Fasano	0.86	−0.84	0.45	0.26	−0.06	0.65
Jason Michaels	1.06	−4.52	0.56	0.16	−0.29	0.43
Michael Aubrey	0.79	−3.30	0.42	0.08	−0.22	0.27
Jorge Velandia	0.14	1.07	0.07	0.03	0.08	0.18
Andy Gonzalez	0.48	−2.77	0.25	0.05	−0.19	0.11
Josh Barfield	0.52	−6.07	0.27	0.10	−0.39	−0.01
Jason Tyner	0.05	−0.80	0.02	0.01	−0.06	−0.02
Colorado Rockies						
Matt Holliday	9.87	46.22	5.16	1.38	5.84	12.39
Chris Iannetta	6.45	10.99	3.37	1.86	0.90	6.13
Garrett Atkins	10.52	−19.31	5.50	1.48	−0.98	6.01
Brad Hawpe	9.01	−4.14	4.72	1.40	−0.27	5.84
Clint Barmes	6.61	5.12	3.46	1.24	0.39	5.08
Willy Taveras	8.52	−22.45	4.46	1.49	−1.07	4.88
Troy Tulowitzki	6.67	−6.55	3.49	1.40	−0.41	4.48
Todd Helton	5.72	7.07	2.99	0.58	0.55	4.12
Ian Stewart	4.82	6.05	2.52	0.83	0.46	3.81
Jeff Baker	5.28	−3.93	2.76	0.75	−0.26	3.25
Ryan Spilborghs	4.36	3.76	2.28	0.56	0.28	3.11
Yorvit Torrealba	4.13	−14.72	2.16	1.28	−0.81	2.64
Omar Quintanilla	3.71	−10.50	1.94	0.78	−0.62	2.10
Scott Podsednik	2.87	−4.18	1.50	0.34	−0.27	1.57
Seth Smith	1.95	−2.60	1.02	0.19	−0.17	1.04
Jonathan Herrera	1.05	−3.35	0.55	0.19	−0.22	0.52
Joe Koshansky	0.63	0.70	0.33	0.06	0.05	0.44
Jayson Nix	1.03	−4.92	0.54	0.21	−0.32	0.43

Player	PA%	Runs Above Average	Average Value Hitting ($)	Fielding ($)	Value Above Average ($)	MRP ($)
Adam Melhuse	0.16	−1.10	0.08	0.05	−0.08	0.06
Dexter Fowler	0.43	−3.70	0.22	0.08	−0.24	0.06
Edwin Bellorin	0.05	−0.14	0.02	0.01	−0.01	0.03
Cory Sullivan	0.38	−4.28	0.20	0.05	−0.28	−0.03
Doug Bernier	0.06	−1.20	0.03	0.02	−0.08	−0.03
Detroit Tigers						
Miguel Cabrera	10.80	17.25	5.65	1.12	1.54	8.32
Placido Polanco	9.94	12.15	5.20	1.75	1.01	7.96
Curtis Granderson	9.94	11.47	5.20	1.78	0.95	7.93
Magglio Ordonez	9.84	13.56	5.15	1.36	1.15	7.66
Carlos Guillen	7.72	3.93	4.04	1.13	0.29	5.47
Edgar Renteria	8.64	−20.17	4.52	1.90	−1.00	5.42
Brandon Inge	6.43	−13.94	3.36	1.66	−0.78	4.25
Ivan Rodriguez	5.18	−1.07	2.71	1.56	−0.07	4.20
Gary Sheffield	7.61	−6.32	3.98	0.05	−0.40	3.64
Matthew Joyce	4.38	8.73	2.29	0.65	0.69	3.63
Marcus Thames	5.40	−9.12	2.83	0.61	−0.55	2.89
Ramon Santiago	2.46	−3.57	1.29	0.57	−0.24	1.62
Clete Thomas	2.10	1.25	1.10	0.35	0.09	1.54
Ryan Raburn	3.14	−11.76	1.64	0.56	−0.68	1.53
Dusty Ryan	0.79	2.71	0.41	0.27	0.20	0.88
Jeff Larish	1.75	−6.91	0.92	0.14	−0.43	0.62
Mike Hessman	0.49	2.21	0.26	0.09	0.16	0.51
Jacque Jones	1.42	−9.30	0.74	0.19	−0.56	0.38
Mike Hollimon	0.39	0.37	0.21	0.09	0.03	0.32
Dane Sardinha	0.77	−6.25	0.40	0.27	−0.40	0.28
Brent Clevlen	0.44	−1.15	0.23	0.09	−0.08	0.24
Florida Marlins						
Hanley Ramirez	11.17	47.09	5.84	2.13	6.01	13.98
Dan Uggla	9.97	24.79	5.22	1.87	2.44	9.52
Jorge Cantu	11.04	2.86	5.77	1.64	0.21	7.63
Cody Ross	8.15	17.64	4.27	1.54	1.58	7.39
Josh Willingham	6.70	15.98	3.51	0.97	1.40	5.88
Jeremy Hermida	9.01	−5.19	4.71	1.31	−0.33	5.69
Mike Jacobs	8.36	−15.45	4.38	0.75	−0.84	4.29
Alfredo Amezaga	5.43	−5.16	2.84	1.04	−0.33	3.55
Luis Gonzalez	6.24	−7.64	3.26	0.75	−0.47	3.54
John Baker	3.75	2.19	1.96	1.10	0.16	3.23
Wes Helms	4.48	−5.45	2.34	0.60	−0.35	2.60
Matt Treanor	3.77	−15.10	1.97	1.17	−0.82	2.32
Mike Rabelo	1.97	−10.52	1.03	0.58	−0.62	0.99
Cameron Maybin	0.58	7.15	0.30	0.10	0.55	0.95
Robert Andino	1.10	−0.79	0.57	0.15	−0.05	0.67
Paul Lo Duca	0.64	−0.68	0.34	0.11	−0.05	0.40
Paul Hoover	0.68	−4.49	0.35	0.23	−0.29	0.29
Dallas McPherson	0.24	0.39	0.13	0.02	0.03	0.18
Gaby Sanchez	0.13	0.71	0.07	0.01	0.05	0.13
Jacque Jones	0.71	−6.11	0.37	0.10	−0.39	0.08
Brett Carroll	0.29	−2.16	0.15	0.05	−0.15	0.05
Jai Miller	0.02	−0.29	0.01	0.00	−0.02	−0.01
Houston Astros						
Lance Berkman	10.99	69.71	5.75	1.07	11.20	18.02
Carlos Lee	7.95	26.65	4.16	1.04	2.68	7.89
Miguel Tejada	11.01	−3.28	5.76	2.23	−0.22	7.77
Hunter Pence	10.61	1.60	5.55	1.65	0.11	7.32
Ty Wigginton	7.09	15.55	3.71	1.15	1.36	6.22
Michael Bourn	8.50	−22.95	4.45	1.54	−1.08	4.90
Kazuo Matsui	6.98	−0.62	3.65	1.19	−0.04	4.80
Geoff Blum	5.88	−2.49	3.08	0.92	−0.17	3.83
Darin Erstad	5.65	−5.86	2.96	0.81	−0.37	3.39
Mark Loretta	4.91	−0.57	2.57	0.76	−0.04	3.29
Brad Ausmus	4.13	−14.60	2.16	1.28	−0.80	2.64
Humberto Quintero	3.02	−11.82	1.58	1.00	−0.68	1.90
J.R. Towles	2.83	−14.03	1.48	0.92	−0.78	1.62
Reggie Abercrombie	0.99	4.45	0.52	0.15	0.33	1.01
David Newhan	1.83	−5.33	0.96	0.26	−0.34	0.88

Player	PA%	Runs Above Average	Average Value Hitting ($)	Fielding ($)	Value Above Average ($)	MRP ($)
Jose Castillo	0.58	−1.49	0.30	0.10	−0.10	0.30
Jose Cruz	0.99	−6.05	0.52	0.09	−0.38	0.23
Mark Saccomanno	0.17	−0.04	0.09	0.00	0.00	0.09
Edwin Maysonet	0.12	−1.25	0.06	0.02	−0.09	0.00
Tomas Perez	0.17	−2.87	0.09	0.02	−0.19	−0.08
Kansas City Royals						
David DeJesus	9.43	12.80	4.93	1.45	1.08	7.46
Mike Aviles	7.21	21.82	3.77	1.42	2.07	7.26
Alex Gordon	9.33	2.62	4.88	1.55	0.19	6.62
Mark Teahen	10.18	−18.08	5.33	1.52	−0.93	5.91
Jose Guillen	10.35	−17.45	5.41	1.06	−0.91	5.56
John Buck	6.83	−20.54	3.57	2.10	−1.01	4.66
Billy Butler	7.81	−8.36	4.09	0.21	−0.51	3.79
Mark Grudzielanek	5.88	−5.27	3.08	1.03	−0.34	3.77
Miguel Olivo	5.18	−3.16	2.71	1.09	−0.21	3.59
Ross Gload	6.83	−19.45	3.57	0.80	−0.98	3.39
Joey Gathright	5.15	−17.36	2.69	1.09	−0.91	2.88
Alberto Callaspo	3.82	−5.28	2.00	0.69	−0.34	2.36
Esteban German	3.96	−12.79	2.07	0.67	−0.73	2.01
Ryan Shealy	1.29	3.89	0.68	0.14	0.29	1.10
Mitch Maier	1.59	−2.09	0.83	0.34	−0.14	1.03
Jason Smith	0.46	−0.09	0.24	0.09	−0.01	0.32
Kila Ka'aihue	0.39	−0.28	0.21	0.01	−0.02	0.20
Matt Tupman	0.02	0.47	0.01	0.00	0.03	0.04
Los Angeles Angels of Anaheim						
Vladimir Guerrero	9.75	19.34	5.10	1.00	1.77	7.87
Torii Hunter	9.88	6.95	5.17	1.78	0.54	7.49
Chone Figgins	8.45	1.67	4.42	1.29	0.12	5.83
Mark Teixeira	3.80	31.08	1.99	0.35	3.30	5.64
Garret Anderson	9.63	−3.45	5.04	0.77	−0.23	5.58
Casey Kotchman	6.47	6.37	3.38	0.69	0.49	4.56
Mike Napoli	4.45	9.21	2.33	1.38	0.74	4.44
Erick Aybar	6.09	−3.98	3.19	1.27	−0.26	4.20
Gary Matthews	7.75	−22.40	4.05	1.09	−1.07	4.08
Howie Kendrick	5.87	−3.19	3.07	1.12	−0.21	3.98
Maicer Izturis	5.22	−3.16	2.73	1.03	−0.21	3.55
Jeff Mathis	5.33	−24.41	2.79	1.75	−1.12	3.42
Juan Rivera	4.55	−12.95	2.38	0.49	−0.73	2.13
Sean Rodriguez	3.04	−10.99	1.59	0.65	−0.64	1.59
Robb Quinlan	2.94	−9.21	1.54	0.44	−0.56	1.43
Brandon Wood	2.55	−18.65	1.33	0.57	−0.95	0.95
Reggie Willits	2.21	−8.47	1.16	0.31	−0.52	0.94
Kendry Morales	1.07	−4.51	0.56	0.10	−0.29	0.37
Bobby Wilson	0.11	−0.68	0.06	0.04	−0.05	0.05
Ryan Budde	0.05	−0.59	0.03	0.04	−0.04	0.02
Freddy Sandoval	0.11	−1.43	0.06	0.01	−0.10	−0.03
Matthew Brown	0.32	−5.63	0.17	0.06	−0.36	−0.13
Los Angeles Dodgers						
Russell Martin	10.49	7.07	5.49	2.82	0.55	8.86
Matt Kemp	10.61	11.50	5.55	1.81	0.95	8.31
Andre Ethier	9.62	17.84	5.03	1.36	1.60	8.00
James Loney	10.51	3.63	5.50	1.10	0.27	6.86
Manny Ramirez	3.70	33.44	1.93	0.49	3.65	6.08
Blake DeWitt	6.80	4.29	3.56	1.24	0.32	5.11
Jeff Kent	7.65	−11.41	4.00	1.29	−0.66	4.63
Juan Pierre	6.55	−4.93	3.43	0.87	−0.32	3.98
Rafael Furcal	2.65	15.56	1.39	0.48	1.36	3.22
Casey Blake	3.76	−0.24	1.97	0.63	−0.02	2.58
Angel Berroa	4.13	−10.27	2.16	0.98	−0.61	2.53
Nomar Garciaparra	2.92	5.63	1.53	0.51	0.43	2.47
Andruw Jones	3.84	−21.93	2.01	0.74	−1.05	1.70
Chin–Lung Hu	2.08	−6.86	1.09	0.53	−0.43	1.19
Delwyn Young	2.31	−6.58	1.21	0.21	−0.41	1.00
Andy LaRoche	1.11	−2.09	0.58	0.16	−0.14	0.60
Luis Maza	1.42	−8.00	0.74	0.34	−0.49	0.59

Player	PA%	Runs Above Average	Average Value Hitting ($)	Fielding ($)	Value Above Average ($)	MRP ($)
Danny Ardoin	0.87	−4.07	0.46	0.32	−0.27	0.51
Mark Sweeney	1.74	−11.20	0.91	0.01	−0.65	0.27
Jason Repko	0.32	0.07	0.17	0.05	0.01	0.23
Gary Bennett	0.37	−1.46	0.19	0.12	−0.10	0.21
Pablo Ozuna	0.53	−3.09	0.28	0.14	−0.21	0.21
Terry Tiffee	0.08	−0.06	0.04	0.00	0.00	0.04
A.J. Ellis	0.05	−0.86	0.03	0.02	−0.06	−0.01
Milwaukee Brewers						
Ryan Braun	10.61	32.24	5.55	1.46	3.47	10.49
J.J. Hardy	10.06	27.23	5.26	2.04	2.76	10.07
Prince Fielder	11.10	21.29	5.81	1.11	2.00	8.92
Corey Hart	10.51	0.20	5.50	1.63	0.01	7.14
Jason Kendall	9.39	−12.39	4.91	2.91	−0.71	7.12
Mike Cameron	8.13	14.57	4.25	1.58	1.25	7.08
Rickie Weeks	8.96	2.69	4.69	1.53	0.20	6.41
Bill Hall	7.17	−11.23	3.75	1.22	−0.65	4.31
Craig Counsell	4.83	2.15	2.53	0.81	0.16	3.49
Gabe Kapler	3.92	8.24	2.05	0.58	0.65	3.28
Russell Branyan	2.43	10.15	1.27	0.38	0.82	2.47
Ray Durham	1.95	1.55	1.02	0.29	0.11	1.43
Mike Rivera	1.10	0.32	0.58	0.30	0.02	0.90
Gabe Gross	0.86	−0.61	0.45	0.16	−0.04	0.57
Joe Dillon	1.44	−4.64	0.75	0.10	−0.30	0.56
Tony Gwynn	0.78	−1.98	0.41	0.08	−0.13	0.36
Brad Nelson	0.13	0.60	0.07	0.00	0.04	0.11
Hernan Iribarren	0.24	−1.08	0.13	0.02	−0.07	0.07
Alcides Escobar	0.06	0.37	0.03	0.00	0.03	0.06
Mat Gamel	0.03	0.57	0.02	0.00	0.04	0.06
Mike Lamb	0.18	−0.91	0.09	0.00	−0.06	0.03
Laynce Nix	0.21	−1.80	0.11	0.01	−0.12	0.00
Minnesota Twins						
Joe Mauer	10.00	31.62	5.23	2.63	3.38	11.25
Justin Morneau	11.25	31.53	5.88	1.09	3.37	10.34
Carlos Gomez	9.70	0.11	5.07	1.89	0.01	6.97
Denard Span	6.49	18.83	3.40	0.98	1.72	6.10
Delmon Young	9.84	−13.44	5.15	1.47	−0.75	5.87
Jason Kubel	8.17	3.27	4.27	0.43	0.24	4.94
Brendan Harris	7.74	−14.12	4.05	1.54	−0.78	4.81
Nick Punto	5.96	3.54	3.12	1.25	0.26	4.63
Alexi Casilla	6.90	−5.72	3.61	1.22	−0.37	4.47
Brian Buscher	3.85	−2.95	2.02	0.69	−0.20	2.51
Michael Cuddyer	4.41	−8.37	2.31	0.62	−0.51	2.41
Mike Lamb	4.12	−18.96	2.16	0.64	−0.96	1.83
Adam Everett	2.37	−7.32	1.24	0.59	−0.46	1.37
Mike Redmond	2.16	−6.05	1.13	0.55	−0.38	1.30
Craig Monroe	2.83	−7.21	1.48	0.11	−0.45	1.15
Matt Tolbert	1.94	−4.98	1.02	0.37	−0.32	1.06
Randy Ruiz	1.07	−1.04	0.56	0.00	−0.07	0.49
Matt Macri	0.57	−1.78	0.30	0.10	−0.12	0.28
Howie Clark	0.13	0.00	0.07	0.02	0.00	0.08
Jason Pridie	0.09	−0.80	0.05	0.01	−0.06	0.01
Ryan Jorgensen	0.02	−0.28	0.01	0.01	−0.02	0.00
New York Mets						
Carlos Beltran	11.06	47.41	5.78	2.08	6.07	13.94
David Wright	11.51	46.79	6.02	1.86	5.95	13.83
Jose Reyes	11.95	23.07	6.25	2.27	2.22	10.75
Carlos Delgado	10.74	13.90	5.62	1.10	1.19	7.90
Brian Schneider	6.01	−6.21	3.15	1.92	−0.39	4.67
Ryan Church	5.62	9.41	2.94	0.85	0.75	4.55
Fernando Tatis	4.79	9.11	2.51	0.70	0.73	3.94
Endy Chavez	4.67	0.62	2.44	0.75	0.04	3.23
Luis Castillo	5.62	−14.99	2.94	0.99	−0.82	3.11
Damion Easley	5.43	−12.05	2.84	0.91	−0.69	3.06
Daniel Murphy	2.36	8.60	1.24	0.28	0.68	2.19
Ramon Castro	2.46	−2.94	1.29	0.77	−0.20	1.86
Nick Evans	1.86	0.97	0.97	0.22	0.07	1.26

Player	PA%	Runs Above Average	Average Value Hitting ($)	Fielding ($)	Value Above Average ($)	MRP ($)
Angel Pagan	1.64	2.14	0.86	0.23	0.15	1.24
Marlon Anderson	2.36	−7.44	1.24	0.21	−0.46	0.99
Argenis Reyes	1.89	−5.60	0.99	0.28	−0.36	0.91
Raul Casanova	0.96	−0.70	0.50	0.26	−0.05	0.71
Moises Alou	0.85	0.14	0.44	0.10	0.01	0.55
Robinson Cancel	0.83	−3.32	0.43	0.20	−0.22	0.42
Trot Nixon	0.64	−0.89	0.34	0.09	−0.06	0.37
Brady Clark	0.17	0.09	0.09	0.02	0.01	0.12
Ramon Martinez	0.28	−1.30	0.15	0.05	−0.09	0.11
Chris Aguila	0.23	−1.28	0.12	0.03	−0.09	0.06
Gustavo Molina	0.13	−1.15	0.07	0.04	−0.08	0.03
Andy Phillips	0.08	−0.68	0.04	0.01	−0.05	0.00
New York Yankees						
Alex Rodriguez	9.49	42.50	4.97	1.48	5.16	11.60
Johnny Damon	9.96	20.34	5.21	1.17	1.89	8.27
Bobby Abreu	10.93	4.51	5.72	1.56	0.34	7.62
Derek Jeter	10.68	−6.30	5.59	2.05	−0.40	7.23
Robinson Cano	10.13	−27.33	5.30	2.01	−1.18	6.13
Jason Giambi	9.03	7.81	4.72	0.73	0.61	6.06
Melky Cabrera	7.24	−15.72	3.79	1.51	−0.85	4.45
Hideki Matsui	6.04	3.38	3.16	0.22	0.25	3.63
Jose Molina	4.75	−16.22	2.48	1.63	−0.87	3.25
Xavier Nady	3.95	0.04	2.07	0.50	0.00	2.57
Jorge Posada	3.12	−3.18	1.63	0.54	−0.21	1.96
Wilson Betemit	3.16	−9.54	1.66	0.43	−0.57	1.51
Brett Gardner	2.25	−4.28	1.18	0.41	−0.28	1.31
Chad Moeller	1.65	−3.84	0.86	0.51	−0.25	1.11
Ivan Rodriguez	1.61	−8.07	0.84	0.50	−0.50	0.84
Cody Ransom	0.82	1.39	0.43	0.19	0.10	0.71
Alberto Gonzalez	0.93	−5.93	0.48	0.22	−0.38	0.32
Richie Sexson	0.56	−0.66	0.29	0.06	−0.05	0.31
Shelley Duncan	1.04	−5.49	0.54	0.11	−0.35	0.31
Justin Christian	0.69	−2.56	0.36	0.11	−0.17	0.30
Juan Miranda	0.22	2.19	0.12	0.03	0.16	0.30
Morgan Ensberg	1.28	−12.34	0.67	0.20	−0.71	0.17
Chris Stewart	0.05	−1.10	0.03	0.02	−0.08	−0.03
Francisco Cervelli	0.08	−1.69	0.04	0.03	−0.11	−0.04
Oakland Athletics						
Kurt Suzuki	9.58	−3.32	5.01	2.70	−0.22	7.50
Mark Ellis	8.26	15.03	4.32	1.48	1.30	7.11
Jack Cust	9.74	14.42	5.10	0.71	1.24	7.05
Jack Hannahan	8.16	5.09	4.27	1.37	0.38	6.02
Bobby Crosby	9.86	−29.07	5.16	2.06	−1.21	6.01
Ryan Sweeney	7.05	5.63	3.69	1.18	0.43	5.30
Daric Barton	8.52	−3.98	4.46	0.91	−0.26	5.11
Emil Brown	7.14	−8.92	3.73	0.99	−0.54	4.18
Carlos Gonzalez	5.15	−6.98	2.69	0.99	−0.44	3.25
Rajai Davis	3.37	−1.36	1.76	0.70	−0.09	2.38
Frank Thomas	3.54	2.09	1.85	0.00	0.15	2.00
Travis Buck	2.80	1.88	1.47	0.40	0.14	2.00
Mike Sweeney	2.22	1.77	1.16	0.07	0.13	1.36
Aaron Cunningham	1.42	2.83	0.74	0.19	0.21	1.14
Chris Denorfia	1.16	1.54	0.61	0.20	0.11	0.92
Eric Chavez	1.55	−1.21	0.81	0.17	−0.08	0.90
Rob Bowen	1.60	−8.44	0.84	0.49	−0.52	0.81
Donnie Murphy	1.91	−10.94	1.00	0.42	−0.64	0.78
Eric Patterson	1.69	−8.04	0.89	0.32	−0.49	0.71
Cliff Pennington	1.91	−13.00	1.00	0.38	−0.73	0.64
Gregorio Petit	0.41	1.75	0.21	0.10	0.13	0.44
Wes Bankston	1.03	−5.25	0.54	0.09	−0.34	0.29
Jeff Baisley	0.77	−4.36	0.40	0.13	−0.28	0.25
Jeff Fiorentino	0.02	0.48	0.01	0.01	0.03	0.05
Brooks Conrad	0.31	−2.73	0.16	0.07	−0.18	0.05
Matt Murton	0.51	−4.70	0.26	0.07	−0.31	0.03
Philadelphia Phillies						
Chase Utley	11.27	73.99	5.90	2.04	12.38	20.32
Jimmy Rollins	9.96	30.64	5.21	1.89	3.24	10.34

Player	PA%	Runs Above Average	Average Value Hitting ($)	Fielding ($)	Value Above Average ($)	MRP ($)
Ryan Howard	11.16	21.87	5.84	1.13	2.07	9.04
Shane Victorino	10.00	14.13	5.23	1.84	1.21	8.27
Pat Burrell	10.28	11.75	5.38	1.34	0.97	7.70
Jayson Werth	7.68	19.60	4.02	1.21	1.80	7.04
Pedro Feliz	7.38	−6.81	3.86	1.28	−0.43	4.72
Carlos Ruiz	5.95	−23.30	3.11	1.83	−1.09	3.85
Chris Coste	4.86	−7.55	2.54	1.36	−0.47	3.43
Geoff Jenkins	5.13	−10.03	2.69	0.76	−0.60	2.85
Greg Dobbs	3.83	0.76	2.00	0.46	0.05	2.51
Eric Bruntlett	3.79	−8.73	1.99	0.75	−0.53	2.21
So Taguchi	1.64	−4.67	0.86	0.20	−0.30	0.75
Matt Stairs	0.30	1.06	0.16	0.02	0.08	0.25
T.J. Bohn	0.08	1.55	0.04	0.02	0.11	0.18
Lou Marson	0.06	1.66	0.03	0.02	0.12	0.17
Tadahito Iguchi	0.11	−0.16	0.06	0.01	−0.01	0.06
Brad Harman	0.18	−1.47	0.09	0.03	−0.10	0.02
Mike Cervenak	0.21	−2.30	0.11	0.01	−0.15	−0.03
Greg Golson	0.10	−2.10	0.05	0.02	−0.14	−0.07
Pittsburgh Pirates						
Nate McLouth	10.91	6.58	5.71	1.97	0.51	8.19
Ryan Doumit	7.41	12.19	3.88	2.00	1.02	6.89
Jason Bay	7.31	19.74	3.83	1.03	1.82	6.67
Adam LaRoche	8.82	10.07	4.62	0.91	0.81	6.34
Freddy Sanchez	9.68	−16.10	5.07	1.64	−0.86	5.85
Xavier Nady	5.73	21.03	3.00	0.84	1.97	5.82
Jack Wilson	5.26	2.43	2.75	1.12	0.18	4.05
Doug Mientkiewicz	5.32	4.47	2.78	0.62	0.33	3.73
Jose Bautista	5.78	−4.94	3.03	0.95	−0.32	3.65
Jason Michaels	4.05	−5.74	2.12	0.52	−0.37	2.27
Nyjer Morgan	2.79	2.91	1.46	0.39	0.21	2.06
Chris Gomez	3.19	−3.94	1.67	0.45	−0.26	1.86
Luis Rivas	3.55	−16.74	1.86	0.64	−0.89	1.61
Brandon Moss	2.82	−5.22	1.48	0.42	−0.34	1.56
Raul Chavez	1.94	−4.41	1.02	0.61	−0.29	1.34
Andy LaRoche	2.91	−17.01	1.53	0.52	−0.90	1.15
Ronny Paulino	2.07	−9.18	1.08	0.57	−0.55	1.10
Steven Pearce	1.90	−2.76	0.99	0.27	−0.18	1.08
Luis Cruz	1.18	−3.50	0.62	0.29	−0.23	0.67
Brian Bixler	1.91	−14.47	1.00	0.45	−0.80	0.65
Robinzon Diaz	0.10	1.17	0.05	0.02	0.08	0.15
San Diego Padres						
Brian Giles	10.46	48.07	5.47	1.49	6.20	13.17
Adrian Gonzalez	11.21	32.43	5.87	1.13	3.50	10.50
Kevin Kouzmanoff	10.70	−0.18	5.60	1.79	−0.01	7.38
Jody Gerut	5.70	22.43	2.98	0.98	2.14	6.10
Chase Headley	5.89	10.62	3.08	0.87	0.87	4.81
Scott Hairston	5.80	9.06	3.03	0.91	0.72	4.67
Khalil Greene	6.77	−19.90	3.54	1.50	−0.99	4.05
Edgar Gonzalez	5.65	1.05	2.96	0.89	0.07	3.92
Tadahito Iguchi	5.29	−11.41	2.77	0.96	−0.66	3.06
Nick Hundley	3.46	−9.83	1.81	1.07	−0.59	2.29
Luis Rodriguez	3.60	−5.64	1.89	0.69	−0.36	2.22
Will Venable	1.99	4.76	1.04	0.35	0.36	1.75
Josh Bard	3.17	−18.16	1.66	0.91	−0.94	1.63
Paul McAnulty	2.63	−2.12	1.37	0.35	−0.14	1.58
Justin Huber	1.07	3.41	0.56	0.16	0.25	0.97
Tony Clark	1.71	0.58	0.90	0.02	0.04	0.96
Luke Carlin	1.68	−11.44	0.88	0.57	−0.66	0.78
Michael Barrett	1.71	−11.90	0.90	0.55	−0.69	0.76
Jim Edmonds	1.65	−10.50	0.86	0.32	−0.62	0.56
Sean Kazmar	0.74	−1.66	0.39	0.16	−0.11	0.44
Chip Ambres	0.77	−0.94	0.40	0.09	−0.06	0.43
Matt Antonelli	1.04	−5.02	0.54	0.20	−0.32	0.42
Drew Macias	0.40	0.75	0.21	0.03	0.05	0.29
Craig Stansberry	0.29	−0.26	0.15	0.04	−0.02	0.17
Brian Myrow	0.38	−1.82	0.20	0.01	−0.12	0.09

Player	PA%	Runs Above Average	Average Value		Value Above Average ($)	MRP ($)
			Hitting ($)	Fielding ($)		
Callix Crabbe	0.62	−6.01	0.33	0.09	−0.38	0.03
Colt Morton	0.29	−3.35	0.15	0.09	−0.22	0.02
San Francisco Giants						
Randy Winn	10.86	22.90	5.68	1.55	2.20	9.43
Bengie Molina	9.26	−1.90	4.85	2.50	−0.13	7.22
Aaron Rowand	9.94	−8.28	5.20	1.92	−0.51	6.61
Fred Lewis	8.48	7.73	4.44	1.15	0.60	6.19
Rich Aurilia	7.16	−9.01	3.75	0.95	−0.54	4.15
Jose Castillo	6.84	−17.74	3.58	1.16	−0.92	3.81
Ray Durham	4.95	0.19	2.59	0.78	0.01	3.38
Emmanuel Burriss	4.46	−6.14	2.33	0.93	−0.39	2.87
Omar Vizquel	4.88	−14.34	2.55	1.07	−0.79	2.83
John Bowker	5.70	−15.26	2.98	0.58	−0.83	2.74
Eugenio Velez	4.75	−14.00	2.49	0.76	−0.78	2.47
Pablo Sandoval	2.51	5.01	1.31	0.40	0.38	2.09
Nate Schierholtz	1.32	10.53	0.69	0.19	0.86	1.74
Travis Ishikawa	1.69	3.14	0.89	0.17	0.23	1.29
Steve Holm	1.60	−3.48	0.83	0.47	−0.23	1.07
Dave Roberts	2.12	−5.25	1.11	0.23	−0.34	1.00
Ivan Ochoa	2.18	−12.68	1.14	0.46	−0.72	0.88
Daniel Ortmeier	1.19	−2.54	0.62	0.14	−0.17	0.59
Brian Bocock	1.51	−10.50	0.79	0.37	−0.62	0.54
Travis Denker	0.68	0.66	0.36	0.10	0.05	0.51
Scott McClain	0.62	0.69	0.32	0.07	0.05	0.44
Brian Horwitz	0.68	−2.08	0.36	0.08	−0.14	0.30
Conor Gillaspie	0.11	−0.05	0.06	0.01	0.00	0.06
J.T. Snow	0.00	0.00	0.00	0.00	0.00	0.00
Rajai Davis	0.31	−3.12	0.16	0.04	−0.21	0.00
Ryan Rohlinger	0.54	−6.20	0.28	0.09	−0.39	−0.02
Clay Timpner	0.03	−0.58	0.02	0.00	−0.04	−0.02
Eliezer Alfonzo	0.18	−3.12	0.09	0.04	−0.21	−0.08
Seattle Mariners						
Adrian Beltre	9.91	30.88	5.18	1.60	3.27	10.06
Ichiro Suzuki	12.13	10.97	6.35	1.86	0.90	9.10
Raul Ibanez	11.45	10.24	5.99	1.52	0.83	8.34
Jose Lopez	11.12	5.42	5.82	1.88	0.41	8.11
Yuniesky Betancourt	9.55	−28.26	5.00	2.16	−1.20	5.96
Kenji Johjima	6.62	−21.85	3.46	1.85	−1.05	4.27
Jeremy Reed	5.05	−8.08	2.64	0.84	−0.50	2.99
Richie Sexson	4.73	−12.20	2.47	0.49	−0.70	2.27
Miguel Cairo	4.05	−6.58	2.12	0.52	−0.41	2.22
Willie Bloomquist	3.11	−1.89	1.63	0.57	−0.13	2.07
Jose Vidro	5.34	−15.19	2.80	0.04	−0.83	2.01
Wladimir Balentien	4.21	−19.88	2.20	0.73	−0.99	1.94
Jeff Clement	3.63	−11.03	1.90	0.65	−0.65	1.90
Bryan LaHair	2.43	−2.62	1.27	0.22	−0.18	1.32
Brad Wilkerson	1.10	−1.18	0.58	0.18	−0.08	0.67
Tug Hulett	0.91	−2.35	0.47	0.05	−0.16	0.37
Greg Norton	0.29	2.03	0.15	0.01	0.15	0.31
Luis Valbuena	0.87	−5.89	0.46	0.19	−0.38	0.27
Matt Tuiasosopo	0.76	−4.20	0.40	0.14	−0.27	0.26
Mike Morse	0.18	−0.59	0.09	0.03	−0.04	0.08
Rob Johnson	0.52	−6.34	0.27	0.14	−0.40	0.01
Charlton Jimerson	0.02	−0.29	0.01	0.00	−0.02	−0.01
St. Louis Cardinals						
Albert Pujols	10.06	93.06	5.26	0.98	18.48	24.72
Ryan Ludwick	9.69	36.22	5.07	1.42	4.09	10.58
Troy Glaus	10.00	27.59	5.23	1.64	2.81	9.69
Skip Schumaker	9.32	5.44	4.88	1.50	0.41	6.79
Yadier Molina	7.61	−2.71	3.98	2.21	−0.18	6.01
Rick Ankiel	7.27	3.71	3.80	1.29	0.27	5.37
Cesar Izturis	7.13	−1.28	3.73	1.63	−0.09	5.28
Adam Kennedy	5.73	8.93	3.00	1.00	0.71	4.71
Chris Duncan	4.03	0.09	2.11	0.49	0.01	2.61
Felipe Lopez	2.65	8.97	1.39	0.45	0.71	2.55
Jason LaRue	2.97	−6.63	1.55	0.91	−0.42	2.05

Player	PA%	Runs Above Average	Average Value Hitting ($)	Fielding ($)	Value Above Average ($)	MRP ($)
Brian Barton	2.81	2.86	1.47	0.29	0.21	1.97
Brendan Ryan	3.42	−8.73	1.79	0.68	−0.53	1.94
Joe Mather	2.31	4.57	1.21	0.33	0.34	1.88
Mark L. Johnson	0.28	−1.22	0.15	0.09	−0.08	0.15
Nick Stavinoha	0.96	−7.05	0.50	0.08	−0.44	0.14
Brian Barden	0.16	−0.32	0.08	0.02	−0.02	0.08
Josh Phelps	0.57	−4.43	0.30	0.05	−0.29	0.06
Rico Washington	0.35	−2.93	0.18	0.03	−0.20	0.02
Tampa Bay Rays						
Carlos Pena	9.62	33.87	5.03	0.94	3.72	9.69
Evan Longoria	8.05	26.47	4.21	1.38	2.66	8.25
B.J. Upton	10.14	10.19	5.31	1.86	0.83	7.99
Akinori Iwamura	11.20	−8.43	5.86	1.93	−0.51	7.28
Dioner Navarro	7.45	−0.45	3.90	2.22	−0.03	6.08
Carl Crawford	7.61	7.24	3.98	1.04	0.56	5.58
Jason Bartlett	7.83	−9.80	4.10	1.76	−0.58	5.27
Eric Hinske	6.85	8.12	3.58	0.83	0.64	5.05
Gabe Gross	5.47	−0.30	2.86	0.94	−0.02	3.78
Willy Aybar	5.74	−0.65	3.00	0.72	−0.05	3.68
Cliff Floyd	4.50	4.75	2.35	0.00	0.36	2.71
Ben Zobrist	3.60	0.25	1.88	0.67	0.02	2.57
Shawn Riggans	2.41	−8.91	1.26	0.75	−0.54	1.47
Fernando Perez	1.14	3.78	0.60	0.22	0.28	1.10
Jonny Gomes	2.81	−9.67	1.47	0.19	−0.58	1.08
Rocco Baldelli	1.43	2.15	0.75	0.04	0.15	0.94
Justin Ruggiano	1.28	−1.86	0.67	0.23	−0.13	0.78
Dan Johnson	0.44	0.79	0.23	0.04	0.06	0.33
Mike Difelice	0.35	−0.35	0.18	0.12	−0.02	0.28
Nathan Haynes	0.74	−5.45	0.39	0.13	−0.35	0.17
Elliot Johnson	0.30	−2.22	0.16	0.06	−0.15	0.06
John Jaso	0.16	−1.39	0.08	0.04	−0.10	0.02
Michel Hernandez	0.24	−2.75	0.12	0.07	−0.18	0.01
Andy Cannizaro	0.02	−0.29	0.01	0.00	−0.02	−0.01
Reid Brignac	0.17	−4.86	0.09	0.03	−0.31	−0.19
Texas Rangers						
Josh Hamilton	10.87	26.36	5.69	1.72	2.64	10.05
Milton Bradley	7.86	44.02	4.11	0.20	5.43	9.74
Ian Kinsler	9.00	18.68	4.71	1.55	1.70	7.96
Michael Young	10.93	−8.06	5.72	2.09	−0.50	7.32
Marlon Byrd	7.13	14.28	3.73	1.25	1.22	6.21
David Murphy	7.01	−2.68	3.67	1.07	−0.18	4.56
Gerald Laird	5.88	−8.97	3.08	1.68	−0.54	4.22
Ramon Vazquez	5.36	−1.57	2.80	1.01	−0.11	3.71
Brandon Boggs	5.16	2.87	2.70	0.68	0.21	3.59
Chris Davis	4.89	0.66	2.56	0.69	0.05	3.30
Hank Blalock	4.34	5.33	2.27	0.59	0.40	3.26
Nelson Cruz	2.05	13.65	1.07	0.33	1.16	2.56
Jarrod Saltalamacchia	3.55	−8.16	1.86	1.03	−0.50	2.39
Frank Catalanotto	4.29	−5.94	2.25	0.37	−0.38	2.24
Chris Shelton	1.81	0.79	0.95	0.20	0.06	1.20
Joaquin Arias	1.85	−1.61	0.97	0.33	−0.11	1.19
Taylor Teagarden	0.82	6.32	0.43	0.22	0.48	1.14
German Duran	2.44	−11.32	1.28	0.49	−0.66	1.10
Max Ramirez	0.85	−2.32	0.44	0.20	−0.16	0.49
Travis Metcalf	0.94	−3.41	0.49	0.17	−0.23	0.44
Jason Botts	0.71	−2.31	0.37	0.05	−0.16	0.27
Ben Broussard	1.37	−11.21	0.72	0.16	−0.65	0.23
Adam Melhuse	0.34	−1.83	0.18	0.10	−0.12	0.15
Jason Ellison	0.22	−0.62	0.11	0.03	−0.04	0.10
Toronto Blue Jays						
Alexis Rios	11.09	28.45	5.80	1.76	2.93	10.49
Marco Scutaro	9.57	14.64	5.01	1.76	1.26	8.02
Lyle Overbay	10.13	16.38	5.30	1.09	1.45	7.84
Scott Rolen	7.55	16.92	3.95	1.32	1.50	6.77
Vernon Wells	7.53	3.86	3.94	1.33	0.29	5.56
Joe Inglett	6.22	11.47	3.26	1.05	0.95	5.25

Player	PA%	Runs Above Average	Average Value Hitting ($)	Fielding ($)	Value Above Average ($)	MRP ($)
Rod Barajas	6.09	-8.13	3.19	1.76	-0.50	4.44
Gregg Zaun	4.65	-6.65	2.44	1.35	-0.42	3.37
Adam Lind	5.64	-7.43	2.95	0.66	-0.46	3.15
Matt Stairs	5.95	-3.06	3.11	0.12	-0.20	3.03
David Eckstein	4.90	-7.43	2.56	0.85	-0.46	2.95
Aaron Hill	3.70	-5.78	1.94	0.70	-0.37	2.26
Brad Wilkerson	3.90	-7.52	2.04	0.61	-0.47	2.19
John McDonald	3.35	-14.81	1.75	0.81	-0.81	1.75
Shannon Stewart	3.23	-6.91	1.69	0.35	-0.43	1.61
Kevin Mench	2.12	-1.38	1.11	0.26	-0.09	1.27
Travis Snider	1.29	1.54	0.68	0.18	0.11	0.97
Frank Thomas	1.16	-2.49	0.61	0.00	-0.17	0.44
Jose Bautista	0.99	-3.14	0.52	0.10	-0.21	0.40
Curtis Thigpen	0.34	-1.51	0.18	0.11	-0.10	0.19
Buck Coats	0.10	0.44	0.05	0.03	0.03	0.11
Jorge Velandia	0.11	-1.63	0.06	0.03	-0.11	-0.02
Robinzon Diaz	0.06	-1.15	0.03	0.00	-0.08	-0.05
Washington Nationals						
Cristian Guzman	9.88	16.41	5.17	1.92	1.45	8.54
Lastings Milledge	9.48	-7.32	4.96	1.79	-0.46	6.30
Willie Harris	6.85	17.70	3.58	1.04	1.59	6.21
Ryan Zimmerman	7.53	9.77	3.94	1.20	0.79	5.93
Elijah Dukes	5.39	20.73	2.82	0.80	1.94	5.56
Ron Belliard	5.44	6.36	2.85	0.84	0.49	4.18
Jesus Flores	5.23	-11.53	2.74	1.50	-0.67	3.57
Austin Kearns	5.77	-13.88	3.02	0.88	-0.77	3.13
Felipe Lopez	5.86	-23.57	3.07	1.06	-1.10	3.03
Nick Johnson	2.37	9.63	1.24	0.24	0.77	2.26
Aaron Boone	4.12	-6.37	2.15	0.43	-0.40	2.18
Wil Nieves	3.17	-11.81	1.66	1.00	-0.68	1.98
Ryan Langerhans	2.24	4.84	1.17	0.26	0.36	1.79
Dmitri Young	2.91	-0.90	1.52	0.24	-0.06	1.70
Emilio Bonifacio	2.81	-5.88	1.47	0.48	-0.37	1.57
Kory Casto	2.94	-7.58	1.54	0.35	-0.47	1.42
Wily Mo Pena	3.33	-15.47	1.74	0.46	-0.84	1.37
Anderson Hernandez	1.47	1.96	0.77	0.24	0.14	1.15
Paul Lo Duca	2.47	-11.25	1.29	0.48	-0.66	1.12
Alberto Gonzalez	0.87	3.57	0.46	0.17	0.26	0.89
Roger Bernadina	1.39	-4.45	0.73	0.23	-0.29	0.66
Pete Orr	1.28	-5.44	0.67	0.17	-0.35	0.49
Luke Montz	0.42	-1.38	0.22	0.12	-0.09	0.25
Rob Mackowiak	1.02	-6.82	0.53	0.10	-0.43	0.20
Johnny Estrada	0.89	-8.38	0.46	0.21	-0.51	0.16

PITCHERS (2008)

Player	BFP %	Runs Above Average	Average Value ($)	Value Above Average ($)	MRP (raw) ($)	MRP (adjusted) ($)
Arizona Diamondbacks						
Danny Haren	14.40	50.49	5.49	6.68	12.18	13.19
Brandon Webb	15.43	44.91	5.89	5.60	11.48	12.63
Chad Qualls	4.90	19.02	1.87	1.74	3.61	9.02
Tony Pena	5.12	14.06	1.95	1.20	3.15	7.88
Randy Johnson	12.71	26.41	4.85	2.65	7.50	7.66
Doug Davis	10.62	10.99	4.05	0.90	4.95	4.95
Brandon Lyon	4.33	8.24	1.65	0.65	2.30	4.60
Juan Cruz	3.51	5.69	1.34	0.43	1.77	3.55
Micah Owings	7.62	4.67	2.91	0.35	3.26	3.26
Max Scherzer	3.87	10.98	1.48	0.90	2.38	2.38
Yusmeiro Petit	3.74	-2.78	1.43	-0.19	1.24	1.24
Edgar Gonzalez	3.61	-3.02	1.38	-0.20	1.18	1.18
Leo Rosales	2.22	1.27	0.85	0.09	0.94	0.94
Doug Slaten	2.40	-0.25	0.92	-0.02	0.90	0.90

Player	BFP %	Runs Above Average	Average Value ($)	Value Above Average ($)	MRP (raw) ($)	MRP (adjusted) ($)
Jon Rauch	1.68	−2.86	0.64	−0.19	0.45	0.45
Brandon Medders	1.44	−1.87	0.55	−0.13	0.42	0.42
Jailen Peguero	0.62	1.33	0.24	0.09	0.33	0.33
Billy Buckner	0.96	−0.73	0.37	−0.05	0.32	0.32
Connor Robertson	0.52	−0.29	0.20	−0.02	0.18	0.18
Wilfredo Ledezma	0.28	0.39	0.11	0.03	0.13	0.13
Atlanta Braves						
Jair Jurrjens	13.02	19.01	4.97	1.74	6.70	6.79
Jorge Campillo	10.49	8.77	4.00	0.70	4.70	4.70
Will Ohman	3.97	8.84	1.52	0.70	2.22	4.44
Tim Hudson	9.18	9.69	3.50	0.78	4.28	4.40
Buddy Carlyle	4.15	5.30	1.58	0.40	1.98	3.97
Jeff Bennett	6.71	3.80	2.56	0.28	2.84	2.84
Jo-Jo Reyes	8.20	−13.98	3.13	−0.78	2.35	2.35
Blaine Boyer	5.01	2.12	1.91	0.15	2.07	2.07
Mike Hampton	5.30	−6.34	2.02	−0.40	1.62	1.62
Charlie Morton	5.53	−8.64	2.11	−0.53	1.58	1.58
John Smoltz	1.87	7.43	0.71	0.58	1.29	1.29
Vladimir Nunez	2.34	2.90	0.89	0.21	1.10	1.10
Julian Tavarez	2.59	0.89	0.99	0.06	1.05	1.05
Manny Acosta	3.62	−7.18	1.38	−0.45	0.93	0.93
Mike Gonzalez	2.27	0.55	0.87	0.04	0.91	0.91
Tom Glavine	4.50	−15.91	1.72	−0.85	0.86	0.86
Royce Ring	1.81	0.80	0.69	0.06	0.75	0.75
Jorge Julio	0.86	3.20	0.33	0.23	0.56	0.56
James Parr	1.63	−3.13	0.62	−0.21	0.41	0.41
Chris Resop	1.31	−1.54	0.50	−0.11	0.40	0.40
Rafael Soriano	0.91	0.28	0.35	0.02	0.37	0.37
Phil Stockman	0.45	1.52	0.17	0.11	0.28	0.28
Peter Moylan	0.40	0.30	0.15	0.02	0.17	0.17
Matt DeSalvo	0.29	0.30	0.11	0.02	0.13	0.13
Jeff Ridgway	0.61	−1.68	0.23	−0.11	0.12	0.12
Chuck James	2.34	−15.31	0.89	−0.83	0.06	0.06
Elmer Dessens	0.42	−2.14	0.16	−0.14	0.01	0.01
Francisley Bueno	0.21	−1.36	0.08	−0.09	−0.01	−0.01
Baltimore Orioles						
Jeremy Guthrie	12.41	1.58	4.73	0.11	4.85	5.12
Jim Johnson	4.38	9.05	1.67	0.72	2.39	4.79
Daniel Cabrera	12.80	−20.25	4.88	−1.00	3.88	3.88
Garrett Olson	9.68	−7.50	3.69	−0.47	3.23	3.23
Brian Burres	9.29	−7.39	3.55	−0.46	3.09	3.09
Chad Bradford	2.49	4.55	0.95	0.34	1.29	2.58
Lance Cormier	4.97	3.41	1.90	0.25	2.15	2.15
Dennis Sarfate	5.60	−5.85	2.14	−0.37	1.76	1.76
Radhames Liz	6.13	−18.26	2.34	−0.94	1.40	1.40
George Sherrill	3.73	−0.41	1.42	−0.03	1.39	1.39
Chris Waters	4.54	−6.60	1.73	−0.42	1.32	1.32
Matt Albers	3.24	−0.90	1.24	−0.06	1.18	1.18
Randor Bierd	2.78	0.50	1.06	0.03	1.09	1.09
Alberto Castillo	1.89	1.83	0.72	0.13	0.85	0.85
Brian Bass	1.33	1.23	0.51	0.09	0.59	0.59
Jamie Walker	2.78	−9.92	1.06	−0.59	0.47	0.47
Kameron Mickolio	0.56	1.72	0.21	0.12	0.34	0.34
Jim Miller	0.61	1.34	0.23	0.10	0.33	0.33
Steve Trachsel	3.02	−16.34	1.15	−0.87	0.28	0.28
Fernando Cabrera	2.06	−8.93	0.79	−0.54	0.24	0.24
Greg Aquino	0.84	−1.36	0.32	−0.09	0.23	0.23
Alfredo Simon	0.92	−2.44	0.35	−0.16	0.19	0.19
Rocky Cherry	1.33	−5.18	0.51	−0.33	0.17	0.17
Bob McCrory	0.58	−1.09	0.22	−0.08	0.15	0.15
Adam Loewen	1.59	−8.81	0.61	−0.53	0.07	0.07
Ryan Bukvich	0.47	−3.59	0.18	−0.24	−0.06	−0.06
Boston Red Sox						
Jonathan Papelbon	4.42	23.73	1.69	2.30	3.99	9.97
Josh Beckett	11.73	36.47	4.48	4.13	8.61	9.21
Jon Lester	14.14	29.37	5.40	3.06	8.45	8.95

Player	BFP %	Runs Above Average	Average Value ($)	Value Above Average ($)	MRP (raw) ($)	MRP (adjusted) ($)
Manny Delcarmen	4.97	12.24	1.90	1.02	2.92	7.29
Daisuke Matsuzaka	11.59	9.38	4.42	0.75	5.17	5.17
Tim Wakefield	12.20	−0.43	4.65	−0.03	4.62	4.65
Hideki Okajima	4.17	7.56	1.59	0.59	2.18	4.37
Justin Masterson	5.91	0.17	2.25	0.01	2.27	2.27
Clay Buchholz	5.78	−1.42	2.20	−0.10	2.11	2.11
Javier Lopez	4.00	2.59	1.52	0.19	1.71	1.71
David Aardsma	3.69	0.01	1.41	0.00	1.41	1.41
Bartolo Colon	2.80	3.11	1.07	0.23	1.30	1.30
Paul Byrd	3.37	0.03	1.28	0.00	1.29	1.29
Mike Timlin	3.67	−4.30	1.40	−0.28	1.12	1.12
Craig Hansen	2.36	−0.98	0.90	−0.07	0.83	0.83
David Pauley	1.08	0.64	0.41	0.05	0.46	0.46
Julian Tavarez	1.04	0.32	0.40	0.02	0.42	0.42
Devern Hansack	0.42	2.17	0.16	0.16	0.32	0.32
Michael Bowden	0.36	1.45	0.14	0.10	0.24	0.24
Charlie Zink	0.40	1.12	0.15	0.08	0.23	0.23
Bryan Corey	0.50	−0.46	0.19	−0.03	0.16	0.16
Chris Smith	1.26	−5.70	0.48	−0.36	0.12	0.12
Kyle Snyder	0.15	−1.90	0.06	−0.13	−0.07	−0.07
Chicago Cubs						
Kerry Wood	4.46	22.01	1.70	2.09	3.79	9.47
Ryan Dempster	13.82	32.35	5.27	3.49	8.76	9.13
Carlos Marmol	5.62	10.34	2.14	0.84	2.98	7.46
Ted Lilly	13.90	9.73	5.30	0.78	6.09	6.11
Carlos Zambrano	12.85	10.80	4.90	0.88	5.79	6.05
Jason Marquis	11.91	3.77	4.55	0.28	4.82	4.82
Bobby Howry	5.02	4.70	1.92	0.35	2.27	4.54
Rich Harden	4.59	12.67	1.75	1.06	2.81	2.81
Jeff Samardzija	2.00	5.29	0.76	0.40	1.16	2.33
Sean Marshall	4.50	3.74	1.72	0.28	1.99	1.99
Sean Gallagher	4.13	5.50	1.58	0.42	1.99	1.99
Michael Wuertz	3.05	1.27	1.16	0.09	1.25	1.25
Jon Lieber	3.29	−0.78	1.26	−0.05	1.20	1.20
Neal Cotts	2.58	1.72	0.99	0.12	1.11	1.11
Kevin Hart	2.29	1.10	0.87	0.08	0.95	0.95
Chad Gaudin	1.92	0.21	0.73	0.01	0.75	0.75
Scott Eyre	0.86	2.75	0.33	0.20	0.53	0.53
Angel Guzman	0.71	1.27	0.27	0.09	0.36	0.36
Rich Hill	1.44	−3.86	0.55	−0.25	0.29	0.29
Jose Ascanio	0.48	−1.24	0.18	−0.08	0.10	0.10
Randy Wells	0.23	−0.01	0.09	0.00	0.09	0.09
Carmen Pignatiello	0.11	−0.65	0.04	−0.04	0.00	0.00
Chad Fox	0.23	−2.11	0.09	−0.14	−0.06	−0.06
Chicago White Sox						
Javier Vazquez	14.31	26.23	5.46	2.63	8.09	8.49
Mark Buehrle	14.76	22.48	5.63	2.15	7.78	8.30
John Danks	12.93	29.48	4.93	3.07	8.01	8.01
Matt Thornton	4.31	15.78	1.64	1.38	3.02	7.56
Gavin Floyd	14.12	−0.86	5.39	−0.06	5.33	5.54
Bobby Jenks	3.91	9.00	1.49	0.72	2.21	4.42
Jose Contreras	8.39	8.34	3.20	0.66	3.86	3.89
D.J. Carrasco	2.54	5.52	0.97	0.42	1.39	2.78
Adam Russell	1.90	5.06	0.72	0.38	1.10	2.21
Octavio Dotel	4.63	4.07	1.77	0.30	2.07	2.07
Clayton Richard	3.46	4.14	1.32	0.31	1.63	1.63
Boone Logan	3.17	2.63	1.21	0.19	1.40	1.40
Nick Masset	3.26	1.58	1.25	0.11	1.36	1.36
Scott Linebrink	2.99	2.57	1.14	0.19	1.33	1.33
Ehren Wassermann	1.62	0.38	0.62	0.03	0.65	0.65
Mike MacDougal	1.25	0.91	0.48	0.06	0.54	0.54
Horacio Ramirez	1.16	0.22	0.44	0.02	0.46	0.46
Lance Broadway	1.06	−3.69	0.40	−0.24	0.16	0.16
Esteban Loaiza	0.21	−0.64	0.08	−0.04	0.04	0.04
Cincinnati Reds						
Edinson Volquez	13.19	23.49	5.03	2.27	7.31	7.31
Jeremy Affeldt	5.27	9.81	2.01	0.79	2.80	7.01

Player	BFP %	Runs Above Average	Average Value ($)	Value Above Average ($)	MRP (raw) ($)	MRP (adjusted) ($)
Bronson Arroyo	13.71	3.81	5.23	0.28	5.51	5.51
Aaron Harang	12.48	−2.84	4.76	−0.19	4.57	4.68
Francisco Cordero	4.83	5.76	1.84	0.44	2.28	4.56
Johnny Cueto	12.11	−2.80	4.62	−0.19	4.43	4.43
Jared Burton	4.05	5.06	1.54	0.38	1.92	3.85
Bill Bray	3.38	5.58	1.29	0.42	1.71	3.43
Dave Weathers	4.90	2.28	1.87	0.17	2.03	2.03
Mike Lincoln	4.68	1.04	1.78	0.07	1.86	1.86
Josh Fogg	5.70	−11.29	2.17	−0.66	1.52	1.52
Gary Majewski	3.02	−0.75	1.15	−0.05	1.10	1.10
Matt Belisle	2.24	1.37	0.85	0.10	0.95	0.95
Ramon Ramirez	1.65	0.10	0.63	0.01	0.64	0.64
Homer Bailey	2.83	−7.86	1.08	−0.48	0.60	0.60
Nick Masset	1.07	−1.14	0.41	−0.08	0.33	0.33
Todd Coffey	1.37	−3.01	0.52	−0.20	0.32	0.32
Danny Herrera	0.58	0.74	0.22	0.05	0.27	0.27
Kent Mercker	0.91	−1.29	0.35	−0.09	0.26	0.26
Josh Roenicke	0.28	1.37	0.11	0.10	0.21	0.21
Daryl Thompson	1.09	−3.39	0.41	−0.22	0.19	0.19
Adam Pettyjohn	0.41	−2.64	0.16	−0.18	−0.02	−0.02
Jon Adkins	0.24	−1.66	0.09	−0.11	−0.02	−0.02
Cleveland Indians						
Cliff Lee	14.45	50.42	5.51	6.67	12.18	14.22
Rafael Perez	5.08	11.86	1.94	0.98	2.92	7.30
C.C. Sabathia	8.23	16.63	3.14	1.47	4.61	5.39
Fausto Carmona	8.91	−8.90	3.40	−0.54	2.86	2.86
Paul Byrd	8.97	−10.59	3.42	−0.62	2.80	2.80
Jeremy Sowers	8.65	−9.39	3.30	−0.56	2.73	2.73
Aaron Laffey	6.64	−2.85	2.53	−0.19	2.34	2.34
Rafael Betancourt	5.01	−0.59	1.91	−0.04	1.87	1.87
Jensen Lewis	4.74	−0.61	1.81	−0.04	1.76	1.76
Masahide Kobayashi	3.96	−0.15	1.51	−0.01	1.50	1.50
Zach Jackson	3.86	−0.06	1.47	0.00	1.47	1.47
Edward Mujica	2.73	1.35	1.04	0.10	1.14	1.14
Anthony Reyes	2.30	0.87	0.88	0.06	0.94	0.94
Jake Westbrook	2.26	−0.54	0.86	−0.04	0.82	0.93
Juan Rincon	1.96	1.44	0.75	0.10	0.85	0.85
Scott Elarton	1.14	2.41	0.43	0.17	0.61	0.61
Matt Ginter	1.41	0.71	0.54	0.05	0.59	0.59
Scott Lewis	1.57	−1.44	0.60	−0.10	0.50	0.50
Jorge Julio	1.27	−3.53	0.48	−0.23	0.25	0.25
Bryan Bullington	0.97	−1.82	0.37	−0.12	0.25	0.25
Rich Rundles	0.36	1.00	0.14	0.07	0.21	0.21
Tom Mastny	1.62	−6.55	0.62	−0.41	0.21	0.21
Craig Breslow	0.65	−0.70	0.25	−0.05	0.20	0.20
Brendan Donnelly	1.12	−3.56	0.43	−0.24	0.19	0.19
Joe Borowski	1.33	−4.95	0.51	−0.32	0.19	0.19
Rick Bauer	0.49	−0.86	0.19	−0.06	0.13	0.13
Jonathan Meloan	0.10	0.27	0.04	0.02	0.06	0.06
Brian Slocum	0.24	−2.44	0.09	−0.16	−0.07	−0.07
Colorado Rockies						
Aaron Cook	13.98	28.87	5.33	2.99	8.32	9.08
Brian Fuentes	4.04	18.13	1.54	1.64	3.18	7.94
Ubaldo Jimenez	13.70	21.12	5.22	1.98	7.21	7.21
Manuel Corpas	5.46	9.16	2.08	0.73	2.81	7.04
Jason Grilli	4.17	11.71	1.59	0.97	2.56	6.40
Taylor Buchholz	4.15	11.40	1.58	0.94	2.52	6.31
Matt Herges	4.64	7.81	1.77	0.61	2.38	4.76
Jorge de la Rosa	9.01	11.52	3.44	0.95	4.39	4.39
Jeff Francis	10.03	1.63	3.83	0.12	3.94	3.94
Ryan Speier	3.42	6.44	1.31	0.50	1.80	3.60
Glendon Rusch	4.34	6.50	1.66	0.50	2.15	2.15
Mark Redman	3.33	−2.00	1.27	−0.14	1.13	1.13
Luis Vizcaino	3.20	−1.71	1.22	−0.12	1.11	1.11
Greg Reynolds	4.64	−12.46	1.77	−0.71	1.06	1.06
Livan Hernandez	2.90	−4.17	1.11	−0.27	0.83	0.83
Kip Wells	1.99	−1.79	0.76	−0.12	0.64	0.64

Player	BFP %	Runs Above Average	Average Value ($)	Value Above Average ($)	MRP (raw) ($)	MRP (adjusted) ($)
Franklin Morales	1.89	−2.65	0.72	−0.18	0.54	0.54
Alberto Arias	0.88	0.82	0.34	0.06	0.40	0.40
Micah Bowie	0.60	0.30	0.23	0.02	0.25	0.25
Jose Capellan	0.14	0.98	0.05	0.07	0.12	0.12
Jason Hirsh	0.73	−2.54	0.28	−0.17	0.11	0.11
Valerio de los Santos	0.63	−2.42	0.24	−0.16	0.08	0.08
Josh Newman	0.77	−3.38	0.29	−0.22	0.07	0.07
Juan Morillo	0.06	0.23	0.02	0.02	0.04	0.04
Cedrick Bowers	0.52	−2.50	0.20	−0.17	0.03	0.03
Steven Register	0.77	−4.42	0.29	−0.29	0.01	0.01
Detroit Tigers						
Justin Verlander	13.73	11.73	5.24	0.97	6.21	6.30
Aquilino Lopez	5.37	7.10	2.05	0.55	2.60	5.20
Bobby Seay	3.84	7.61	1.46	0.59	2.06	4.12
Nate Robertson	11.87	−7.54	4.53	−0.47	4.06	4.06
Armando Galarraga	11.64	−6.56	4.44	−0.41	4.03	4.03
Kenny Rogers	12.20	−11.20	4.65	−0.65	4.00	4.00
Zach Miner	7.94	1.79	3.03	0.13	3.16	3.16
Jeremy Bonderman	4.98	−5.71	1.90	−0.36	1.53	1.53
Freddy Dolsi	3.40	−0.95	1.30	−0.07	1.23	1.23
Fernando Rodney	2.93	1.33	1.12	0.10	1.21	1.21
Casey Fossum	2.79	0.43	1.07	0.03	1.10	1.10
Todd Jones	3.01	−3.86	1.15	−0.25	0.89	0.89
Eddie Bonine	1.82	0.94	0.70	0.07	0.76	0.76
Clay Rapada	1.47	1.24	0.56	0.09	0.65	0.65
Chris Lambert	1.59	0.57	0.61	0.04	0.65	0.65
Gary Glover	1.34	−0.27	0.51	−0.02	0.49	0.49
Kyle Farnsworth	1.19	−0.58	0.45	−0.04	0.41	0.41
Jason Grilli	0.92	0.27	0.35	0.02	0.37	0.37
Joel Zumaya	1.78	−4.95	0.68	−0.32	0.36	0.36
Denny Bautista	1.29	−2.14	0.49	−0.14	0.35	0.35
Freddy Garcia	0.95	−1.78	0.36	−0.12	0.24	0.24
Francis Beltran	0.87	−2.77	0.33	−0.19	0.15	0.15
Francisco Cruceta	0.87	−2.80	0.33	−0.19	0.15	0.15
Yorman Bazardo	0.31	−0.84	0.12	−0.06	0.06	0.06
Dontrelle Willis	1.90	−13.92	0.73	−0.77	−0.05	−0.05
Florida Marlins						
Ricky Nolasco	13.84	23.41	5.28	2.26	7.54	7.84
Scott Olsen	13.63	−13.99	5.20	−0.78	4.42	4.50
Kevin Gregg	4.72	5.02	1.80	0.38	2.18	4.36
Matt Lindstrom	3.91	7.86	1.49	0.62	2.11	4.21
Joe Nelson	3.67	7.00	1.40	0.54	1.94	3.88
Andrew Miller	7.85	6.13	2.99	0.47	3.46	3.46
Mark Hendrickson	9.41	−2.97	3.59	−0.20	3.39	3.39
Josh Johnson	5.82	12.32	2.22	1.03	3.25	3.37
Chris Volstad	5.82	7.62	2.22	0.60	2.82	2.82
Doug Waechter	4.39	3.00	1.67	0.22	1.89	1.89
Justin Miller	3.22	3.94	1.23	0.29	1.52	1.52
Anibal Sanchez	3.84	−1.03	1.47	−0.07	1.40	1.40
Logan Kensing	4.05	−2.35	1.55	−0.16	1.39	1.39
Arthur Rhodes	0.86	4.75	0.33	0.36	0.68	1.37
Renyel Pinto	4.53	−7.13	1.73	−0.44	1.28	1.28
Burke Badenhop	3.48	−2.78	1.33	−0.19	1.14	1.14
Rick VandenHurk	1.18	1.84	0.45	0.13	0.58	0.58
Ryan Tucker	2.84	−9.39	1.08	−0.56	0.52	0.52
Taylor Tankersley	1.34	−6.60	0.51	−0.42	0.10	0.10
Lee Gardner	0.61	−2.50	0.23	−0.17	0.06	0.06
Jesus Delgado	0.16	−1.12	0.06	−0.08	−0.02	−0.02
Eulogio De La Cruz	0.85	−5.54	0.32	−0.35	−0.03	−0.03
Houston Astros						
Roy Oswalt	14.07	21.23	5.37	2.00	7.36	7.95
Wandy Rodriguez	9.58	15.46	3.66	1.35	5.00	5.00
Jose Valverde	4.95	7.12	1.89	0.55	2.44	4.88
Doug Brocail	4.67	5.78	1.78	0.44	2.22	4.44
Chris Sampson	7.80	13.61	2.98	1.16	4.13	4.13
Brian Moehler	10.61	−0.39	4.05	−0.03	4.02	4.02

Player	BFP %	Runs Above Average	Average Value ($)	Value Above Average ($)	MRP (raw) ($)	MRP (adjusted) ($)
Brandon Backe	12.34	−34.41	4.71	−1.28	3.43	3.43
Randy Wolf	4.91	4.67	1.87	0.35	2.22	2.22
LaTroy Hawkins	1.29	7.89	0.49	0.62	1.11	2.22
Geoff Geary	4.28	4.11	1.63	0.31	1.94	1.94
Shawn Chacon	6.11	−18.20	2.33	−0.94	1.39	1.39
Wesley Wright	4.08	−5.45	1.56	−0.35	1.21	1.21
Tim Byrdak	3.87	−9.41	1.48	−0.57	0.91	0.91
Jack Cassel	2.16	−2.83	0.82	−0.19	0.63	0.63
Dave Borkowski	2.82	−8.48	1.08	−0.52	0.56	0.56
Fernando Nieve	0.80	1.09	0.31	0.08	0.38	0.38
Runelvys Hernandez	1.60	−4.28	0.61	−0.28	0.33	0.33
Alberto Arias	0.64	0.68	0.24	0.05	0.29	0.29
Oscar Villarreal	2.74	−16.51	1.05	−0.88	0.17	0.17
Chad Paronto	0.67	−1.47	0.26	−0.10	0.15	0.15
Kansas City Royals						
Zack Greinke	13.69	25.12	5.22	2.48	7.71	8.10
Gil Meche	14.26	20.82	5.44	1.95	7.39	7.61
Ramon Ramirez	4.75	12.85	1.81	1.08	2.89	7.23
Joakim Soria	4.18	11.63	1.60	0.96	2.56	6.40
Brian Bannister	13.05	−9.78	4.98	−0.58	4.39	4.39
Luke Hochevar	9.11	1.63	3.47	0.12	3.59	3.59
Leo Nunez	3.30	5.65	1.26	0.43	1.69	3.38
Kyle Davies	7.84	2.88	2.99	0.21	3.20	3.20
Horacio Ramirez	1.54	5.59	0.59	0.42	1.01	2.03
Ron Mahay	4.47	0.88	1.71	0.06	1.77	1.77
Brett Tomko	4.36	−1.34	1.66	−0.09	1.57	1.57
Robinson Tejeda	2.53	3.16	0.96	0.23	1.20	1.20
Brandon Duckworth	2.69	−0.11	1.03	−0.01	1.02	1.02
John Bale	1.77	4.31	0.68	0.32	1.00	1.00
Yasuhiko Yabuta	2.70	−4.38	1.03	−0.29	0.75	0.75
Joel Peralta	3.60	−11.59	1.38	−0.67	0.70	0.70
Jimmy Gobble	2.56	−5.98	0.98	−0.38	0.60	0.60
Jeff Fulchino	1.16	−0.98	0.44	−0.07	0.37	0.37
Carlos Rosa	0.19	1.40	0.07	0.10	0.17	0.17
Kip Wells	0.80	−2.88	0.31	−0.19	0.11	0.11
Tony Pena	0.05	0.42	0.02	0.03	0.05	0.05
Josh Newman	0.56	−2.70	0.21	−0.18	0.03	0.03
Devon Lowery	0.34	−1.83	0.13	−0.12	0.00	0.00
Neal Musser	0.05	−0.40	0.02	−0.03	−0.01	−0.01
Hideo Nomo	0.43	−5.11	0.17	−0.33	−0.16	−0.16
Los Angeles Angels of Anaheim						
Ervin Santana	14.56	39.00	5.55	4.55	10.10	11.35
Darren Oliver	4.72	10.82	1.80	0.88	2.69	6.72
Francisco Rodriguez	4.67	9.88	1.78	0.80	2.58	6.45
Jered Weaver	12.09	16.02	4.61	1.41	6.02	6.02
Jose Arredondo	3.96	10.13	1.51	0.82	2.33	5.83
Joe Saunders	13.10	5.61	5.00	0.43	5.42	5.75
Jon Garland	14.02	−1.32	5.35	−0.09	5.26	5.38
John Lackey	10.96	4.32	4.18	0.32	4.50	5.03
Scot Shields	4.38	4.99	1.67	0.38	2.05	4.09
Darren O'Day	3.15	6.83	1.20	0.53	1.73	3.46
Dustin Moseley	3.85	1.22	1.47	0.09	1.55	1.55
Justin Speier	4.95	−9.09	1.89	−0.55	1.34	1.34
Shane Loux	1.07	1.80	0.41	0.13	0.54	0.54
Chris Bootcheck	1.46	−1.51	0.56	−0.10	0.45	0.45
Jason Bulger	1.18	−0.89	0.45	−0.06	0.39	0.39
Kevin Jepsen	0.58	1.53	0.22	0.11	0.33	0.33
Nick Adenhart	1.02	−2.76	0.39	−0.18	0.21	0.21
Rich Thompson	0.19	−0.20	0.07	−0.01	0.06	0.06
Alex Serrano	0.06	0.47	0.02	0.03	0.06	0.06
Los Angeles Dodgers						
Derek Lowe	13.89	31.89	5.30	3.42	8.72	9.01
Jonathan Broxton	4.65	19.02	1.77	1.74	3.51	8.78
Chad Billingsley	14.02	26.60	5.35	2.68	8.02	8.02
Hiroki Kuroda	12.67	23.19	4.83	2.24	7.07	7.07

Player	BFP %	Runs Above Average	Average Value ($)	Value Above Average ($)	MRP (raw) ($)	MRP (adjusted) ($)
Takashi Saito	3.22	15.15	1.23	1.31	2.54	6.35
Cory Wade	4.49	6.63	1.71	0.51	2.22	4.45
Hong-Chih Kuo	5.27	23.08	2.01	2.22	4.23	4.23
Joe Beimel	3.49	7.23	1.33	0.56	1.89	3.79
Ramon Troncoso	2.61	7.87	1.00	0.62	1.61	3.23
Clayton Kershaw	7.67	1.16	2.93	0.08	3.01	3.01
Chan Ho Park	6.72	0.09	2.57	0.01	2.57	2.57
Brad Penny	6.95	−12.09	2.65	−0.69	1.96	1.96
Greg Maddux	2.71	2.10	1.03	0.15	1.18	1.18
Eric Stults	2.73	−1.59	1.04	−0.11	0.93	0.93
Scott Proctor	3.00	−4.55	1.15	−0.30	0.85	0.85
Esteban Loaiza	1.68	−0.57	0.64	−0.04	0.60	0.60
Jason Johnson	2.12	−3.83	0.81	−0.25	0.56	0.56
Brian Falkenborg	0.80	−0.94	0.31	−0.06	0.24	0.24
James McDonald	0.39	1.17	0.15	0.08	0.23	0.23
Yhency Brazoban	0.26	−0.13	0.10	−0.01	0.09	0.09
Tanyon Sturtze	0.15	0.14	0.06	0.01	0.07	0.07
Scott Elbert	0.51	−2.12	0.19	−0.14	0.05	0.05
Milwaukee Brewers						
C.C. Sabathia	8.31	35.46	3.17	3.97	7.14	8.35
Ben Sheets	13.08	26.89	4.99	2.71	7.70	8.18
Manny Parra	11.93	2.73	4.55	0.20	4.75	4.75
David Bush	12.29	−9.83	4.69	−0.59	4.10	4.10
Jeff Suppan	12.56	−26.57	4.79	−1.17	3.63	3.63
Carlos Villanueva	7.47	0.04	2.85	0.00	2.85	2.85
Seth McClung	7.34	−2.42	2.80	−0.16	2.64	2.64
Salomon Torres	5.54	1.77	2.11	0.13	2.24	2.24
Brian Shouse	3.41	2.87	1.30	0.21	1.51	1.51
Guillermo Mota	3.93	−2.40	1.50	−0.16	1.34	1.34
David Riske	3.11	−7.66	1.19	−0.47	0.71	0.71
Mitch Stetter	1.76	−0.52	0.67	−0.04	0.63	0.63
Yovani Gallardo	1.56	0.49	0.60	0.03	0.63	0.63
Eric Gagne	3.27	−11.13	1.25	−0.65	0.60	0.60
Mark DiFelice	1.26	0.09	0.48	0.01	0.49	0.49
Julian Tavarez	0.66	1.88	0.25	0.13	0.39	0.39
Todd Coffey	0.47	2.18	0.18	0.16	0.34	0.34
Tim Dillard	1.05	−2.26	0.40	−0.15	0.25	0.25
Zach Jackson	0.29	0.03	0.11	0.00	0.11	0.11
Derrick Turnbow	0.71	−5.58	0.27	−0.36	−0.09	−0.09
Minnesota Twins						
Joe Nathan	4.20	13.56	1.60	1.15	2.75	6.88
Scott Baker	11.30	13.02	4.31	1.10	5.41	5.54
Nick Blackburn	13.23	3.15	5.05	0.23	5.28	5.28
Kevin Slowey	10.50	12.64	4.00	1.06	5.06	5.06
Livan Hernandez	10.08	−3.21	3.85	−0.21	3.63	3.63
Boof Bonser	8.55	3.26	3.26	0.24	3.50	3.50
Glen Perkins	10.63	−14.21	4.05	−0.79	3.27	3.27
Craig Breslow	2.40	7.81	0.91	0.61	1.53	3.05
Francisco Liriano	5.29	3.35	2.02	0.25	2.26	2.26
Jesse Crain	4.31	2.16	1.64	0.16	1.80	1.80
Matt Guerrier	5.53	−9.76	2.11	−0.58	1.53	1.53
Dennys Reyes	3.02	4.01	1.15	0.30	1.45	1.45
Brian Bass	4.87	−8.62	1.86	−0.52	1.33	1.33
Jose Mijares	0.55	3.01	0.21	0.22	0.43	0.43
Juan Rincon	2.14	−6.15	0.82	−0.39	0.43	0.43
Pat Neshek	0.90	0.97	0.34	0.07	0.41	0.41
Bobby Korecky	1.19	−2.92	0.45	−0.19	0.26	0.26
Eddie Guardado	0.53	0.05	0.20	0.00	0.21	0.21
Philip Humber	0.80	−5.85	0.31	−0.37	−0.07	−0.07
New York Mets						
Johan Santana	15.21	27.30	5.80	2.77	8.57	9.68
Mike Pelfrey	13.43	14.70	5.12	1.27	6.39	6.67
Billy Wagner	2.90	10.30	1.11	0.84	1.94	4.86
Oliver Perez	13.36	−10.34	5.10	−0.61	4.49	4.49
John Maine	9.59	−2.56	3.66	−0.17	3.49	3.49
Pedro Martinez	7.78	−9.59	2.97	−0.57	2.39	2.39

Player	BFP %	Runs Above Average	Average Value ($)	Value Above Average ($)	MRP (raw) ($)	MRP (adjusted) ($)
Aaron Heilman	5.62	−4.11	2.14	−0.27	1.87	1.87
Joe Smith	4.28	2.88	1.63	0.21	1.84	1.84
Duaner Sanchez	4.01	1.05	1.53	0.07	1.60	1.60
Pedro Feliciano	3.74	−1.58	1.43	−0.11	1.32	1.32
Nelson Figueroa	3.33	0.23	1.27	0.02	1.29	1.29
Scott Schoeneweis	3.83	−3.79	1.46	−0.25	1.21	1.21
Claudio Vargas	2.37	−0.27	0.90	−0.02	0.88	0.88
Brian Stokes	2.18	0.69	0.83	0.05	0.88	0.88
Luis Ayala	1.23	1.32	0.47	0.09	0.56	0.56
Carlos Muniz	1.58	−1.55	0.60	−0.11	0.50	0.50
Brandon Knight	0.90	1.51	0.34	0.11	0.45	0.45
Jorge Sosa	1.69	−4.47	0.64	−0.29	0.35	0.35
Jonathon Niese	1.09	−1.56	0.42	−0.11	0.31	0.31
Tony Armas	0.58	−0.54	0.22	−0.04	0.19	0.19
Bobby Parnell	0.30	0.60	0.11	0.04	0.16	0.16
Matt Wise	0.54	−1.80	0.20	−0.12	0.08	0.08
Ricardo Rincon	0.25	−0.67	0.10	−0.05	0.05	0.05
Eddie Kunz	0.22	−1.29	0.08	−0.09	0.00	0.00
New York Yankees						
Mariano Rivera	4.19	23.70	1.60	2.30	3.90	9.75
Mike Mussina	13.26	37.06	5.06	4.23	9.29	9.29
Andy Pettitte	14.27	25.92	5.44	2.59	8.03	8.26
Joba Chamberlain	6.75	22.88	2.58	2.20	4.77	4.77
Chien-Ming Wang	6.51	9.49	2.48	0.76	3.25	3.42
Darrell Rasner	8.31	−0.05	3.17	0.00	3.17	3.17
Sidney Ponson	5.83	−8.14	2.22	−0.50	1.72	1.72
Edwar Ramirez	3.77	3.82	1.44	0.28	1.72	1.72
Jose Veras	4.10	2.15	1.56	0.15	1.72	1.72
Dan Giese	3.01	4.72	1.15	0.35	1.50	1.50
Phil Coke	0.84	5.28	0.32	0.40	0.72	1.44
LaTroy Hawkins	2.80	0.83	1.07	0.06	1.13	1.13
Brian Bruney	2.22	3.69	0.85	0.27	1.12	1.12
Philip Hughes	2.54	1.08	0.97	0.08	1.05	1.05
David Robertson	2.12	3.03	0.81	0.22	1.03	1.03
Ross Ohlendorf	3.03	−2.83	1.16	−0.19	0.97	0.97
Ian Kennedy	3.14	−5.29	1.20	−0.34	0.86	0.86
Carl Pavano	2.49	−1.72	0.95	−0.12	0.83	0.83
Damaso Marte	1.30	3.29	0.49	0.24	0.74	0.74
Kyle Farnsworth	3.00	−6.68	1.14	−0.42	0.72	0.72
Alfredo Aceves	1.94	−1.62	0.74	−0.11	0.63	0.63
Jonathan Albaladejo	0.94	1.48	0.36	0.11	0.46	0.46
Chris Britton	1.70	−4.00	0.65	−0.26	0.39	0.39
Billy Traber	1.30	−1.73	0.49	−0.12	0.38	0.38
Kei Igawa	0.39	1.28	0.15	0.09	0.24	0.24
Scott Patterson	0.11	−0.21	0.04	−0.01	0.03	0.03
Humberto Sanchez	0.13	−0.41	0.05	−0.03	0.02	0.02
Oakland Athletics						
Joey Devine	2.78	13.00	1.06	1.10	2.16	5.39
Dana Eveland	12.06	4.86	4.60	0.37	4.97	4.97
Justin Duchscherer	9.11	13.52	3.48	1.15	4.62	4.94
Huston Street	4.70	6.30	1.79	0.48	2.27	4.55
Greg Smith	13.09	−19.82	4.99	−0.99	4.00	4.00
Joe Blanton	9.00	1.58	3.43	0.11	3.55	3.55
Rich Harden	5.09	13.30	1.94	1.13	3.07	3.07
Jerry Blevins	2.55	6.00	0.97	0.46	1.43	2.86
Chad Gaudin	4.30	4.13	1.64	0.31	1.95	1.95
Dallas Braden	4.92	−3.23	1.88	−0.21	1.66	1.66
Brad Ziegler	3.75	2.80	1.43	0.20	1.63	1.63
Santiago Casilla	3.75	2.21	1.43	0.16	1.59	1.59
Alan Embree	4.42	−3.27	1.69	−0.22	1.47	1.47
Sean Gallagher	4.35	−6.07	1.66	−0.39	1.27	1.27
Josh Outman	1.90	4.38	0.72	0.33	1.05	1.05
Kirk Saarloos	1.93	3.11	0.74	0.23	0.96	0.96
Andrew Brown	2.41	−2.96	0.92	−0.20	0.72	0.72
Lenny DiNardo	1.87	−4.26	0.71	−0.28	0.43	0.43
Dan Meyer	2.16	−7.16	0.82	−0.45	0.38	0.38
Keith Foulke	2.18	−7.48	0.83	−0.46	0.37	0.37

Player	BFP %	Runs Above Average	Average Value ($)	Value Above Average ($)	MRP (raw) ($)	MRP (adjusted) ($)
Gio Gonzalez	2.67	−13.72	1.02	−0.77	0.25	0.25
Kiko Calero	0.33	1.14	0.12	0.08	0.21	0.21
Jeff Gray	0.39	−0.11	0.15	−0.01	0.14	0.14
Fernando Hernandez	0.31	−1.50	0.12	−0.10	0.02	0.02
Philadelphia Phillies						
Cole Hamels	14.67	23.38	5.60	2.26	7.86	8.87
Brad Lidge	4.69	16.55	1.79	1.46	3.25	8.13
Ryan Madson	5.46	12.68	2.08	1.06	3.15	7.87
Jamie Moyer	13.50	9.19	5.15	0.73	5.89	5.89
Chad Durbin	5.86	8.09	2.24	0.64	2.87	5.74
Brett Myers	13.12	1.64	5.00	0.12	5.12	5.39
Clay Condrey	4.86	4.49	1.86	0.34	2.19	4.38
Kyle Kendrick	11.59	−13.35	4.42	−0.75	3.67	3.67
Adam Eaton	7.67	−8.83	2.93	−0.54	2.39	2.39
Joe Blanton	4.90	−4.72	1.87	−0.31	1.56	1.56
J.C. Romero	4.09	−2.18	1.56	−0.15	1.41	1.41
Scott Eyre	0.85	4.11	0.32	0.31	0.63	1.26
Rudy Seanez	3.03	0.75	1.16	0.05	1.21	1.21
J.A. Happ	2.22	1.37	0.85	0.10	0.94	0.94
Tom Gordon	2.23	−0.21	0.85	−0.01	0.84	0.84
Les Walrond	0.79	0.75	0.30	0.05	0.35	0.35
Andrew Carpenter	0.08	−0.03	0.03	0.00	0.03	0.03
R.J. Swindle	0.39	−2.09	0.15	−0.14	0.01	0.01
Pittsburgh Pirates						
Paul Maholm	13.07	7.52	4.99	0.59	5.57	6.12
Zach Duke	12.70	5.15	4.84	0.39	5.23	5.23
Matt Capps	3.23	9.08	1.23	0.72	1.96	4.89
Ian Snell	11.73	−6.82	4.48	−0.43	4.05	4.05
Damaso Marte	2.94	5.87	1.12	0.45	1.57	3.14
Tyler Yates	5.07	−0.23	1.93	−0.02	1.92	1.92
Phil Dumatrait	5.38	−4.24	2.05	−0.28	1.77	1.77
John Grabow	4.93	−3.66	1.88	−0.24	1.64	1.64
Tom Gorzelanny	7.51	−30.22	2.86	−1.23	1.63	1.63
Franquelis Osoria	4.23	−1.81	1.61	−0.12	1.49	1.49
Jeff Karstens	3.37	−2.15	1.29	−0.14	1.14	1.14
Sean Burnett	3.88	−7.13	1.48	−0.44	1.03	1.03
T.J. Beam	3.05	−5.05	1.16	−0.33	0.84	0.84
Jason Davis	2.34	−1.86	0.89	−0.13	0.77	0.77
Denny Bautista	2.88	−5.74	1.10	−0.37	0.73	0.73
Yoslan Herrera	1.53	0.82	0.58	−0.06	0.53	0.53
Ross Ohlendorf	1.73	−2.71	0.66	−0.18	0.48	0.48
Jesse Chavez	1.13	−0.56	0.43	−0.04	0.39	0.39
Romulo Sanchez	0.87	0.24	0.33	0.02	0.35	0.35
Matt Morris	1.81	−5.68	0.69	−0.36	0.33	0.33
Ty Taubenheim	0.41	0.68	0.16	0.05	0.21	0.21
John Van Benschoten	1.91	−10.99	0.73	−0.64	0.09	0.09
Marino Salas	1.35	−7.64	0.51	−0.47	0.04	0.04
Craig Hansen	1.19	−6.96	0.46	−0.44	0.02	0.02
Jimmy Barthmaier	0.81	−5.19	0.31	−0.33	−0.02	−0.02
Evan Meek	0.93	−6.72	0.36	−0.42	−0.07	−0.07
San Diego Padres						
Jake Peavy	11.28	8.82	4.30	0.70	5.00	5.34
Heath Bell	5.15	7.20	1.97	0.56	2.53	5.05
Mike Adams	4.12	7.23	1.57	0.56	2.13	4.27
Greg Maddux	10.15	3.27	3.87	0.24	4.11	4.11
Cha Seung Baek	7.56	0.71	2.88	0.05	2.93	2.93
Randy Wolf	8.30	−3.58	3.17	−0.24	2.93	2.93
Chris Young	6.90	−9.47	2.63	−0.57	2.07	2.07
Cla Meredith	4.80	0.46	1.83	0.03	1.87	1.87
Josh Banks	5.92	−14.76	2.26	−0.81	1.45	1.45
Trevor Hoffman	2.86	0.14	1.09	0.01	1.10	1.10
Wilfredo Ledezma	3.96	−6.71	1.51	−0.42	1.09	1.09
Justin Hampson	2.00	2.62	0.76	0.19	0.96	0.96
Clay Hensley	2.75	−4.67	1.05	−0.30	0.75	0.75
Josh Geer	1.86	0.11	0.71	0.01	0.72	0.72
Shawn Estes	3.15	−8.87	1.20	−0.54	0.66	0.66

Player	BFP %	Runs Above Average	Average Value ($)	Value Above Average ($)	MRP (raw) ($)	MRP (adjusted) ($)
Bryan Corey	2.66	−6.70	1.01	−0.42	0.59	0.59
Justin Germano	3.09	−10.27	1.18	−0.61	0.57	0.57
Joe Thatcher	2.04	−5.43	0.78	−0.35	0.43	0.43
Dirk Hayhurst	1.34	−2.47	0.51	−0.17	0.34	0.34
Glendon Rusch	1.46	−3.35	0.56	−0.22	0.34	0.34
Chad Reineke	1.24	−2.37	0.47	−0.16	0.31	0.31
Brett Tomko	0.57	0.99	0.22	0.07	0.29	0.29
Kevin Cameron	0.73	−0.39	0.28	−0.03	0.25	0.25
Jared Wells	0.22	0.54	0.09	0.04	0.12	0.12
Carlos Guevara	0.95	−3.72	0.36	−0.25	0.12	0.12
Sean Henn	0.75	−2.95	0.29	−0.20	0.09	0.09
Brian Falkenborg	0.84	−3.67	0.32	−0.24	0.08	0.08
Enrique Gonzalez	0.24	−0.34	0.09	−0.02	0.07	0.07
Scott Patterson	0.24	−0.42	0.09	−0.03	0.06	0.06
Michael Ekstrom	0.75	−4.47	0.29	−0.29	−0.01	−0.01
Charlie Haeger	0.45	−4.59	0.17	−0.30	−0.13	−0.13
Wade LeBlanc	1.65	−14.24	0.63	−0.79	−0.16	−0.16
San Francisco Giants						
Tim Lincecum	14.63	52.48	5.58	7.09	12.68	13.96
Matt Cain	14.71	16.63	5.61	1.47	7.09	7.53
Jonathan Sanchez	10.96	13.38	4.18	1.13	5.31	5.31
Keiichi Yabu	4.76	6.06	1.82	0.46	2.28	4.56
Barry Zito	12.90	−6.82	4.92	−0.43	4.49	4.49
Brian Wilson	4.32	5.00	1.65	0.38	2.02	4.05
Kevin Correia	8.11	−5.48	3.09	−0.35	2.74	2.74
Sergio Romo	2.05	5.99	0.78	0.46	1.24	2.48
Tyler Walker	3.56	1.72	1.36	0.12	1.48	1.48
Jack Taschner	3.58	0.91	1.37	0.06	1.43	1.43
Patrick Misch	3.63	−4.03	1.38	−0.26	1.12	1.12
Billy Sadler	3.11	−3.13	1.19	−0.21	0.98	0.98
Alex Hinshaw	2.82	−2.30	1.08	−0.15	0.92	0.92
Brad Hennessey	3.09	−5.23	1.18	−0.34	0.84	0.84
Vinnie Chulk	2.19	−2.56	0.84	−0.17	0.66	0.66
Osiris Matos	1.55	−0.44	0.59	−0.03	0.56	0.56
Merkin Valdez	1.09	1.55	0.42	0.11	0.53	0.53
Erick Threets	0.79	−2.25	0.30	−0.15	0.15	0.15
Matt Palmer	1.06	−4.22	0.40	−0.28	0.13	0.13
Geno Espineli	1.09	−6.63	0.42	−0.42	0.00	0.00
Seattle Mariners						
Felix Hernandez	13.46	13.60	5.13	1.16	6.29	6.75
Sean Green	5.62	8.28	2.14	0.65	2.80	5.60
Carlos Silva	10.82	−0.47	4.13	−0.03	4.10	4.10
Jarrod Washburn	10.60	−4.83	4.04	−0.31	3.73	3.73
Ryan Rowland-Smith	7.95	−4.32	3.03	−0.28	2.75	2.75
R.A. Dickey	7.85	−14.66	3.00	−0.81	2.19	2.19
Roy Corcoran	4.96	3.61	1.89	0.27	2.16	2.16
Miguel Batista	8.73	−30.50	3.33	−1.23	2.10	2.10
Erik Bedard	5.45	−0.37	2.08	−0.03	2.05	2.05
Mark Lowe	4.76	−0.18	1.82	−0.01	1.80	1.80
J.J. Putz	3.31	2.39	1.26	0.17	1.44	1.44
Brandon Morrow	4.16	−3.56	1.59	−0.23	1.35	1.35
Cesar Jimenez	2.21	2.95	0.84	0.22	1.06	1.06
Arthur Rhodes	1.44	3.97	0.55	0.29	0.85	0.85
Ryan Feierabend	2.87	−4.06	1.10	−0.27	0.83	0.83
Randy Messenger	0.90	0.09	0.34	0.01	0.35	0.35
Cha Seung Baek	1.99	−7.39	0.76	−0.46	0.30	0.30
Justin Thomas	0.35	0.47	0.13	0.03	0.16	0.16
Eric O'Flaherty	0.66	−2.56	0.25	−0.17	0.08	0.08
Jamie Burke	0.06	0.19	0.02	0.01	0.04	0.04
Jake Woods	1.37	−8.08	0.52	−0.50	0.02	0.02
Jared Wells	0.47	−4.52	0.18	−0.29	−0.11	−0.11
St. Louis Cardinals						
Kyle Lohse	13.39	15.77	5.11	1.38	6.49	6.55
Braden Looper	13.44	3.47	5.13	0.26	5.38	5.41
Todd Wellemeyer	12.88	−1.01	4.91	−0.07	4.85	4.85
Kyle McClellan	5.22	5.61	1.99	0.43	2.42	4.84

Player	BFP %	Runs Above Average	Average Value ($)	Value Above Average ($)	MRP (raw) ($)	MRP (adjusted) ($)
Adam Wainwright	8.68	12.04	3.31	1.00	4.31	4.71
Joel Pineiro	10.30	−2.90	3.93	−0.19	3.73	3.73
Russ Springer	3.27	5.32	1.25	0.40	1.65	3.30
Ryan Franklin	5.52	−2.81	2.11	−0.19	1.92	1.92
Brad Thompson	4.36	3.12	1.66	0.23	1.89	1.89
Ron Villone	3.66	−2.77	1.39	−0.19	1.21	1.21
Jason Motte	0.64	4.53	0.24	0.34	0.58	1.16
Jason Isringhausen	3.19	−1.21	1.22	−0.08	1.14	1.14
Chris Perez	2.83	−0.81	1.08	−0.06	1.02	1.02
Chris Carpenter	1.01	2.78	0.38	0.20	0.59	0.59
Mike Parisi	1.93	−2.24	0.74	−0.15	0.59	0.59
Randy Flores	2.09	−3.48	0.80	−0.23	0.57	0.57
Mitchell Boggs	2.62	−9.03	1.00	−0.55	0.45	0.45
Anthony Reyes	0.97	0.65	0.37	0.05	0.42	0.42
Josh Kinney	0.40	2.80	0.15	0.20	0.36	0.36
Kelvin Jimenez	1.82	−8.18	0.69	−0.50	0.19	0.19
Mark Mulder	0.19	0.01	0.07	0.00	0.07	0.07
Mark Worrell	0.43	−1.51	0.16	−0.10	0.06	0.06
Jaime Garcia	1.10	−5.64	0.42	−0.36	0.06	0.06
Aaron Miles	0.05	0.15	0.02	0.01	0.03	0.03
Tampa Bay Rays						
James Shields	14.27	25.45	5.44	2.52	7.97	8.60
Andy Sonnanstine	13.33	19.72	5.08	1.82	6.90	6.95
Grant Balfour	3.65	14.82	1.39	1.28	2.67	6.68
J.P. Howell	6.02	11.74	2.30	0.97	3.27	6.54
Matt Garza	12.56	9.37	4.79	0.75	5.54	5.68
Edwin Jackson	12.89	−11.58	4.92	−0.67	4.25	4.25
Scott Kazmir	10.43	−0.56	3.98	−0.04	3.94	3.94
Trever Miller	3.04	6.86	1.16	0.53	1.69	3.38
Jason Hammel	5.63	−8.25	2.15	−0.51	1.64	1.64
Dan Wheeler	4.30	−1.32	1.64	−0.09	1.55	1.55
Gary Glover	2.60	−0.88	0.99	−0.06	0.93	0.93
Al Reyes	1.56	1.09	0.60	0.08	0.67	0.67
Troy Percival	3.16	−10.05	1.20	−0.60	0.61	0.61
David Price	0.93	2.23	0.35	0.16	0.52	0.52
Chad Bradford	1.32	−0.81	0.50	−0.06	0.45	0.45
Scott Dohmann	1.07	−0.65	0.41	−0.04	0.36	0.36
Jeff Niemann	1.24	−1.84	0.47	−0.13	0.35	0.35
Kurt Birkins	0.60	1.00	0.23	0.07	0.30	0.30
Juan Salas	0.44	1.29	0.17	0.09	0.26	0.26
Jae Kuk Ryu	0.08	−0.03	0.03	0.00	0.03	0.03
Mitch Talbot	0.88	−7.03	0.34	−0.44	−0.10	−0.10
Texas Rangers						
Kevin Millwood	11.79	15.47	4.50	1.35	5.85	5.85
Jamey Wright	5.83	7.73	2.22	0.61	2.83	5.66
Frank Francisco	4.06	9.04	1.55	0.72	2.27	4.54
Vicente Padilla	11.64	−5.52	4.44	−0.35	4.09	4.09
Scott Feldman	10.01	−12.83	3.82	−0.73	3.09	3.09
Josh Rupe	6.03	−3.79	2.30	−0.25	2.05	2.05
Sidney Ponson	3.87	5.81	1.48	0.44	1.92	1.92
Luis Mendoza	4.86	0.49	1.85	0.03	1.89	1.89
Matt Harrison	5.72	−5.98	2.18	−0.38	1.80	1.80
Dustin Nippert	5.24	−4.35	2.00	−0.28	1.72	1.72
Eddie Guardado	2.98	3.08	1.14	0.23	1.36	1.36
Kason Gabbard	4.04	−6.84	1.54	−0.43	1.11	1.11
Kameron Loe	2.06	2.78	0.79	0.20	0.99	0.99
C.J. Wilson	3.29	−5.85	1.26	−0.37	0.88	0.88
Warner Madrigal	2.37	−0.43	0.90	−0.03	0.87	0.87
Joaquin Benoit	3.21	−6.63	1.23	−0.42	0.81	0.81
Franklyn German	1.43	1.60	0.55	0.11	0.66	0.66
Wes Littleton	1.23	1.73	0.47	0.12	0.59	0.59
Brandon McCarthy	1.43	−1.75	0.55	−0.12	0.43	0.43
Doug Mathis	1.72	−4.16	0.66	−0.27	0.38	0.38
Eric Hurley	1.64	−3.98	0.63	−0.26	0.37	0.37
A.J. Murray	0.58	1.58	0.22	0.11	0.34	0.34
Tommy Hunter	0.95	−2.53	0.36	−0.17	0.19	0.19
Brian Gordon	0.25	1.06	0.09	0.08	0.17	0.17

Player	BFP %	Runs Above Average	Average Value ($)	Value Above Average ($)	MRP (raw) ($)	MRP (adjusted) ($)
Jason Jennings	2.08	−12.23	0.79	−0.70	0.09	0.09
Jose Diaz	0.09	0.27	0.04	0.02	0.05	0.05
Robinson Tejeda	0.45	−1.74	0.17	−0.12	0.05	0.05
Elizardo Ramirez	0.29	−1.41	0.11	−0.10	0.01	0.01
Kazuo Fukumori	0.40	−3.68	0.15	−0.24	−0.09	−0.09
Bill White	0.46	−5.55	0.18	−0.36	−0.18	−0.18
Toronto Blue Jays						
Roy Halladay	16.27	51.74	6.21	6.94	13.15	15.39
A.J. Burnett	15.77	27.66	6.02	2.82	8.84	9.29
Scott Downs	4.78	9.16	1.82	0.73	2.56	6.39
Jesse Litsch	12.11	5.97	4.62	0.46	5.08	5.14
Shaun Marcum	10.38	−1.00	3.96	−0.07	3.89	3.93
B.J. Ryan	4.10	4.99	1.57	0.38	1.94	3.88
Brian Tallet	3.96	5.04	1.51	0.38	1.89	3.78
Dustin McGowan	7.81	9.04	2.98	0.72	3.70	3.70
Jesse Carlson	3.91	4.11	1.49	0.31	1.80	3.59
Shawn Camp	2.74	6.91	1.04	0.53	1.58	3.16
David Purcey	4.76	−2.47	1.82	−0.17	1.65	1.65
Scott Richmond	1.86	6.50	0.71	0.50	1.21	1.21
Jason Frasor	3.43	−3.85	1.31	−0.25	1.05	1.05
Brandon League	2.32	1.09	0.89	0.08	0.96	0.96
John Parrish	2.95	−2.87	1.13	−0.19	0.93	0.93
Brian Wolfe	1.42	1.12	0.54	0.08	0.62	0.62
Jeremy Accardo	0.92	0.08	0.35	0.01	0.36	0.36
Randy Wells	0.07	−0.39	0.03	−0.03	0.00	0.00
Armando Benitez	0.43	−2.72	0.16	−0.18	−0.02	−0.02
Washington Nationals						
Saul Rivera	5.88	11.39	2.24	0.94	3.18	7.96
Joel Hanrahan	5.77	4.42	2.20	0.33	2.53	5.06
Odalis Perez	11.27	0.07	4.30	0.01	4.30	4.30
John Lannan	12.35	−7.97	4.71	−0.49	4.22	4.22
Tim Redding	12.54	−9.38	4.78	−0.56	4.22	4.22
Jon Rauch	3.04	8.93	1.16	0.71	1.87	3.74
Jay Bergmann	9.73	−11.36	3.71	−0.66	3.05	3.05
Shawn Hill	4.69	4.17	1.79	0.31	2.10	2.10
Collin Balester	5.67	−4.21	2.16	−0.28	1.89	1.89
Jesus Colome	4.94	−1.35	1.89	−0.09	1.79	1.79
Luis Ayala	4.07	0.30	1.55	0.02	1.58	1.58
Steven Shell	3.15	1.39	1.20	0.10	1.30	1.30
Garrett Mock	2.85	1.71	1.09	0.12	1.21	1.21
Matt Chico	3.47	−6.81	1.32	−0.43	0.90	0.90
Mike Hinckley	0.78	3.16	0.30	0.23	0.53	0.53
Charlie Manning	3.00	−11.16	1.14	−0.65	0.49	0.49
Shairon Martis	1.46	−4.29	0.56	−0.28	0.28	0.28
Brian Sanches	0.86	−0.75	0.33	−0.05	0.28	0.28
Chad Cordero	0.35	0.76	0.13	0.05	0.19	0.19
Marco Estrada	1.00	−3.61	0.38	−0.24	0.14	0.14
Tyler Clippard	0.76	−2.66	0.29	−0.18	0.11	0.11
Levale Speigner	0.67	−2.56	0.25	−0.17	0.08	0.08
Ray King	0.52	−1.92	0.20	−0.13	0.07	0.07
Chris Schroder	0.43	−4.47	0.16	−0.29	−0.13	−0.13
Mike O'Connor	0.76	−7.54	0.29	−0.47	−0.18	−0.18

Endnotes

1. Rickey (1955, p. 250).

2. Mark Bradley (2002), "Estrada the Result of Bad Economics." In: *Atlanta Journal-Constitution*, December, 21.

3. Hendricks (1994, pp. 190–220) describes the strategy used in Drabek's arbitration hearing in explicit detail. It is an enlightening introduction to the way arbitration hearings work.

4. Associated Press, "Arroyo Agrees to Three-Year, $12 M Deal," *ESPN.com*, January 19, 2006 (http://sports.espn.go.com/mlb/news/story?id=2298402).

5. A common belief in baseball is that good players can "protect" each other in the lineup, which induces pitchers to throw more easy-to-hit pitcher. My research with Doug Drinen indicates that this is not the case. See Bradbury and Drinen (2008) and Chapter 2 of *The Baseball Economist*.

6. For further discussion see my essay "Statistical Analysis in Sport," (Bradbury 2009).

7. "Chat with Joe Morgan," *ESPN.com*, July 7, 2009 (http://espn.go.com/sportsnation/chat/_/id/27305/hall-of-famer-joe-morgan).

8. The correlation between winning and run differential is 0.93.

9. See Albert and Bennett (2003, pp. 178–189) for an explanation of regression-estimated runs, which they refer to as least squares linear regression (LSLR). The ordinary least squares regression estimate for 2003–2007: Runs = (0.62 × hits) + (0.14 × doubles) + (0.93 × triples) + (0.89 × home runs) + (0.3 × walks) + (0.43 × hit-by-pitch) − 557.72. Because the impacts are not statistically significant and of

J.C. Bradbury, *Hot Stove Economics*, DOI 10.1007/978-1-4419-6269-0,
© Springer Science+Business Media, LLC 2011

counterintuitive signs, I exclude stolen base attempts in trying to achieve the best fit with runs scored.

10. Linear weights = (0.47 × hits) + (0.38 × doubles) + (0.55 × triples) + (0.93 × home runs) + (0.33 × walks) + (0.33 × hit-by-pitch) + (0.22 × stolen bases) – (0.38 × caught stealing) – [0.29 × (at-bats – hits)] (Palmer and Gillette 2005).

11. "Best fit" means that the prediction minimizes the variance of the prediction error. The differences between the predictions and the observations are squared, because squaring errors has the benefit of preventing positive and negative errors from canceling out and punishing bigger errors more than smaller errors. For example, the equation for the best-fit line for batting average is runs scored = –690 + (5476 × AVG).

12. In some cases, even persistent performance in an area may not indicate true talent. For example, an average player who consistently bats after three hitters with excellent on-base percentages may have above-average RBI totals for many years. We know that his high RBI totals are not likely due to RBI skill, but instead the product of the situation that he is put in that allows him to benefit from his teammates excellent performance. Were he to move to another slot in the lineup or to an inferior team, we would expect his RBI numbers to drop.

13. The correlation coefficient has a hypothetical range from –1 to 1, where 0 equals no correlation, 1 equals a perfect positive correlation, and –1 equals a perfect negative correlation.

14. For further analysis of how BABIP pollutes ERA see Bradbury (2008) and Chapter 12 of *The Baseball Economist*.

15. Pitchers do appear to have some impact on the hitting power allowed on balls hit into play. However, the control over this factor is so small that this effect is meaningless for practical purposes. For further discussion see "Extra Base Hits on Balls in Play and Pitcher Skill," *Sabernomics.com,* June 23, 2008 (http://www.sabernomics.com/sabernomics/index.php/2008/06/extra-base-hits-on-balls-in-play-and-pitcher-skill/).

16. For example, range factor is biased by fielding opportunities, and zone rating doesn't properly reward players for making plays outside of their

assigned zones—see "Thoughts on Zone Rating," July, 19, 2004, *Sabernomics.com* (http://www.sabernomics.com/sabernomics/index.php/2004/07/thoughts-on-zone-rating/).

17. Dewan (2009, p. 83).

18. Albert and Bennett (2003, p. 108).

19. Data acquired from Retrosheet with the assistance of Doug Drinen and covers the 1989 through 1992 seasons. Hits and on-base are estimated using probit regression estimation. Total bases are estimated using negative binomial regression. Full results are available at *Sabernomics.com*, "A Little Clutch Hitting Study," October 12, 2009 (http://www.sabernomics.com/sabernomics/index.php/2009/10/a-little-clutch-hitting-study/) and "Does Clutch Pitching Exist?" October 12, 2009 (http://www.sabernomics.com/sabernomics/index.php/2009/10/does-clutch-pitching-exist/). The data were obtained free of charge from and is copyrighted by Retrosheet. Interested parties may contact Retrosheet at "www.retrosheet.org".

20. Bill Ladson, "Notes: Nationals Sign Gonzalez: Sixteen-Year-Old Shortstop Thought to Have Bright Future in DC," *MLB.com*, July 2, 2006 (http://washington.nationals.mlb.com/news/article.jsp?ymd=20060702 &content_id=1534629).

21. Month of birth data in baseball from Baseball-Databank.org (http://baseball-databank.org). General population data from National Center for Health Statistics Vital Stats averaged from 1990, 1995, 2000, and 2005 (http://www.cdc.gov/nchs/datawh/vitalstats/VitalStatsbirths.htm).

22. In the mid-1950s, Little League Baseball and other youth baseball organizations agreed to standardize the age-determination date at July 31. Thus, by 1970 nearly every American major-league player would have faced the cutoff rule in their youth.

23. See Ericsson et al. (1993) for a discussion of the role of practice on performance.

24. The correlation between the percentage of All-Star and entire-league birth-month percentages is 0.36, which is not statistically significant (p value $= 0.26$).

25. See http://www.socialproblemindex.ualberta.ca/relage.htm for a survey of relative-age effects across sports. Chapter 1 of Malcom Gladwell's *Outliers*, provides a summary of relative-age effects in several areas.

26. Texas A&M motor development expert Carl Gabbard (2004) provides an excellent summary of the medical evidence on when humans reach peak physiological output.

27. Mark Zuckerman, "Thoughts from Riggleman," *The Washington* Times, September 9, 2009 (http://washingtontimes.com/weblogs/chatter/2009/sep/09/thoughts-from-riggleman/).

28. See Schulz and Curnow (1988), and Schulz et al. (1994).

29. The detailed results of my study are available in Bradbury (2009).

30. Five thousand is the career cutoff used by Albert (2002). Schell (2005) identifies the average age at which long-time players reach 5,000 plate appearances is 30.

31. The park factors are from Baseball-Databank.org (http://baseball-databank.org).

32. The following equation was estimated using the Baltagi and Wu (1999) random effects method, which corrects for detected first-order serial correlation. Performance $= (W_1 \times \text{Age}) + (W_2 \times \text{Age}^2) + (W_3 \times \text{Career}$ performance$) + (V \times \text{League-season indicators})$. The model also includes player-specific and random error terms. W's represent coefficient weights, and V is a vector of coefficient weights. Indicator (or "dummy") variables are equal to one in the year and league of observation, and zero otherwise.

33. The formula for the maximum or minimum of a quadratic function is $- W_1/(2 \times W_2)$. A potential problem with the quadratic function is that it imposes a symmetric improvement and decline in performance. I estimated several alternate specifications with higher-order polynomials that were not statistically significant. Rudimentary fractional polynomial model estimates—adjustments for serial correlation and random effects

estimation were not feasible—which do not impose symmetry yielded peak age estimates similar to the quadratic estimates.

34. Schulz and Curnow (1988, p. 118).

35. Baker et al. (2007) find some evidence of compensation among professional golfers; though the compensation is not sufficient to explain completely the low rate of decline in performance in golf.

36. Interpreting linear weights is difficult because its reference point for average is zero, and thus is probably best ignored for our purposes.

37. "Nationals' Pride Takes Another Hit," *ESPN.com*, February 18, 2009 (http://sports.espn.go.com/espn/blog/index?entryID=3916915&name=law_keith).

38. James (1982, p. 191).

39. James (2003, p. 338).

40. For examples of both methods see Keith Woolner, "Peak Ages for Hitters," *StatHead.com*, April 16, 1997 (http://www.stathead.com/bbeng/woolner/peakage.htm).

41. James (1982, p. 205).

42. Sommers and Quinton (1982) noted "the first family of free agents received salaries commensurate with their ability to 'put fannies in the seats.'" Scully (1989) reported free agent wages were well below players' estimated marginal revenue products during the collusion years of the 1980s.

43. Krautmann (1999) used multiple regression analysis to compare free-agent player performance and salaries. In his paper, Krautmann looked only at position players, but the concept could easily applied to pitchers. Krautmann used the slugging average and total bases—in separate estimates—to proxy player quality, and included dummy variables for catchers and shortstops. I do not approve of his exact specification choice, but I think the methodology underpinning his estimation strategy is satisfactory.

44. As the difference between the number of observations and the included explanatory variables shrinks—known as "degrees of freedom"—the likelihood that a few odd contracts can bias the estimates increases.

45. Scully's model also included explanatory variables to control for league and proximity to being in the playoff hunt.

46. In 2008, the report's coauthor Kurt Badenhausen explained the method that *Forbes* uses to generate its estimates. "We contact every team as well as investment bankers, consultants and other baseball people. The level of cooperation varies significantly amongst teams. Some teams won't confirm the name of their stadium, while others will provide us with their revenue and operating income . . .. We contact all of the teams each year and ask for certain pieces of information. This year we heard back from all 30 teams and all but two cooperated to some degree." Maury Brown, *The Biz of Baseball*, "Interview—Kurt Badenhausen—Senior Editor Forbes", May 4, 2008 (http://www.bizofbaseball.com/index.php?option=com_content&task=view&id=2151&Itemid=81).

47. Best fit estimated using fractional polynomial regression of run differential on total revenue. Revenue estimates converted to dollars in terms of what teams would be earning in 2007.

48. Current reported national television, radio, and online broadcast rights approach $28 million per team. Associated Press, "Fox, TBS have seven-year, $3 billion TV deal with MLB," *ESPN.com*, July 11, 2006. (http://sports.espn.go.com/mlb/news/story?id=2516552) and Eric Fisher, *Sports Business Journal*, "Special Report: MLB Season Preview," April 03, 2006 (http://www.sportsbusinessjournal.com/article/50067). Jeff Passan reported central revenue shares per team to be $33 million per team in 2006. "Bargaining Power," *Yahoo!Sports*, October 25, 2006 (http://sports.yahoo.com/mlb/news?slug=jp-newcba102506&prov=yhoo&type=lgns).

49. Monte Burke and Mike Ozanian at *Forbes* provided this figure to me.

50. A "honeymoon effect" indicator variable records whether or not a team is playing in a stadium no more than eight years old.

51. Estimates are park-adjustment with park factors from Baseball-Databank.org (http://baseball-databank.org) using the method detailed in Palmer and Gillette (2005, p. 1711).

52. Bradbury (2007a) finds evidence that DIPS performance is correlated with batting average on balls in play.

53. Bradbury (2007a) compares the R^2 values of models that include and exclude performance on balls in play. When fielders are included the $R^2 = 0.76$, with fielders excluded the $R^2 = 0.56$ (0.56/0.76 = 73 percent).

54. Estimates based on data published by *The Hardball Times* (http://www.hardballtimes.com/thtstats/main/index.php?view=fielding& linesToDisplay=1000&orderBy=balls_in_zone&direction=DESC& qual_filter=ignore&season_filter[]=2007&league_filter[]=All& pos_filter[]=All&Submit=Submit). Catchers and pitchers are excluded from fielding because they field a small percentage of balls and are normally valued for their other contributions to preventing runs.

55. Approximately 6.1 percent of all plate appearances result in a stolen base attempt; therefore, I estimated that average play at catcher is worth $2.93 million a season (0.061 × $48 million). Catchers then were awarded a percentage of $2.93 million according to their playing time—for example, a catcher who catches 75 percent of his team's batters faced would be worth $2.2 million (0.75 × $2.93 million). As catchers prevented steals above/below the break-even value for stolen bases, they received additional credit for preventing runs. The Thorn and Palmer (1984) "Basestealing Runs" denominate stolen base attempts in runs according to the formula: (0.22 × stolen bases) – (0.38 × caught stealing). These additional runs were converted into dollars using the estimates in Equation 4.1.

56. The exact formula is: runs allowed = (3463.1 × Walks per batters faced) + (10470.0 × Home runs allowed per batters faced) – (1618.6 × Strikeouts per batters faced) + 449.4. The team estimate includes a control variable for league (add 22.4 for playing in the AL), but is removed for player estimates because it is the league, not the player that is responsible for the additional runs. The R^2 of the estimate is 0.62. I conducted several estimations using differing specifications, which produced similar results. Park factors acquired from Baseball-Databank.org (http://baseball-databank.org). The league average runs allowed during this period was 771 runs per team.

57. Lindsey (1961, p. 717).

58. Win probability added (WPA) is a popular metric used to measure the win probability impact associated with all players, not just pitchers. It looks at

the team's win probability before and after events, and credits the player for the change in win probability.

59. This includes pitchers who average more than four outs per appearance.

60. "Introduction to VORP: Value Over Replacement Player," *StatHead.com* (http://www.stathead.com/bbeng/woolner/vorpdescnew.htm).

61. Minimum 100 plate appearances for batters, minimum 100 batters faced for pitchers. Lower cutoffs yielded similar results.

62. Rottenberg (1956, p. 253) states: "while each player has a monopoly to his own services, he is not truly unique, and there are more or less good substitutes for him. His salary is, therefore, partially determined by the difference between the value productivities and costs of other players by whom he may be replaced."

63. Baseball's talent pool obviously extends beyond America, which expands the baseball-age population, so this estimate is conservative.

64. For an explanation of a popular wins-to-dollars conversion method see David Cameron, "Win Values Explained: Part Six," *Fangraphs,* January 2, 2009 (http://www.fangraphs.com/blogs/index.php/win-values-explained-part-six).

65. Identifying when a free agency begins is complicated; therefore, I use players with at least seven years beyond their debuts to proxy free agency. Some players who have been in the league for six seasons are not yet free agents, while most players with seven years experience are free agents. The sample includes players with more than two percent of his team's plate appearances (to provide a large-enough sample to proxy performance) and who played for only one team during the season (to fully capture the non-linear impact of performance on revenue).

66. As measured by R^2. The regression-estimated equations are as follows: Hitters: Salary = (0.98 × MRP) + 1.16; Pitchers: Salary = (0.91 × MRP) + 2.00. The samples include 565 hitter and 449 pitcher observations. Equations estimated using ordinary least squares, and all estimates are statistically significant at the one-percent level.

67. Zimablist (1992) and Krautmann (2000) criticized Scully-based estimates for their low correlations with salaries; however, the analysis here

indicates the low correlations are a product of the inherent instability of performance, not a poor fit of the estimates to salaries.

68. The median difference is preferred to the mean difference, because the mean is more affected by exceptionally high salaries, which will be exacerbated by winning teams (who generate higher returns from improved performance) being especially active in the top-end of the free-agent market.

69. The low salaries of fourth-year players likely is influenced by the fact that many players in their fourth year in the majors (the proxy I use for service time) lack four years of service time.

70. The difference for hitters is similar to my estimate in *The Baseball Economist*, which used a different and less-inclusive estimation method. However, my previous estimates for pitchers indicated they earned 19 percent less than their marginal revenue products. I believe much of this difference results from crediting fielders for defense. However, it is curious that this does not result in hitters earning a greater share of their marginal revenue products; therefore, I believe that some of the difference is still explained by more precise estimates of marginal revenue products in the models presented in this book.

71. The list does not include players who did not play baseball in a given season, because outside insurance typically covers a large portion of these salaries.

72. The sample included 146 position players who were on the free-agent market and ultimately signed major-league contracts and played in the following season. Because outfielders frequently play multiple outfield positions, all outfielders were treated as competing for three slots of the same position. The model is estimated using ordinary least squares. More complicated models that included non-linear transformations of the number of free agents by position and other controls (including age) yielded similar results. The basic results are reported for parsimony. The fit of the model: $R^2 = 0.44$.

73. The loss trap extends from the peak of the bump (−170 runs) until the returns to winning become positive (−41 runs). The runs-to-wins conversion is based on the "Pythagorean" method developed by Bill James.

The conversion is consistent with Thorn and Palmer's rule of thumb that every ten runs approximate one win.

74. Only five teams in the ten-year sample had run differentials below this level: 2002 Detroit Tigers (–289 runs), 2002 Tampa Bay Devil Rays (–245 runs), 2003 Detroit Tigers (–337 runs), 2004 Arizona Diamondbacks (–284 runs), and 2005 Kansas City Royals (–234 runs).

75. Dollar values are expressed in 2007 terms, so that performance value is equivalent across the decade.

76. Example from Mlodinow (2008, pp. 70–71).

77. Albert and Bennett (2003, p. 378).

78. *The Report of the Independent Members of the Commissioner's Blue Ribbon Panel on Baseball Economics*, p. 5.

79. The Noll-Scully measure is the ratio between the standard deviation in winning percentage in the league and the hypothetical ideal standard deviation in the league. See Quirk and Fort (1997) for further explanation of the metric.

80. Rickey (1965, p. 200).

81. Salary data from Baseball-Databank.org (http://baseball-databank.org). Performance value in current dollars is based on annual discounting of player values of nine percent per year from 2007. For players who played for more than one team in a season, the compensation is apportioned to each team based on a percentage of total playing time. Players with salaries not reported are assigned the league minimum salary for that season.

82. You could argue that the Blue Jays were a better team than some of the clubs who made the playoffs, because they averaged more wins than the Brewers, Padres, Rays, and Rockies.

83. "An Interview with Farhan Zaidi of the Oakland A's," *Sabernomics.com*, May 25, 2005 (http://www.sabernomics.com/sabernomics/index.php/2005/05/an-interview-with-farhan-zaidi/).

84. Valuing Sabathia's performance in 2008 is complicated because he was traded by the Cleveland Indians to the Milwaukee Brewers halfway through the season. The values in Appendix D are determined according to

the runs saved above average for each team. Thus, his value for the Indians is determined by the 16.63 runs above average he prevented for the team. For the Brewers, he is valued according to the 35.46 runs above average for the Brewers. In total, Sabathia saved 52.09 runs above average, which is the number that should be used to measure his value as a player. A mid-season trade sends a player's starting point back to average; thus, additional runs added to his new team are not valued the same as if he remained on a single same team for the entire season. This means summing the estimated value of the performances for each team understates the potential value that Sabathia would generate over the course of a season. Estimating Sabathia's worth for the entire 2008 season requires summing the runs saved above average for both teams before applying the run-value weights to estimate his marginal revenue product. Simply summing the 2008 dollar estimates of his separate production Cleveland and Milwaukee generate an estimated worth of $12.61 million; however, the marginal revenue product of Sabathia's performance for a single team would be worth $14.27 million—a difference of $1.66 million.

85. Sabathia does have the option to exit his contract after the 2011 season.

86. Another estimate by David Pinto pegged the growth rate to be nearly twelve percent. "Money Can Buy Hope for All Baseball Fans" *Sporting News*, November 11, 2007 (http://www.sportingnews.com/mlb/article/2007-11-28/money-can-buy-hope-all-baseball-fans).

87. Ken Belson, "Apples for a Nickel, and Plenty of Empty Seats," *The New York Times*, January 6, 2009 (http://www.nytimes.com/2009/01/07/sports/baseball/07depression.html).

88. The future value of a dollar amount $= \text{Principle} \times (1 + g)^n$, where g is the annual growth rate and n is the number of years compounded. In this example, the revenue-growth conversion is calculated by multiplying each value times $1.09^{(\text{year}-2007)}$.

89. In addition, the Red Sox would pay the $3 million buyout of an optional fifth-year that would pay Renteria $11 million, if the Braves did not exercise the option. "Red Sox Deal Renteria to Braves for Marte" *ESPN.com*, 12/08/2005 (http://sports.espn.go.com/mlb/news/story?id=2252297).

90. "2005 Top 100 Prospects: 1–25," *Baseball America*, March 3, 2005 (http://www.baseballamerica.com/today/features/040228top1004.html).

91. The criterion for identifying when to include a performance metric in the prediction model was if it was statistically significant at better than the ten-percent level for any minor-league level.

92. Runs scored = $(2865 \times \text{OBP}) + (1740 \times \text{SLG}) + (20 \times \text{AL}) - 934$. Adj. $R^2 =$ 0.92. All estimates are significant at the five-percent level. To estimate runs above average the predicted runs scored are subtracted from the average runs scored over the sample, 771 runs. Converting the team estimates to player estimates requires projecting playing time, as better players ought to play more than worse players. The estimated runs above average were multiplied times the percent of his team's plate appearances that he is expected to take. Predicted plate appearances for five-season peak = (Predicted OPS $\times$ 2178) + 410. The estimate is then divided by the average number of team plate appearances over five seasons (31,325), which generates a percentage of team plate appearances the player will be expected to take.

93. Defensive playing time is estimated to be 7.77 percent for every one-percent of a team's plate appearance. This value is multiplied times $1.86 million (in 2007 dollars), which is the value expected from the average defender at any position who played all his team's innings.

94. I do not use the expected value of his marginal revenue product because he is producing the full value of his projection if he plays. His projected marginal revenue products for his anticipated arbitration years (2009, 2010, and 2011) are $6.57, $7.35, and $8.7 million, respectively.

95. I was unable to conduct a similar analysis for pitchers because the necessary minor league data were not available to me.

96. The minimum salary is subject to a cost-of-living increase in 2011; therefore, beyond 2010, I add a three-percent cost-of-living adjustment to the league minimum salary. Arbitration-eligible salaries are determined according to league-average in this service-class, adjusted for league revenue growth.

97. Rottenberg (1956, pp. 253–254).

98. Kerrane (1989, p. 227).

99. Helyar (1994, pp. 171–197) reports Miller's thoughts on optimal service-time requirements for free agency.

100. Reported in Lewis (2003) as a quote from "a newsletter he wrote for eighteen months in the mid-1980s."

101. "Breaking Down the 1990–1997 Drafts," *Baseball America*, 2006 (http://www.baseballamerica.com/today/draft/90–97draftbreakdown.html).

102. Burger and Walters (2009).

103. Helyar (1994, p. 529).

104. Vince Gennaro (2007) used a model that values wins differently across markets using time-series data for each team; however, I am worried that going far enough back in time to generate a sufficient sample size picks up outdated information on factors that affect revenue in the present. In addition, the specifics of the model are not presented for analysis.

105. Burger and Walter (2003) used interaction terms to find some impact of wins impacting large markets more than small markets. One specification included population times wins and population times wins above a minimum threshold. The model did not include population, wins, and population times wins; thus, it is unclear what the interaction term picked up. I estimated the non-linearity of wins in a different manner—as a continuous function.

106. Isolated power was excluded for High-A because the relationship was not statistically significant and was negative when it was included in the model; a counterintuitive result—hitting power should not be negatively correlated with major-league success—that was likely the result of multicollinearity.

References

Albert, Jim (2002), "Smoothing Career Trajectories of Baseball Hitters." Unpublished manuscript, Bowling Green University.

Albert, Jim and Bennett, Jay (2003), *Curve Ball: Baseball, Statistics, and the Role of Chance in the Game*. New York, NY: Copernicus.

Baker, Joseph, Deakin, Janice, Horton, Sean, and Pearce, G. William (2007), "Maintenance of Skilled Performance with Age: A Descriptive Examination of Professional Golfers." In: *Journal of Aging and Physical Activity*, 15, pp. 300–317.

Baltagi, Badi H. and Wu, Ping X. (1999), "Unequally Spaced Panel Regressions with AR(1) Disturbances." In: *Econometric Theory*, 15, pp. 814–823.

Berri, David J., Schmidt, Martin B., and Brook, Stacey L. (2006), *The Wages of Wins*. Stanford: Stanford University Press.

Bradbury, John C. (2007a), "Does the Baseball Labor Market Properly Value Pitchers?" In: *Journal of Sports Economics*, 8, pp. 616–632.

Bradbury, John C. (2007b), *The Baseball Economist: The Real Game Exposed*. New York, NY: Dutton.

Bradbury, John C. (2008), "Statistical Performance Analysis in Sport." In: *The Business of Sports* (edited by Brad R. Humphreys and Dennis R. Howard), 3, pp. 41–56. Westport, CT: Praeger.

Bradbury, John C. (2009), "Peak Athletic Performance and Ageing: Evidence from Baseball." In: *Journal of Sports Sciences*, 27, pp. 599–610.

Bradbury, John C. and Drinen, Douglas J. (2008), "Pigou at the Plate: Externalities in Major League Baseball." In: *Journal of Sports Economics*, 9, pp. 211–224.

Burger, John D. and Walters, Stephen K. (2003), "Market Size, Pay, and Performance: A General Model and Application to Major League Baseball." In: *Journal of Sports Economics*, 4, 2, pp. 108–125.

Burger, John D. and Walters, Stephen K. (2009), "Uncertain Prospects: Rates of Return in the Baseball Draft." In: *Journal of Sports Economics*, 10, pp. 485–501.

Dewan, John (2009), *The Fielding Bible: Volume II*. Skokie, IL: ACTA Sports.

Ericsson, K. Anders, Krampe, Ralf, and Tesch-Romer, Clemens (1993), "The Role of Deliberate Practice in the Acquisition of Expert Performance." In: *Psychological Review*, 100, pp. 363–406.

Fair, Ray C. (2008), "Estimated Age Effects in Baseball." In: *Journal of Quantitative Analysis in Sports*, 4, http://www.bepress.com/jqas/vol4/iss1/1. Accessed October 15, 2009.

Gabbard, Carl (2004), *Lifetime Motor Development*. San Francisco, CA: Benjamin Cummings.

Gennaro, Vince (2007), *Diamond Dollars: The Economics of Winning in Baseball.* Hingham, MA: Maple Street Press.

Gladwell, Malcolm (2008), *Outliers: The Story of Success.* New York, NY: Little, Brown and Company.

Hakes, Jahn and Clapp, Christopher (2005), "How Long a Honeymoon? The Effect of New Stadiums on Attendance in Major League Baseball." In: *Journal of Sports Economics*, 6, pp. 237–263.

Hakes, Jahn and Sauer, Raymond (2006), "An Economic Evaluation of the Moneyball Hypothesis." In: *The Journal of Economic Perspectives*, 20, pp. 173–186.

Helyar, John (1994), *The Lords of the Realm: The Real History of Baseball.* New York, NY: Villard.

Hendricks, Randal (1994), *Inside the Strike Zone.* Austin, TX: Eakin Press.

James, Bill (1982), *The Bill James Baseball Abstract.* New York, NY: Ballantine Books.

James, Bill (2001), *The New Bill James Historical Abstract.* New York, NY: Free Press.

Kerrane, Kevin (1989), *Dollar Sign on the Muscle.* New York, NY: Fireside.

Krautmann, Anthony C. (1999), "What's Wrong with Scully-Estimates of a Player's Marginal Revenue Product." In: *Economic Inquiry*, 37, pp. 369–381.

Krautmann, Anthony C., Hadley, Lawrence, and Gustafson, Elizabeth (2000), "Who Pays for Minor League Training Costs?" *Contemporary Economic Policy*, 18, pp. 37–47.

Lewis, Michael (2003), *Moneyball: The Art of Winning an Unfair Game.* New York, NY: W. W. Norton & Company.

Lindsey, George R. (1961), "The Progress of the Score During a Baseball Game." In: *Journal of the American Statistical Association*, 56, pp. 703–728.

Miller, Marvin (1991), *A Whole Different Ball Game: The Sport and Business of Baseball.* New York, NY: Birch Lane Press.

McCracken, Voros (2001), "Pitching and Defense: How Much Control Do Hurlers Have?" In: *Baseball Prospectus*, January, 23. http://www.baseballprospectus.com/article.php?articleid=878. Accessed October 15, 2009.

Mlodinow, Leonard (2008), *The Drunkard's Walk: How Randomness Rules Our Lives.* New York, NY: Pantheon Books.

Palmer, Pete and Gillette, Gary (2005), *The 2005 ESPN Baseball Encyclopedia.* New York, NY: Sterling.

Poitras, Marc and Hadley, Lawrence (2006), "Do New Major League Ballparks Pay for Themselves?" In: *The Journal of Business*, 79, pp. 2275–2299.

Quirk, James and Fort, Rodney (1997), *Pay Dirt: The Business of Professional Team Sports.* Princeton, NJ: Princeton University Press.

Rickey, Branch (1955), "What is Amateur Sport?" In: *Journal of Educational Sociology*, 28, pp. 249–253.

Rickey, Branch and Riger, Robert (1965), *The American Diamond.* New York, NY: Simon and Schuster.

Rottenberg, Simon (1956), "The Baseball Players' Labor Market." In: *Journal of Political Economy*, 64, pp. 242–258.

Saint, Onge, Jarron, Rogers, Richard, and Krueger, Patrick (2008), "Major League Baseball Players' Life Expectancies." In: *Social Science Quarterly*, 89, pp. 817–830.

Schell, Michael J. (2005), *Baseball's All-Time Best Sluggers: Adjusted Batting Performance from Strikeouts to Home Runs.* Princeton, NJ: Princeton University Press.

Schulz, Richard and Curnow, Christine (1988), "Peak Performance and Age Among Superathletes: Track and Field, Swimming, Baseball, Tennis, and Golf." In: *Journal of Gerontology*, 43, pp. 113–120.

Schulz, Richard, Musa, Donald, Staszewski, James, and Siegler, Robert S. (1994), "The Relationship Between Age and Major League Baseball Performance: Implications for Development." In: *Psychology and Aging*, 9, pp. 274–286.

Schwarz, Alan (2004), *The Numbers Game: Baseball's Lifelong Fascination with Statistics*. New York, NY: Thomas Dunne Books.

Scully, Gerald W. (1974), "Pay and Performance in Major League Baseball." In: *American Economic Review*, 65, 915–930.

Scully, Gerald W. (1989), *The Business of Major League Baseball*. Chicago, IL: The University of Chicago Press.

Sommers, Paul and Quinton, Noel (1982), "Pay and Performance in Major League Baseball: The Case of the First Family of Free Agents." In: *The Journal of Human Resources*, 17, pp. 426–436.

Thorn, John and Palmer, Pete (1984), *The Hidden Game of Baseball: A Revolutionary Approach to Baseball and Its Statistics*. New York, NY: Doubleday.

Turocy, Theodore (2005), "Offensive Performance, Omitted Variables, and the Value of Speed in Baseball." In: *Economics Letters*, 89, pp. 283–286.

Zimablist, Andrew (1992), *Baseball and Billions: A Probing Look Inside the Big Business of Our National Pastime*. New York, NY: Basic Books.

Index